25 WOODWORKING PROJECTS

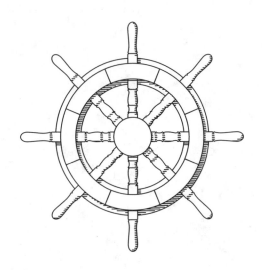

FOR SMALL *and* LARGE BOATS

Series Editor, Peter H. Spectre

Text design by Richard Gorski and Lindy Gifford
Cover design by Richard Gorski
Printed in the United States of America
Cover photographs by Kip Brundage and Stephen Rubicam

Published by WoodenBoat Publications
P.O. Box 78, Naskeag Road
Brooklin, Maine 04616-0078

Introduction

*I*f you are of a practical mind, perhaps the most satisfying aspect of owning a boat, after actually using it, is working on it. And of all the work to be done on a boat — and there is plenty of it — perhaps the most satisfying is making your own accessories and modifications.

Large or small, sail or power: there's always something that can be done to improve a boat. For a skiff, it could be a new pair of spoon-bladed oars. For a canoe, a custom paddle designed for your grip, your reach, your paddling style. Larger craft can be upgraded with a new locker to fit an odd space, a new door to fit an old locker, a leakproof icebox, or a table that stows out of the way when not in use.

The off season is an ideal time for this sort of work, as much can be done away from the boat. She might be laid up under a winter tarp or inside a storage shed. The cold winter winds might be blowing; the snow might be two feet deep. But if you have a heated workshop, you can still be in business. You can build that mahogany skylight you've always wanted, or a grate for the cockpit sole, or a traditional steering wheel with turned spokes. Actual installation can be saved for later, when the tarp comes off at spring fit-out time.

Even if you don't have an ideal workshop, there are many projects that can be done in the smallest of spaces. You don't need much room to make a set of hand planes for woodworking or a pattern for casting a bronze cleat. Many are the canoe paddles that have been carved in the kitchen or the wooden bilge pumps made in the basement, or in the corner of a heated garage.

The projects in this book are designed for woodworkers, amateur or professional, with a wide range of skills. While the ship's wheel requires a substantial level of expertise with stationary shop tools, as well as precision in layout and planning, and the louvered doors require the ability to make and bring together a large number of parts all at once, many of the projects are quite simple in concept and execution. An icebox, after all, is only a modified rectangle; a canoe paddle is nothing more than a stick of wood that can be carved to shape with the simplest of hand tools.

None of the projects described here are based on untested theory. All of the items have been built by the people doing the describing, and over the years they been built more than once. These are time-tested designs laid down and executed by woodworkers and boatbuilders who know what they are doing. There's no blind leading the blind in this book.

Furthermore, none of these projects have been designed simply for the sake of doing them. All were created to fill a need. As a result, they exhibit that most elegant characteristic — functionality — and as a consequence they have a beauty all their own.

Pick a project. Follow it through. You will have the pleasure of working with your hands and the satisfaction of having produced the best.

—Peter H. Spectre
Spruce Head, Maine

About the Authors

TIM ALLEN is a professional cabinetmaker in Blue Hill, Maine.

MAYNARD BRAY, the author of numerous articles and books on wooden boat building and repair, and *WoodenBoat* magazine's contributing editor, lives in Brooklin, Maine.

JIM BROWN, multihull pioneer, designer, and builder, lives in North, Virginia.

GEORGE CADWALADER, a retired marine officer, and founder and former director of Penikese Island School, is now a lobster fisherman out of Woods Hole, Massachusetts.

RICH CAHOON, professor of psychology at Cape Cod Community College, is an avid sailor, and a freelance writer/photographer specializing in boats and woodworking.

JAMES CURRY, is a professional boatbuilder who works at Essex Boat Works, Essex, Connecticut.

ARCH DAVIS is a New Zealander transplanted to Maine; he builds, designs, and writes about boats in Morrill, Maine.

ED FROST, a retired industrial designer, has had a life-long affair with the sea, including World War II service in the U.S. Coast Guard.

BEN FULLER, former curator at Mystic Seaport Museum, is a researcher, writer, and consultant.

RICHARD JAGELS, the author of *WoodenBoat* magazine's "Wood Technology" column, is a professor at the University of Maine at Orono.

MICHAEL KORTCHMAR, sometime charter skipper, is the owner of Kortchmar and Willner, Inc., a boatyard in Greenport, New York, specializing in restorations.

PAUL LAZARUS, editor of *Professional BoatBuilder* magazine, lives in Alna, Maine.

DONALD MACKENZIE makes violins and bows in Brewster, Massachusetts.

The late **DAVID C. "BUD" MCINTOSH,** author of *How to Build a Wooden Boat,* designed and built boats in Dover, New Hampshire.

MICHAEL SANDOR PODMANICZKY, founder of Challenge, a boat-building program for youths, is the head of furniture conservation at Winterthur Museum in Delaware.

RICH SHEW, a boatbuilder and freelance writer, lives in South Bristol, Maine.

PETER H. SPECTRE, *WoodenBoat*'s contributing editor, is a writer and editor specializing in nautical subjects.

PHILIP TEUSCHER, is a professional mariner, writer, and filmmaker specializing in maritime subjects.

RICK WATERS builds and restores boats in Noank, Connecticut.

ALDREN WATSON, illustrator, freelance writer, and woodworker, is the author of *Hand Tools: Their Ways and Workings,* as well as other books about tools and methods used in the manual trades.

JOEL WHITE, a frequent contributor to *WoodenBoat* magazine, designs and builds boats in Brooklin, Maine.

KENDALL WILLIAMS is a cruising sailor.

Table of Contents

A Traditional Ship's Wheel

by Michael Sandor Podmaniczky

A ship's wheel must function on two levels: It must be visually correct, as it is a focal point of the vessel and is symbolic of its quality, and it must be well engineered, as the lives of the crew and the ship depend upon it.

Design Considerations

The design of a steering wheel is restricted by functional requirements, such as the diameter of the wheel and the placement of the handles. Also, on a boat where hard sailing is expected and lives depend on maintaining control, it is crucial from an engineering standpoint that the wheel be designed to withstand the shock of a body being thrown against it; conversely, the handles should be shaped so as to minimize the damage done to that body. These requirements for utility, strength, and user-friendship practically predetermine wheel design, as you shall see.

The overall diameter of the wheel can be determined by considering the waterline length of the vessel (see Figure A); this, in turn, will determine the length of the spokes. The number of spokes, and how closely they are spaced, are determined by the control and comfort that the relative proximity of adjacent handles provide the helmsman. In order for the spokes to be supported with maximum strength, the actual wheel, or rim, should be as far out along the spokes as possible, while still allowing adequate length of handle for a comfortable grip.

The rim is a three-layer composite of thick inner members, or felloes, lapped over by thinner, outer felloes, much like the overlapping futtocks in sawn frames (see Photo 1), creating a very strong wheel. The total thickness of the outside felloes should equal the thickness of the inside felloes. This ensures that the built-up rim is equally strong throughout, despite the inherent, though unavoidable, weakness of the butt joints between felloes in the same layer.

The dimensions of the square blanks that the spokes are turned from are determined by the square openings in the hub. The actual working dimension of the spokes — that is, the minimum thickness after all turning and joining is done — is unavoidably less, since the outer felloes are halved, or notched into, the spoke

A

Length of waterline	Radius of quadrant or drive wheel	Steering wheel size	Theoretical tiller length
17–23′	6.5″	18–22″	4½′
17–25′	8″	18–22″	6′
26–29′	10″	24–28″	9′
30–34′	12″	26–30″	12′
33–34′	14″	26–30″	15′
34–35′	16″	32–36″	18′
37–40′	18″	32–36″	20′
46–55′	20″	36–40″	25′
56–70′	24″	36–40″	38′
60–75′	30″	40–48″	43′
65–85′	36″	44–54″	68′

This chart is the result of research by Edson Corporation and is intended as a guide. Variations in hull shape, horsepower, rig, and steering machinery will alter these figures. The final design of a steering system should be approved by a naval architect.

squares, reducing the spoke squares in that area to the thickness of the inner felloes. Therefore, to maximize the strength of the spokes, it is good practice to limit the depth of the decorative turnings to the thickness of the inner felloes.

Once all the utilitarian and structural requirements have been satisfied, the designer is left with a somewhat narrow parameter for aesthetic enrichment. However, the wheel can be enhanced by the quality of the decorative turnings, the exactness of turning and joint execution, and variations in inlaid details.

One major decision in wheel design is the choice of a hub: either a stock or a custom-made hub may be employed. In the project described here, I use a bronze Edson hub for my wheel; if you'd like to use a custom hub, the accompanying sidebar describes how to make the wood pattern for a casting.

There are two traditional methods of building wheels; both methods call for lathe-turned spokes. The first way is to work small wheels on a faceplate lathe after the felloes have been rough cut and joined up into circles. However, properly aligning everything for turning and assembly is a bit ticklish — never mind that faceplate turning of a piece this large is not the easiest thing to do without some experience. The other way is to cut, shape, and join everything by hand, assembling the finished product on a solid, dead-flat work surface.

I have updated the latter technique for shaping and joining the rim elements with a device I call a compass router — that is, a router mounted on the end of an arm that pivots on the center of the wheel. All of the wheel's curves, as well as a number of the joints, can be cut with this jig. The nicest thing about this technique is that once you have locked that machine where you want it, you have to be a pretty sloppy craftsman to make a mistake.

Making a Pattern for a Custom Hub

Although stock wheel hubs, such as the one I have used in this example, are available from Edson, you may wish to make your own custom casting. A hub of smaller diameter allows for longer spokes and changes some of the overall proportions of the wheel. The detailing that you can add to the surface of a custom hub — for example, extra beads, coves, or lips — is particularly rewarding, since the rest of the wheel is your own custom work as well. But, unless you have more extensive facilities than the average woodworker, you will have to draw on the expertise of a few other craftsmen. Making a custom hub involves three different processes: patternmaking, casting, and machining. You can easily take care of the first, and if you have access to a machine shop, you could probably handle the third, but you will have to find a traditional, non-ferrous foundry for the second.

For a pattern as simple as this one, you need very little in the way of a layout — in fact, you can use the same layout on which you make the rest of the wheel. When making the initial drawing, instead of laying down the dimensions of the stock hub, you are free to substitute the dimensions of your own. There is some leeway here, but I suggest that you examine a few other wheels for guidance. Draw the inside detailing of the hub, defined by the intersection of the eight spokes. This results in eight pie-shaped wedges that fill in between the spokes around the perimeter of the hub (see photo). Although metal shrinks slightly when cooled, this need not concern you for this particular casting. With a compass, draw the hole that must be fitted to the shaft on your steering gear. Increase the compass radius by about 5/16 inch and strike the outside of this inner hub. The inner hub and wedges are projections from one face of the overall hub. The other face will be a separate cast plate screwed to the main casting.

To make the pattern, begin with the plates for the outside faces. Bandsaw two slightly oversized discs from a piece of tight-grained mahogany, pine, or tulipwood. Screw these in turn (from behind) to the faceplate of your lathe and turn them true, to the dimension of the outer hub. Decorate the faces with beads or other raised portions, being sure not to go too thin — say, no less than ⅛ inch. For looks and strength, I suggest leaving a thick lip around the outside perimeter. Remember that the "loose" face will be screwed to the main casting where it lies on the filler wedges, so leave this area flat and undecorated.

Next, get out wedges from stock that is approximately ⅛ inch thicker than the spoke heels. This extra dimension is called the "finish," and will be machined off the rough casting for a good mating surface. Make the wedges 1/32 inch larger (all around) in plan view than the layout calls for. Finish the vertical faces with a disc or upright belt sander, tapering all three vertical sides say from top to bottom. Thus, the top face will end up being exactly what the layout calls for. This taper is called draft, and it allows for the pattern to be drawn out of the mold without hanging up on exactly vertical (or, saints preserve us, undercut!) surfaces. Glue these wedges to the flat side of one of the plates, positioned exactly as you have drawn them.

To complete the main casting, turn the inner hub (on the lathe) to the same 1/32-inch taper (1/16 inch overall) that you gave the wedges. Since this slightly tapered cylinder projects through the loose plate, make it about 1/16 inch longer than the inside dimension of the hub (wedge height) plus the thickness of one faceplate. Although this inner-hub cylinder can be cast with a hole through it, this operation takes a bit more experience with patternmaking. So, I suggest you leave everything solid, and drill out the cylinder once the casting has been made (this includes the loose faceplate). Glue the big end on the center of the plate to which you have assembled the wedges.

Wipe a little plastic wood or surfacing putty into and along all corners of the pattern where the wedges and the inner hub meet the faceplate, then sand smooth. The slight radius (1/16 inch) that this forms is called a fillet — it allows the casting to cool without stress cracks at these points. Finally, sand and varnish all surfaces until they are very smooth. Traditionally, shellac, rather than varnish, is used because it dries quickly.

These two patterns will now be sent to the foundry and cast in the particular bronze alloy that the rest of the hardware on the boat has been made of. The castings will be polished by the foundry and sent to a machine shop for finishing — but if you are lucky, the foundry will do the machining, too.

The machined surfaces are: the tops of the wedges, to bring their heights down to the dimension of the spoke heels; and the flat face of the loose plate, for a good mating with the wedge tops. In addition, the inner hub needs to be turned smooth and true down to a point just below the tops of the wedges, and the loose plate must be bored out to slide snugly onto the end of the inner hub. With the loose plate clamped in place, holes will be drilled and tapped for the screws that will fasten everything together when the wheel is built. These can be flathead machine screws, countersunk flush, round-head machine screws standing proud, or, for a very snappy look, bronze threaded lugs with bronze acorn nuts.

Finally, the inner hub will be bored out to fit the steering gear, and a keyway broached to match (this is best done on a machinist's lathe to ensure that everything is true). If you want, you can have the inside faces of the wedges machined true and vertical on a milling machine, but if you patronize a good foundry, the faces will be smooth enough. The slight draft you made makes for a nice, tight fit when you get around to installing the spokes.

If you have had patternmaking experience, you might want to try making a pattern for a single-piece casting, but this is substantially trickier work. Whatever you decide, talk to the foundry and the machine shop first — tell them what you are planning to do and what you expect them to provide. Their advice will be quite valuable as you proceed.

With the faceplate removed, the inner-hub cylinder and inter-spoke wedges are clearly visible. These pieces project from the face of the hub that is obscured by the spokes.

The rim of this wheel is composed of thin outer felloes overlapping thicker inner felloes. The joints have been staggered for maximum strength.

The Drawing

As with any joined wooden object, unless you know exactly what it is you want to end up with and are loaded with justifiable confidence that you can pull it off with your eyes closed, you had better do a full-sized drawing before you start chopping wood. The boatbuilder will be comfortable with this principle, since few boats are ever built without at least some lofting being done in advance.

The basic drafting tools that you will need are a trammel, or beam compass, that will take either a sharp steel scribe or a pencil point, a 24-inch straight-edge, a smaller compass that will also take both kinds of points, a drafting triangle, a selection of French curves, and a good drafting pencil. I prefer a pencil with an F lead, but you should use what suits you.

To start with, I like to make a barebones drawing on drafting vellum, and then develop a working "lofting" or layout by putting down more extensive lines and details drawn and/or cut into a flat piece of wood. For me, "wood" means a good, smooth piece of birch-faced, lumber-core plywood.

On your drafting vellum, you need only to establish a few key dimensions and the plan for your turnings; save the real construction details for the layout. As in Figure B, draw just a portion of the hub, a single spoke, and the adjacent felloes. I have struck my various radii, and planned where my turnings will be and what they will look like.

Start your drawing with a straight line indicating the center of the spoke. Along this line, strike the hub radius and an arc of the desired overall radius (to the tip of the spoke) with a pencil point in one of the trammel heads. The Edson hub that I am using for our example gives some predetermined design

specifications, such as the overall wheel diameter (28 inches), hub diameter (6 inches), and spoke dimensions (1⅜ inches square).

I began my design by drawing 2-inch-long arcs of 3-inch and 14-inch radii. I then shortened the greater radius by 4 inches and struck another short arc to indicate where the spoke handle ends and the transition to the square portion of the spoke begins. Keep in mind that at these transitions there are actually three important points: (1) where the adjacent, fully turned shape ends, (2) where the flat face of the square begins, and (3) where the spoke is completely square in section. The second point is the most important, since it is from this point that you will measure back to the rim. Done properly, this transitional region should show an arc on the face of the square that can vary from a bold half-circle (sloping shoulders) to just a slight curve (broad shoulders). I favor the latter — not only for appearance, but because broad shoulders are easier to turn!

The transition between square and round on a turning is always an opportunity for visually exciting detail and should be sharp and bold without being overdone. Decide what you like and draw it in.

Shorten the trammel setting to indicate the outside radius of the rim. The dimension from the rim to the ends of the flat face on the spoke can vary, depending on what appeals to you, but I recommend something between 3/16 inch and ½ inch. Much less, and you run the risk of accumulated error in construction, pushing the rim past the end of the square. On the other hand, a square section that protrudes much more than ½ inch starts to look chunky.

In order to establish the next important radius — the width of the rim — you need to do a little tangential figuring, since this dimension is somewhat dependent on the thickness of the inner felloe. The rim is made up of inner and outer felloes. The outer felloes are usually half the thickness of the inner ones, with their butt joints landing on the centers of the inner felloes. For both increased stability and strength as well as for a more attractive assembly, the outer felloes should be halved or notched into the squares of the spokes. The thickness of the spoke square after notching both sides is the same as the thickness of the inner felloes, in this case 1 inch (which in turn means that the notches will be 3/16 inch deep). The outer and inner edges of the inner felloes will be rounded to a full radius, which terminates ½ inch back from the edge of the inner felloe. Add another ⅛ inch to this figure to ensure a flat surface for the outer felloes to laminate to, and strike a radius at this point (in short, ⅝ inch from the arc that indicates the outside of the rim). This is the outside edge of the outer felloes.

Reduce the radius by the width of the outer felloes, and strike another short arc. The edges of the outer felloes are also rounded, and there must be room for two sets of inlaid stringing, which will be described later. I have found that a 2-inch-wide outer felloe makes for proper proportions and still provides enough strength, so strike the inner edge radius accordingly. Strike the radius of the innermost edge of the composite rim — ⅝ inch less than the outer felloes. Reduce the radius again by another ½ inch, and strike an arc where the spoke square ends and the turned portion begins again.

Now strike a radius at about ½ inch to ¾ inch greater than the hub to indicate where the turning stops. At this point the spoke must again become square to enter the square hub socket. (I'll develop this area on the layout shortly.) As you can see, the radius of the stock hub determines the length of turning between the hub and the rim. A custom wheel can include a smaller hub to give a longer turning on the inner spoke. Next, using your compass, set off the maximum width of the spoke by marking a half-width on either side of the centerline and drawing lines tangent to these arcs.

All the dimensions necessary for fabrication of the wheel are now defined, so you can turn your attention to the decorative elements. As for the turned details, I would suggest not trying to make them up on your own, since there really hasn't been an improvement on classical design since Palladio published *The Four Books of Architecture* in 1570. But, don't despair — one of the best sources for this sort of design is the Windsor chair leg.

Examine a few Windsor chairs, and you will notice that there are only two or three primary designs for the arrangement of the turned elements on traditional chair legs. These individual elements are the full vase, the partial vase, the reel, the bead, and the cylinder, which are all three-dimensional shapes developed from two-dimensional antecedents: the S-curve, the C-curve, the straight line, and combinations of each. Almost every design for a spoke (or leg) is composed of an arrangement or repetition of these basic lines. The S- or cyma curve is what William Hogarth, the 18th-century artist/philosopher, referred to as the "curve of beauty." He saw the undulation of the cyma as primarily attractive to the human eye and wrote extensively on the use of this element in decorative design.

I have provided a few examples of turned spokes in Photo 2; feel free to copy any of them. If you don't like any of these patterns, or if none of the wheels you

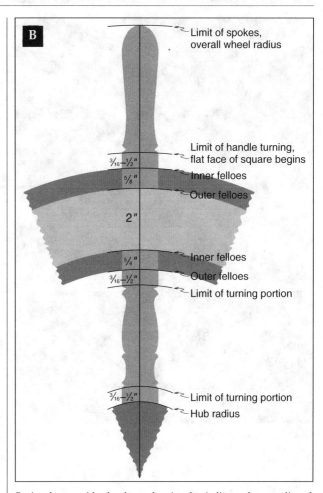

Begin a layout with a barebones drawing that indicates the centerline of a spoke and the critical points along the line. Dimensions will be lifted directly from this drawing to create the working layout. The dimensions shown here are for the wheel designed for this chapter and may be altered for individualized designs.

have seen do much for you, there are a couple of guidelines for design that I can suggest:

As you can see with a few of our examples, the design of the handle (a vase) is repeated inside the rim as a mirror image. If you like, you can break the inner element down into a smaller vase and add a reel (cove) or a bead the way I have. This is an old design trick that makes for nice visual modulation: the eye starts outside at the periphery, moving from the larger, more separated elements in toward the more complex and tightly grouped details at the center.

Construct your chosen design on the drawing using a compass, a straightedge, and French curves. As I have already mentioned, where the square portions begin or end is very important and should be clearly drawn. If you are comfortable with this process, you really only have to draw one side of the profile. However, to best visualize the design, I suggest that you do a full rendering of the spoke.

2

Winterthur Museum

Look to a Windsor chair leg for inspiration when designing the spokes of a wheel. Traditional turnings are composed of just a few individual elements in different arrangements.

The Layout

The next step is to make the working layout of the entire wheel. You will do this on a 3-foot-square sheet of ¾ inch birch- or paper-faced plywood. Veneer-faced particleboard is also an option, but be sure that there are multiple veneers so the sheet will not dent or break up easily. This will not only be your layout, but also your work surface and router jig as well (Photo 3).

The tools you will need for your layout are: the trammel with sharp scribe points (instead of the pencil point you used on the previous drawing), a layout knife, a steel rule/straightedge (preferably 24 inches long), a pair of dividers, and a No. 2 wood pencil. Sharpen the pencil to a spade tip — that is, it should be flat on two sides so in one view you have a broad, flat tip, but when it is turned 90 degrees, it comes to a point. This will stay sharper longer and is less prone to break during the sometimes rough treatment it gets in the boatshop. Just be sure to orient the tip so as to draw the narrowest line possible.

Setting your trammel directly from the previous drawing, scribe onto the plywood the full circles that correspond to the hub, all edges of the inner and outer felloes, and the overall 28-inch diameter. Divide the concentric circles into 16 equal parts with lines drawn through the center point; knife these lines into the surface of the plywood.

To divide your circle, you will want to dredge up what you learned in your old high-school geometry lessons. Start by drawing a line through the circle, intersecting the center point. Set the trammel to approximately three-fourths of the circle's diameter, locate the pivot point at the two points where the centerline intersects the circle, and swing intersecting arcs above and below the line. Knife in a line that intersects the points defined by the intersecting arcs, and you'll have a line 90 degrees to the centerline; the circle will be divided into quarters. Use these same mechanical principles to divide the 90-degree angles into 45-degree angles, and so on until you have 16 parts. (This sort of trammel play will quickly become second nature, and you will no longer have to rely on a framing square or a protractor.) Every other one of these lines is a centerline of a spoke, while the other eight lines indicate the joints between outer felloes on the rim.

Lay off and knife in half-breadths on either side of the spoke centerlines to establish the 1⅜-inch width of a turning blank. Picking up the dimensions from the drawing with your trammel, tick off on each of the centerlines all the points of transition between square and turned elements on the spokes, and with the end of your steel rule as a square, knife in perpendicular lines across the spokes at these points.

Now draw the inside of the hub, where you'll note that the sides of each spoke remain parallel until they converge, at which point the butt end of the spoke must be beveled on either side. This will be a tricky fit when you come to assemble the wheel parts to the hub; the straight sides must be tight against the sides of the square sockets, the beveled ends must be tight against each other, and the heel of the spoke must seat hard against the inner hub. Lay it all out carefully, taking the inside dimensions directly from the hub.

Your layout is now complete, but it is a little confusing because of all the undifferentiated overlapping lines. Take your pencil and darken all the lines that correspond directly with an edge or an interface (joint) on the wheel. For example, you'll darken the entire circle that indicates the edges of the outer rim felloes, but when you darken the outside edge of the inner felloes, you'll stop at each spoke interface. You won't darken any of the 28-inch-diameter circle, since it only corresponds with the tips of the handles.

What you now have is a very readable working layout that gives you ample information for making templates, cutting, shaping, and assembling. All measuring and assembling will be done on this board, so the cleaner you make the layout at this time, the easier it will be for you to use it as the job goes along.

Although you don't have to include the turned

portions of the spokes on the layout, you'll want something to use as a guide at the lathe. A template laid out on a ³⁄₁₆-inch piece of softwood batten will do nicely. Cut this to the overall length of a spoke, and half again as wide. Using a marking gauge, strike lines indicating the width and the centerline of the spoke blank at 1³⁄₈ inches and ¹¹⁄₁₆ inch from one edge of the batten. Lay the edge of this template on your drawing and tick off a mark for each important point on the turning. These are the points of transition, such as the extremes of a cove, the edges of a bead, the bottom of a vase, etc. The shoulder areas between square and turned portions should be correctly represented on your drawing, and these points of transition should be transferred to the batten.

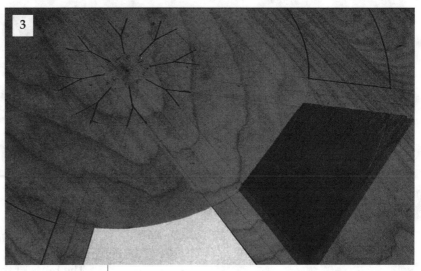

The working layout has been developed from the barebones drawing. The lines have been knifed in, and those that correspond to an edge or a joint have been darkened with a pencil.

Once you have all the crucial points indicated on the template, knife them in across its width with a square, and darken the lines. Then draw in the curved profile of the turned areas. You can draw this the same way you did the original drawing, or trace the original with carbon paper, or, if you have a copy machine, make a one-to-one copy of the initial spoke layout and paste it onto the template. If you go the latter route, you can omit drawing anything. I prefer leaving this template as a layout, rather than cutting it to shape.

Turning the Spokes

Get out enough spoke blanks for what you will need plus a few flubs, keeping in mind that you'll want to have at least one extra-perfect turning for show and tell later on. These blanks must all be square in section and of the same dimensions. Whether you cut them on a table saw to dimension, or saw close to the line and then reduce the thickness with a planer, you must clean up the sawn blanks with a hand plane, since all power machines leave unacceptable surface markings. A cabinet scraper will work for this, but be careful; if you are not, you will round the edges.

Saw and plane or scrape carefully, checking with parallel-jaw calipers to ensure exact uniformity. Then cut the blanks to the same length — about an inch more than the finished turnings require.

Draw crossed diagonals from the corners on both ends of each blank to locate dead center. Either by laying the template against the blank, or by laying the blank on your drawing, tick off the transitional points from square to round, working out from the butt.

I do not make cuts in blanks for the spur drive, because unless they are perfectly positioned, they can throw the alignment slightly off. This is disastrous when you are turning something with transitions from square to round and back again, since the misalignment shows up at the shoulder areas of the squares.

Chuck the blank between centers, making sure that the points are sharp and properly aligned with your cross marks. Tighten up the tail stock, and the spur will grab effectively. If the spur shears the end-grain after you have started turning, pull the tail stock out of the way and tap the end of the blank onto the spur with a mallet.

First establish the shoulders of the squares with a skew chisel, keeping in mind all three points of transition and the semicircular profile you have designed on the face of the flats where they become rounds. This is one of the most difficult cuts to execute on the lathe because of the tendency to break off edges of the square, or to produce an unfair curve at the shoulder. If you have never cut this shape, I suggest you study one of the many good turning books available and turn enough practice pieces so you feel comfortable with the techniques. Once the squares and their shoulders are established, round the handle and the area between the squares to the maximum diameter.

If your design calls for square portions that are smaller in section than the turned portions, the job is considerably trickier. You must start with a blank large enough to accommodate the rounds, and reduce the appropriate portions to the required, lesser squares (this must be done before turning). Probably the easiest way to do this is to strike lines around the blank indicating the points at which the adjacent rounds terminate (the first of the three transition points I mentioned previously), then mark the width of the smaller

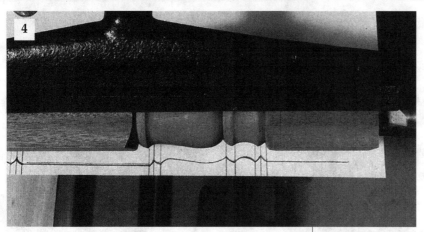

Matching the shapes by eye is surprisingly easy if you have taken the time to make a good template.

square with a marking gauge on two opposite sides. Cut close to all the lines on the bandsaw, and after removing this waste, finish the two surfaces on a router table with a square bit in the tool. Mark the depth of the other two sides on these new surfaces and repeat the cutting and routing. This will only be necessary for the squares out at the rim. You can reduce the dimension at the heel by standing the blank on end and cutting it on the table saw.

Once these squares have been reduced, chuck the blank in the lathe and cut the shoulders. Then round the thicker material in between — and be careful not to lose control and hit the squares.

Stop the lathe, and with a sharp, black pen transfer all the important points from the template to the round areas. When you turn the lathe back on, these black marks will be just visible. If you wish, you can make them clearer by just touching them with a pencil while the blank spins. These marks will guide you as you shape the rest of the spoke.

If you are new to duplicate turning, you may want to use calipers to be sure that you are keeping your dimensions correct. At least use calipers and a parting tool to establish minimum and maximum dimensions before you start to shape the piece. I like to jig the turning template just behind the work and cut by eye, lining up the top profile of my turning with the layout just behind it (see Photo 4). After all, if it looks right, it is right. You'll be surprised by how easy it is to match shapes by eye if you have taken the time to make a good template.

Once the spokes are turned, you can either cut them out of the lathe by completing the radius at the end of the handle, or you may choose to leave the waste attached for the moment. There is no turning back once you've removed the waste, so be sure the turnings meet your highest standards before doing this. With the waste intact, you can always re-chuck the

piece and continue turning.

Next, fit the heels to the hub and to each other within the hub. Take the angle of the butt bevels from your layout, set the table saw to this angle, and run the spokes vertically over the blade. Although a cool hand can do this unassisted, you might want to jig up something to help you push or hold. This wheel will not be much fun to use if you are reduced to nine fingers while making it. You'll be happier if you leave everything an eyelash strong, and do the final fitting with a block plane and chisel.

The butts of the spokes land against a compound shape: the concave radius of the inner hub, and the fillet that the patternmaker put where the inner hub joins the outside hub cheek. This gives you a little leeway; you don't have to fit the spoke perfectly against the inner hub. But if you have taken a trifle too much off the bevels on the heels of the spokes, you can tighten everything up again by fitting the heels closer to the inner hub using a fine (patternmaker's) rasp on the end-grain of the spoke.

Since all the bevels have been cut exactly the same, you will have to dress all the heels. This keeps the positions of the spokes from changing relative to each other. The open face of a stock hub allows you to see just what is going on inside. If you are using a custom hub, it is not much trickier. You can chalk the inside of either casting so that when the spoke is tapped into place and removed, you will see where it is proud and a whisker more wood must be removed.

As for "tapping" into place, I suggest a dead-blow hammer or a carver's mallet of something like soft maple, so you are striking the end-grain of the mahogany spoke with the side-grain of a wood of comparable density. Be wary of doing too much tapping. You will be looking at the ends of those spokes for a long time, and you don't want them to look beat-up. Before you do the final bedding of the spokes into the hub, you'll need to make the inner felloes of the rim to ensure exact alignment.

Making the Rim

The steps for making all the felloes are the same. Start with parallel-sided stock of the desired thickness (1 inch for the inner felloes, ½ inch for the outer felloes) and wide enough to contain an individual felloe. Lift the spoke angle from the layout, set the table saw miter gauge precisely, and cut a test angle. Check this against the layout for accuracy. When you are happy with how the table saw is set up, clamp a stop to the miter gauge and cut enough felloe blanks for at least one extra — just in case. Leave these blanks with straight sides for the moment. You will now permanently set the spokes into the hub, and at the same time locate the inner rim felloes by jigging and fastening the hub, spokes, and felloes onto the layout board — on center and in plane.

In order for your layout board to also become a building jig and router table, you must drill a shallow, flat-bottomed hole of the same diameter as the wheel shaft. This will also double as router arm pivot. Since this hole must be exactly on center, take extra precautions to ensure that the drill bit does not slip off-center while drilling. On the drill press, using an appropriate bit (e.g., Forstner, Powerbore, or Speedbore), drill a hole of the required diameter through a small piece of scrap wood, say 3 inches by 3 inches; this will serve as the jig's pivot bearing. As you will soon see, the pivot bearing must be the same thickness as the inner felloes so the router arm remains parallel to the layout board while you are shaping these pieces.

Likewise, you will need a new pivot bearing for shaping and rounding the outer felloes. Take the bit out of the drill press, locate the center point in the little hole your trammel point has made in the center of the layout, and slip the pivot bearing over the drill bit. Fasten the bearing to the layout with a couple of sheetrock screws. This will hold your Forstner bit on center while you drill out the center of the layout to a depth of about ³⁄₁₆ inch. Remove the pivot bearing.

Locate the wheel hub on the layout with a dowel that just fits the hole in the hub. (I am using 1-inch electrical conduit in the photographs.) With the spokes temporarily in the hub, and using the layout to keep them lined up, screw locating blocks to the board on either side of the fat portion of each handle. Measure the distance between the layout board and the lower edge of the hub's spoke openings. Get out eight shims of this thickness, and cut them slightly smaller than the square portions of the spokes. Placed under the squares, these will keep the spokes in plane. Remove the spokes, apply bedding compound to all the inside surfaces of the hub, and reset the spokes, tapping them into place soundly and making sure that all shims and locating blocks are in place.

Now retrieve your inner felloe blanks and snug them into place against the spoke squares (see Photo 5).

Align the blanks for the inner felloes for final shaping and rounding over by snugging them in place against the spoke squares. The blanks need not be in the correct plane relative to the spokes. The spokes will be removed before routing the felloes.

For the moment, it's okay that they are not in plane with the spokes, but you should make any slight corrections necessary to get them to butt perfectly against the spoke sides. It is best to do this on the table saw again, so corrections are consistent and accumulated error is minimized. A fine adjustment with a block plane on one or two of the felloe blanks will probably be unavoidable. For this reason, you should number the blanks and keep them in order. When you are satisfied they fit, fasten them down to the layout board with two screws per piece. Final shaping and rounding over will be done with a router, with all of the felloe blanks screwed down.

Since the router can only do the edges of one side at a time, the felloes will have to be flipped over and screwed down again to get at the other side. Therefore, the screw holes must be exactly symmetrical. This requires a stop on the drill press table that allows you to drill a pilot hole through the exact same relative location in either end of each felloe blank. I used a piece of scrap pine, with a bandsawn notch matching the end angle of the felloe blank. With this jig clamped to the drill press table, bore all blanks with two pilot holes.

Trace a template for the finished felloe shape from the layout, or make one from your drawing on the copy machine and rough-cut the felloes to the curve of the rim. Return them to their positions on the layout and, using four bar clamps, pull them tightly into place against the spokes by cross-clamping to the other side of the wheel and screw them down to the layout board. Now, carefully remove the hub/spoke assembly, and you're ready to round the felloe edges. But first you will have to set up a compass router.

6

With the spokes removed and the inner felloe blanks securely fastened to the layout board, the edges are shaped and rounded over with a compass router.

Rounding Over the Edges

Depending on your level of expertise, you should feel free to use any shortcuts you want. However, I will show you, paraphrasing teacher/philosopher/woodturner David Pye, how to minimize the "workmanship of risk" by maximizing the "workmanship of certainty" in using a router and a well-designed jig.

A compass router consists of a piece of ½-inch plywood with a hole at one end for pivoting on the wheel "shaft" and a clamping system at the other end to hold your router in place while you run it around the rim (see Photo 6).

It is important to keep in mind that jigs need not be inordinately elaborate. They must only get the job done properly — period. So don't go overboard wasting time on a fancy-looking rig that will be going into the woodstove once this project is done.

Rough-cut a piece of flat ½-inch plywood into a two-pronged fork shape. It can be narrower at the non-forked end, but it should be able to receive a hole for the pivot shaft there. The business end should be shaped such that the router bit has plenty of clearance to be moved in and out within the slot, and that the prongs are wide enough to receive the router — with enough additional room for the stops and hold-downs required to locate and stabilize the machine. Screw runners to the prongs parallel to the radius and just wide enough apart to allow the router to slide between them without any slop. The runners and the slot should be long enough to allow the round-over bit to work the inside and the outside of the rim.

To position the router properly, you need to set up the jig on the layout board. Slide the pivot shaft through the pivot bearing, locating it to the board in the shallow hole, and screw the bearing down. As you can see, this is a repeatable and entirely accurate procedure. Slide the pivot end of the jig over the shaft and into place. It should now be apparent why the bearing is the same thickness as the inner felloes: the router, the felloes, and the layout board must be in parallel planes.

Cut a rectangular piece of plywood that just fits between the runners on the jig to act as a stop. About ¾ inch from either side of the stop, drill oversize holes for screws (with washers); ¼-inch should be large enough. The large holes will allow some adjustment when the stop is screwed down to the jig.

Before rounding the edges over, I first routed the felloes to their exact shape with a straight bit. Since two quarter radii equal a complete half radius (with nothing left over), you may feel that this step is unnecessary and may want to skip it and go directly to the rounding-over step. Suit yourself.

Chuck a straight bit in the router and pivot the jig so it is centered over one of the spaces left by the spokes that were removed. Wind the bit down until it just touches the outside layout line of the felloes on the board; this line is otherwise hidden under the rough-cut felloes. Slide the stop against the inside edge of the router and, with washers under the heads of sheetrock screws, screw it down hard. (You will note that I am a sucker for the versatile sheetrock screw.) Turn on the router, and with the base plate held tightly against the stop, pivot the arm slightly. The track left by the cutter on the layout will show you if your setting is correct; if not, the jig allows for a little "microadjustment."

To microadjust, slightly loosen one screw and push the stop to where you want it; the oversize pilot hole will allow for ⅛ inch of throw. If this is not quite enough, tighten this screw and loosen the other for another increment of adjustment. If this is still not enough, well, you were too far off at the initial setting, and you must start over. With stops on only three sides, you can back the router away from the work in order to take as light a cut as you want. The spaces between felloes will give you relaxing breaks from white-knuckle routing as you work your way around the perimeter. Don't worry about short-grain breakout on the outside edges.

Reset your stop and repeat the process to shape the inside edges. Here, to avoid breaking off grain on the following corners, you may want to back off a little and come into them from the reverse direction with two or three shallow cuts. Once you have bottomed out on the stop, back off again, swing over to the leading corner, and complete the cut along the entire edge. Those of you who routinely use a router will probably have your own working methods when these fine points come up.

Now repeat the process, only this time with a ¼-inch rounding bit. If you have carried out the preceding steps instead of skipping right to here, you have spent a little extra time, but you'll be happier with this step, since the material to be removed has been minimized. Once you've rounded the edges on one face, flip the felloes over and round the edges on the other side. The care with which you drilled the screw holes will ensure that everything stays properly located.

When gluing the inner felloes to the spokes, the felloes must be held in the correct plane with shims. Oversize holes, not visible here, allow the hold-down screws to pass through the shims without interference.

Gluing the Felloes

When rounding is complete, it is time to glue the felloes to the spokes. So take them up from the board again, remove the router jig and the bearing, and, using the pivot shaft, relocate the hub assembly onto the board and shim the spokes into plane. The felloes must now also be shimmed up off the board to be exactly in plane with the wheel and centered on the side faces of the spokes. Get out shims to the correct thickness, roughly the shape of the felloes and with oversize clearance holes for the hold-down screws to pass through them without interference (see Photo 7).

My adhesive of choice is Weldwood plastic resin glue, since it is reasonably gap-filling, waterproof, very strong, and doesn't leave a black glue line like most epoxies. Apply adhesive to the end-grain of the felloes so they are well sealed, but with not so much that there is a lot of squeeze-out. With shims in place under them, slide the felloes into place and screw them down to the board. Again, cross-clamp everything tightly into place. (The screws will hold everything down and in plane, but the clamps will easily overcome them in sheer, pulling everything together good and tight.) Check to make sure that all the joints fit correctly and that everything is pulled tightly down to the board.

This assembly step is crucial to a successful job, so don't overlook anything. To avoid inadvertently pulling the layout board out of plane, it is wise to clamp the board down to a good, flat surface. Once the glue is hard, unclamp, unscrew, and remove the wheel from the board.

The Outer Felloes

From ½-inch stock, get out the individual outer felloe blanks on the table saw the same way that you did the inner ones, and, again, wait to cut them to their final, curved shape. The difference between the inner and outer rims is that the outer felloes pass over the spokes and butt-join to each other in the middle of the inner felloes. This overlapping of the joints is what makes the structure so sound and strong. In order to ensure tight joints, you will make up the outer rims into separate rings before assembling them on the wheel.

Since there are two rings, I made up a second layout board so I could glue up and rout both rings simultaneously. This meant boring a hole for the pivot shaft and scribing the two circles copied from the original layout, to help align the ring. This also required two new shaft bearings the thickness of the felloes to keep the router arm level.

Start by laying eight of the trapezoidal blanks in place on the layout board. Correct any misalignments, so the blanks all butt perfectly. With a piece of waxed paper under each joint, apply epoxy to the joints and clamp them together. Since the surface of these will be seen, you will have to screw them down to the board from underneath, but you can cross-clamp as before. Repeat with the other rim members (see Photo 8).

When the glue is hard, but before you remove the rings from the boards, clean up any glue or slight misalignments with a smooth plane. This is the surface that the router jig has to ride on, and it should be flat and smooth.

Now scribe the inner and outer circumferences on each ring. The layouts are covered by the felloe blanks

The outer felloe blanks are screwed to the layout board from underneath and cross-clamped to tighten the joints.

The compass router is also used to shape the outer rim. Since only one side is rounded over, the shape of the rim must first be established with a straight bit.

you can't skip shaping them first with a straight bit. Set your router stop so you just cut to the scribed line on the outside of the ring, and take your finish cut. Before resetting for the inside, use the same setup to cut the ring that is on the other board. Reset for the inside, and again cut both rings. Substitute a ¼-inch radiusing bit for the straight cutter and round all the edges over. (If your radiusing bit has a follower bearing, this can be done without the pivoting jig.) Remove the rings from the boards.

Joining the Outer Rings to the Wheel

The next step is to let the rings into the faces of the spokes, flush with the inner felloes. This is done with a large, straight router bit. However, in this case, the jig, which now pivots with the hub as the bearing, cannot ride on the spokes. The jig must be supported by the adjacent inner felloes, so you must screw two shims to the underside of the router arm. These must be thick enough to just raise the jig off the spoke, and far enough apart to ensure that they don't fetch up against the spoke while you are cutting the joint. Set the depth of the cutter so it just touches the surface of the inner felloes.

Make a second stop for the router, and fasten both stops to the jig, setting them so the cutter will stop just shy of the width of cut needed to let in the rings. Rout out the joint on all spokes, working the arm back and forth and sliding the router in and out until you fetch up against each stop in turn. Lift the jig off, flip the wheel over, and cut the other sides of the spokes.

Lay a ring on the joint and observe how much more you need to take off for a good press-fit. Micro-set the stops to give yourself the added dimension, and finish up the cutting. The rings should just press into place, not showing any gaps.

Apply adhesive to all mating surfaces, but make it lean enough at the edges to minimize squeeze-out. Align the joints between the outer felloes exactly between the spokes, and clamp everything together. The rest is all downhill — you've done it!

at this point, but you can set the trammel from your original drawing. Although the layouts have been bored for the pivot shafts, the center point of the Forstner bit has left you a center for the trammel point to locate to. When the circumferences are scribed, unscrew the rings from the boards and clean up any glue on the backsides.

Cut the outsides of the rings close to the line on the bandsaw, and on the insides with a sabersaw, and screw them back in place on the layout boards. They are now ready to be shaped with the router (see Photo 9).

Since the ½-inch-thick rings will only be rounded off on one side, and with only a ¼-inch radius at that,

Decorative Stringing

To compensate for non-weatherproof adhesives, early wheels needed rivets or screws to hold everything together. Modern adhesives reduce the need for mechanical fastenings; however, I decided to put them in this wheel. Also, as is seen on the bellies and backs of stringed instruments, I let two bands of multiple laminate stringing into the faces of the outer rims, near the edges. This stringing, or purfling as it is usually called, adds a very decorative touch and strengthens the butt joints between felloes. Again, modern adhesives reduce the need for structural reinforcement, but the decorative character of the detail certainly remains. Instead of riddling the faces of the rim with bungs, follow the best wheelmaking traditions and hide the screws behind the stringing. Start by cutting the purfling groove, which must match the width of the stringing.

For stringing, a holly/ebony/holly combination is usual. Individual lengths of each can be purchased in various thicknesses, which have to add up to the width of a groove cut by a standard router bit. You can go with an odd dimension of stringing, but you will have to either have a bit custom ground to match for a one-pass cut, or cut the groove in two passes with an undersize bit. In keeping with the off-the-shelf approach, I used a ¼-inch router bit and stringing purchased to match.

Remount the wheel to the layout board to hold it steady. Fix the router in position on the jig to cut a ¼-inch groove about ⅜ inch in from one of the edges of the outer felloes. Cut this groove on both sides of the wheel, reset the router, and cut grooves ⅜ inch in from the other edge.

Carefully drill countersunk holes to receive No. 6 screws in the bottom of the groove. These should be spaced so as to put screws about ¾ inch in from the corners of each felloe on both sides of the wheel (see Photo 10). Stagger the holes just enough so they don't run up against the screws coming from the opposite side. For good measure, I also put one screw into each spoke — but I can't, for the life of me, justify it!

The stringing and the groove are "buttered up" with glue, and the laminates are pressed into place. These pieces are not full length; they are simply butt joined to complete the full circumference.

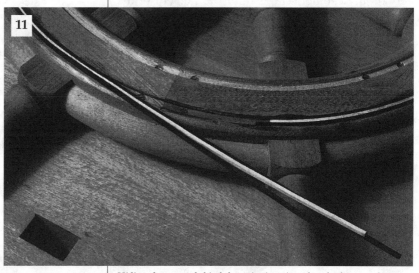

Hiding the screws behind the stringing gives the wheel a very clean appearance. Be sure to stagger the screws so they don't interfere with those on the other side.

The stringing can now be glued into place. All three laminates have to go in at the same time, but you should stagger the (butt) joints by a few inches. Butter up the groove and the stringing with glue, and begin pressing it into place (see Photo 11). The strings will not be full length, so just butt another length to the first and continue till you're back to the starting line. Trim the end square and tap it into place, butted tightly against the other end. When the glue has dried, you have the pleasant job of cutting the stringing down flush with the surface of the felloes. This is almost as much fun as opening Christmas presents, because with the stringing proud of the surface, and with glue all over it, you can't really tell what the stringing is going to look like when it has been cleaned up.

Because the ebony and holly have brash grain that is running every which way, trying to cut it down with a chisel or plane is just asking for trouble. So, to eliminate tear-out, take it down with a sharp cabinet scraper. When you take the final stroke with the scraper and remove the last bit of excess glue, the beautiful fit that is revealed will make all of this work worthwhile.

Finishing

Go over the entire wheel and clean up any glue squeeze-out that you may have missed earlier, and sand everything smooth. I don't like to use sandpaper coarser than 180 grit, and if I've done well with my surfacing up to this point, I may even start with 220. Be careful when sanding around the stringing, because you can drive ebony dust into the mahogany and holly grain, and give these woods a dark hue. I rely on my cabinet scraper to do 95 percent of the work, and then I seal just the stringing with a thin coat of shellac or sanding sealer. With 220-grit sandpaper, I give the stringing a quick rubdown before tackling the surrounding mahogany.

Once everything is sanded, you can apply a paste wood filler to get a leg up on filling the grain. Be sure the stringing is well sealed before you do this — otherwise, the holly would be readily stained by the mahogany-colored filler. I chose to skip the filler on this job, so I needed a few extra coats of varnish to get a good, even surface.

When the surface meets your approval, you can start building up the finish. Although polyurethane makes a fine finished surface, I prefer the way alkyd resin spar varnishes wear. Be sure to sand well between coats to ensure good adhesion. You will find that with an object as complex as this wheel, you cannot avoid leaving holidays or losing your wet edge, so try to work as systematically as possible.

Hang the wheel by inserting a dowel or broom pole through the hub and supporting it on a pair of horses. Start by coating the inner spokes, turning the wheel as you finish each one. Next, do one side of the wheel, then the other, and finish up with the handles. Make sure that the last coat goes on like glass, and you will have one heck of a fine wheel on your boat next summer!

Suggested Reading:

F. Pain, *The Practical Wood Turner*, NY : Sterling, 1990.

David Pye, *The Nature and Aesthetics of Design*, NY : Van Nostrand, 1982.

Edson Corporation offers three sizes of hubs for wheels ranging from 20 inches through 42 inches. The smallest is for a six-spoke wheel; the larger two are for eight-spoke wheels. Edson Corporation, 146 Duchaine Blvd., New Bedford, MA 02745; 508-995-9711.

A Skylight

by Paul Lazarus
Drawings by Samuel F. Manning

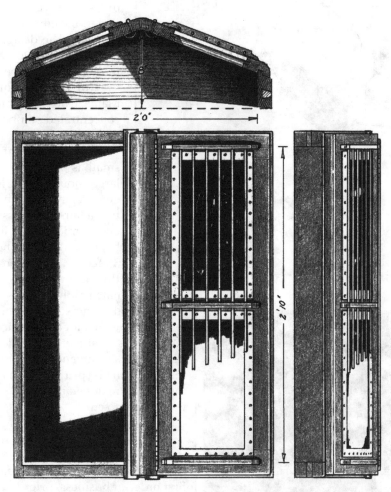

On the subject of deck furniture, veteran builder/designer David C. "Bud" McIntosh once wrote, "The skylight might well be considered the crowning glory of a proper yacht."

Certainly a ridged skylight rendered in the classic style sets off a traditional vessel — much as a march of gable dormers enhances the architectural character of an old country estate. There are, of course, easier, though less elegant, ways to add fenestration to buildings and boats: a residential roof window can do the job; likewise, a regular marine hatch.

But this is about a crowning glory and nothing less — a small, practical, and handsome deck structure for the well-appointed yacht. Still, there's a lot of work involved in fashioning just this single piece of furniture, so let's briefly review the fundamentals of a good

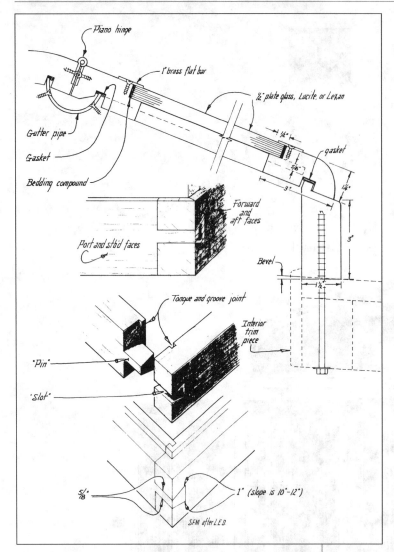

Piano hinge
1" brass flat bar
½" plate glass, Lucite, or Lexan
Gutter pipe
Gasket
Bedding compound
gasket
Forward and aft faces
Port and stb'd faces
Bevel
Tongue and groove joint
Interior trim piece
"Pin"
"Slot"
5/8"
1" (slope is 10°-12°)
SFM after L.E.D.

A Dodge-built skylight on the cabintop of the 53-foot cutter
Saskianna.

Stephen Rubicam

skylight, before proceeding to the particulars of the design shown here.

Any skylight is potentially vulnerable to a mishap at sea, precisely because it is such a prominent feature on deck; by contrast, a conventional hatch offers only a low profile. A skylight's construction, too, is more complex than that of a hatch, so it follows that since a skylight represents a comparatively exposed and elaborate subassembly, the numerous parts involved in the overall piece increase the chances for leakage below.

Being a functional adornment — with the emphasis on function — a sensible skylight ought to be not just attractive, but structurally secure against solid water, inclement weather, and physical damage. The design presented here — unique in the marine literature — meets those criteria. It is the creation of Lawrence E. (Duffy) Dodge of North Edgecomb, Maine, whose long professional career has concentrated on fine yacht joinery above and below deck.

Duffy's skylight is dimensioned as small as possible — meaning it remains large enough, at the least, to double as an emergency exit if necessary. Note, too, that a fair-sized vessel is needed to carry even a minimal skylight; in this case, the boat would likely be a cruiser of about 35 feet. A bigger boat might easily add this unit to its inventory, without even replacing a hatch in the process.

The literal cornerstone of Duffy's skylight is the locking dovetail joint that connects the side and end base pieces. Just as the late Pete Culler modestly claimed to have invented merely the snotter arrangement seen on his sprit rigs, Duffy takes credit only for this signature dovetail and the simple jig he devised with which to cut it.

Specifications

Duffy's dovetail comes at an early stage in the construction sequence and will be described later. But the first order of business, prior to any milling or fabrication of parts, is to take careful measurements aboard the boat in order to ensure that the skylight as designed can be accommodated in its intended location by the existing deck or cabintop framing schedule. Since Duffy's skylight is essentially a generic model, it may be found necessary or desirable to slightly enlarge this design for a given yacht; any reduction, though, compromises the unit's usefulness as an escape hatch.

The inside edge of the completed fixture should finish flush with the deck opening prepared to receive it, because a final, interior trim piece (not shown) will be fitted to cover the seam between the deck or cabintop and the base frame of the skylight.

A materials list for Duffy's design depends on the actual boat and compatible woods. Duffy is not dogmatic about this or other elements of his design, believing instead in the principle of "builder's choice." If the existing deck is dressed in mahogany, then clearly the new skylight should be of similar material. Duffy himself usually builds with, and favors, teak or mahogany. The latter wood, by the way, is typically an African or Honduran species, as distinct from so-called Philippine mahogany, which is technically lauan, a lesser hardwood.

Additional choices are present for the builder. Shatter-proof glass may be installed as lights in conjunction with a set of traditional, protective bars made from uniformly spaced brass rods. Alternatively, a modern, hard plastic, such as Lucite or Lexan, may be substituted, in which case the metal-rod system can be dispensed with. Duffy does stress, however, that ordinary plexiglass is unsuitable in this application: it tends to expand and contract with the weather, and it is too easily scratched.

Hardware is another category for exercising one's choice. The full-length piano hinge, for example, can be purchased pre-drilled, if desired, or the leaves can be obtained as blanks for in-shop countersinking and boring. Hardware for raising, lowering, or locking the sash should preferably conform with patterns found elsewhere on the boat.

Construction

In his shop, Duffy "lofts" the location of the skylight on an oversized sheet of plywood. He draws the predetermined deck aperture in plan view at full scale, and the deck camber as an elevation; the latter is either lifted directly off the boat or taken from blueprints of it.

Duffy's full-scale sketch serves as a shop reference for the skylight's construction, while the plywood panel itself functions as a convenient work surface for

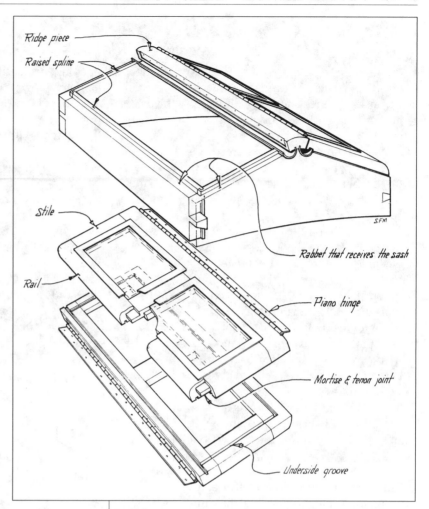

Ridge piece
Raised spline
Stile
Rail
Rabbet that receives the sash
Piano hinge
Mortise & tenon joint
Underside groove

A 10-sided skylight built by Duffy Dodge for the 90-foot sloop Whitefin.

The Duffy Dovetail

Although he performs many woodworking operations by machine (and often with clever contrivances, given the degree of difficulty of the pieces he builds), Duffy prefers to cut his dovetails by hand.

Working in teak, for example, in a test run prior to glue-up, he can get the dovetail's pin to slide in the slot between the tails on what seems like a molecular film of the wood's own oil. Duffy works to close tolerances.

The simple jig he uses to achieve a tight fit like that is similar to a shop-made spar clamp: two pieces of squared scrap wood held together with carriage bolts. This clamp functions as a handy guide and tool rest, helping to maintain accuracy in both the marking and cutting procedures involved.

1. The inside walls of the slot are cut first, care being taken to saw squarely and smoothly to the marked line. For the slot floor, or base between tails, the jig is clamped flush with the base line, front and rear; then a sharp chisel, whose flat lower surface is resting on the top edge of the jig, is used to clean and true the base of that

opening. Besides keeping the chisel honest, the little jig helps prevent tear-out.

2. To mark the adjoining pin stock, the piece is temporarily held in position behind the slot or tail, using the jig, whose top edge is clamped flush with the base of the slot. The whole works is kept rigid in a bench vise. The pin will be cut to conform to the tail, as made, by marking the pin stock with the slot's profile. Duffy places the bottom of a regular plane iron against each of the inside surfaces of the slot in turn, using the jig as a wing extension to keep the plane blade square to the task. By giving the iron a sharp rap, he transfers in one motion the information from each faying surface of the slot to the end-grain of the pin blank. The lines thus etched indicate the absolute edge for each corresponding surface of the pin.

3. Next, after the pin stock is released from the jig setup, the pin is cut as marked by first chiseling enough

assembling the entire piece. Duffy delays cutting, for as long as possible, the camber and bevel required along the bottom edges of the base frame. He is thus able to work comfortably on a flat plane, which facilitates operations such as clamping, scribing, and sanding. After ripping, jointing, and planing dry, clear stock so it is trued and smoothed to its finished thickness, Duffy begins construction.

The base frame is built first. Once the dovetailed corners are satisfactorily joined and the entire base squared (the latter procedure being best accomplished by checking diagonal measurements across the frame), the base can be knocked down in order to cut the deck crown on the end pieces, and the corresponding bevel on the side pieces. Duffy cautions here that the bevel should be undercut, rather than overcut, insisting that you can always remove wood later, as needed, whereas it's a lot harder to put it back on.

The ridge piece is of the same thickness as the base-frame stock; it laps the tops of the ends, to which it will be glued and

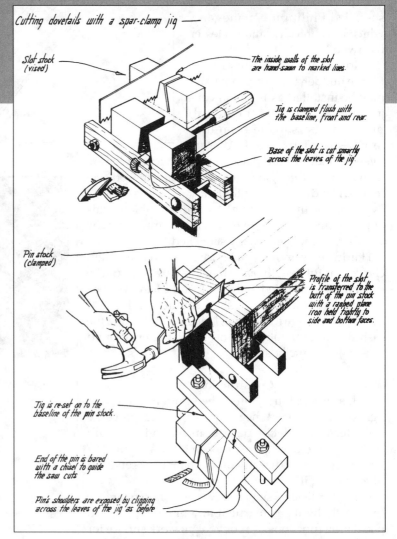

Cutting dovetails with a spar-clamp jig —

Slot stock (vised)

The inside walls of the slot are hand-sawn to marked lines.

Jig is clamped flush with the baseline, front and rear.

Base of the slot is cut smartly across the leaves of the jig.

Pin stock (clamped)

Profile of the slot is transferred to the butt of the pin stock with a rapped plane iron held tightly to side and bottom faces.

Jig is re-set on to the baseline of the pin stock.

End of the pin is bared with a chisel to guide the saw cuts

Pin's shoulders are exposed by clipping across the leaves of the jig as before

wood away from the scribed line to eliminate the possibility of the ripsaw slipping to the wrong side of that line. The pin is then hand-sawn nearly to the end of the line, at which point Duffy clamps on his jig again to complete the cuts and keep the pin's shoulders square to the sides of the piece.

4. The tongue-and-groove joint — which adds a measure of insurance to the dovetail and, not incidentally, shows off a crisp joint line to the cabin interior — is cut on the table saw. The small amount of material that is left standing around the pin after this operation can be removed at the bench by hand.

For the finished through-dovetail, plan on allowing the pin to emerge from the slot by about ³⁄₁₆ inch once all cutting operations are concluded. This excess is later cut away, upon satisfactory assembly of the base frame.

Note that the completed joint calls for the pins to be oriented fore-and-aft with the boat's centerline, a marine convention Duffy cites as traditional.

The resulting, locking dovetail, if ever sawn free of all surrounding wood, resembles one of those exquisite examples of Japanese joinery — demonstrating, for true believers, Zen in the art of marine joinery.

Paul Lazarus

Using the dovetail jig, a simple device that is the key to precision joinery in the base frame.

screwed. The outermost ends of the ridge may finish proud of the end pieces on the base frame, if desired. Inside — that is, viewed from the cabin interior — the builder may choose to leave the underside of the ridge either square (with visible edges stop-chamfered), or coved (with the curve echoing that of the top outside edge when finished).

Note that the skylight is built square to an imaginary level line running across the deck, conveniently represented by the plane of the temporary plywood work surface. The top edge of each base piece may be completed separately, and then "fined up" at assembly. Duffy mills the raised spine so that it is integral with the base; other builders may choose a less difficult course and affix instead a narrow wood strip with epoxy adhesive.

Duffy recommends epoxy, by the way, for its reliability in exterior applications. But though epoxy resin is gap-filling and thus forgiving, Duffy's own joinery throughout strives for superior dry fits. According to Duffy's way of thinking, "If you've got room for the glue, you don't have a good joint. Some of the old-timers said that you want wood-to-wood, with nothing piled up in between. Then the glue goes into the wood in both joining parts."

With the base frame set up and squared away, the builder can move on to the upper, or sash, frame. Duffy sees this portion of the skylight's construction as conventional cabinetry, more or less. The joinery employed here is standard for door-and-panel work.

Rails and stiles are connected with a haunched mortise-and-tenon joint. Duffy bores the mortise first, then shapes the tenon to suit. His dovetail joint follows a similar sequence: he prepares the "slot," or cutaway portion between tails, prior to making a matching pin.

The rabbet that receives the sash can be cut with a router after the frame has been assembled and glued. Likewise, the underside groove — which receives the top spine in the base frame — can be scribed for and routed after assembly. Note that this groove is made oversize both to allow for the sash swinging up, and also to accept a compressible, synthetic gasket.

The shop-built gutter arrangement in this skylight consists of split, yellow-metal (copper or brass) pipe of a generous radius, screwed into the end pieces of the base frame, and allowed to extend "out by" the exterior face of the base by about ⅛ inch to ensure adequate drainage.

If the protective bars are added — and they lend a nice touch, even when plastic lights are selected — then Duffy likes to finish the ends of the wood retainers in a decorative ogee pattern, fastening these strips with ovalhead screws. The brass flat bar, though, which keeps the lights in their place, is countersunk for flathead screws. Bedding compound, where called for, should be a high-grade, durable, marine polysulfide or equivalent material.

A skylight such as this is customarily finished bright, and deservedly so; you can always paint it later, but the reverse is not readily done. The completed structure is then bedded and fastened in position. Long screws or lags extend through the deck carlins and beams to grip the skylight's base all around.

For added security at sea, and privacy at the dock, a fitted, waterproofed canvas cover can be slipped over the skylight, but otherwise kept stowed.

A skylight such as Duffy's dramatically alters the sense of space down below, admitting light and air not obtainable with a more modest hatch in the same location. On deck, a unit like this is a showpiece, adaptable virtually without further modification to any yacht of traditional appearance. Best of all, if you've done it right, and tend to maintenance — this is one skylight that will give years of service, without a leak.

Traditional Teak Grates

by Maynard Bray
Photographs by Phil Hall

Ken Woisard

There are various places in a boat where gratings, rather than a solid sole, make sense: A small one at the base of the companionway ladder for drainage and bilge ventilation, and another on the foredeck where the ground tackle can be stored. And then there's the familiar cockpit grating. As a unit that can be built apart from the boat, a grating makes a fine winter project.

The Henry R. Hinckley Co. of Southwest Harbor, Maine, has been building boats for years. They turn out excellent work and have been doing enough of it to have attained proficiency and efficiency in their methods. Here is how they make custom teak grates for their yachts:

Ken Woisard

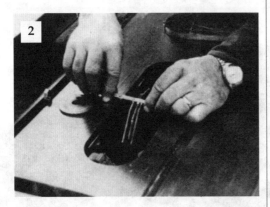

Build It by the Numbers

1
The project is begun by milling the stock to the desired thickness and to the rough length. For reasons that will be obvious later, these pieces must be cut square and to equal lengths.

2
The notches that enable the grating crosspieces to interlock with those going the other way are cut with a dado blade mounted in a table saw.

3
To save time, the notched strips used in making up this grating start out as wider planks with grooves cut in them. Lines marking the groove boundaries have been carefully drawn on the plank edges, and the table saw's fence has been adjusted to index all the planks identically for each cut. Note that the fence is used for indexing only — not as a guide in the usual sense. The plank is held firmly against the miter guide (set for 90 degrees) while it passes across the blade: this eliminates the risk of the plank jamming between the fence and the blade and kicking back at the operator.

4
The center groove in each plank is made first, followed by the adjacent grooves on each side. The idea is to make all cuts for a given fence setting as a single operation.

5
Two passes over the dado blade are required for each groove, because the grooves are somewhat wider than the blade. This photo shows the start of a second pass. (The extreme end of the plank will be dadoed to half its thickness for fitting the grating's margin piece.)

6

With the grooving complete and a regular blade installed in the table saw, the grooved planks are cut into 1-inch strips from which the grating's cross-pieces will be made.

7

The other set of strips — that is to say, those that run at 90 degrees to the first ones and seat in their notches — are likewise cut from a plank. They measure 1 inch by ½ inch.

8

The thickness of this second set of strips is fine-tuned by checking the fit in one of the notches.

9

As a guide in assembly, the outline of the finished grating is marked on the assembly table, using an accurate pattern — upside down, because the grating will be built that way.

10

The grating is put together on this marked outline, starting with three thin strips and the wide notched one that will serve as a margin piece for one side of the grating.

11

One end of each remaining thin strip is tucked into a notch until all the notches are filled. (Margin pieces for the remaining sides will be installed later after the basic grating has been completed.)

12

Now the notched strips are laid in place and pushed firmly down over the intersecting strips, one by one, using one of the loose notched strips as a spacer.

13

Flathead wood screws, driven from what will be the underside of the grating, hold things together permanently — there is no glue used here.

14

Because a screw goes into each crossing, a power screwdriver is a big timesaver.

15

The basic grating is now complete and can be turned right-side up to have its edges trimmed and margin pieces fitted. The two side margins are being positioned here for marking.

16

Once again the plywood pattern is used, this time to determine the cut lines for the grating's edges.

17

For a guide in cutting a line that falls across the grating on the bias, a parallel-sided guide plank is temporarily nailed so one of its edges is on the marked line.

18

The other edge of the guide plank runs against and is guided by the table saw, which has been set to match the width of the guide plank.

19

Thus the cut is made, accurately and smoothly at the marked line. Note the parallel line representing the inside edge of the margin piece. To make this cut, the grating will be turned over, the saw blade adjusted for half-thickness, and the fence reset for the proper alignment of the blade with the line.

20

Because this is a small grating, it can be easily flopped upside down or turned on its edge for making the margin plank cuts. A larger grating would be best left in one position, with these kinds of cuts made by portable tools, such as a router and a Skilsaw.

21
Here's our grating with its edges cut back for the margin pieces.

22
But while it is still possible to do so on the table saw, the sides of the grating have to be cut to the marked outline. The fence ensures that opposite sides will be parallel.

23
Now for the two final margins. First, their ends are cut to fit against each other and against those margins already in place. Then they are securely clamped in position so they won't shift while the grating is turned upside down...

24
...for drilling and fastening.

25
At the pointed end, a separate piece is attached to hold the ends of the margins together and to give them support.

26
Although there are other ways to give a grating's top surface a smooth and finished appearance, this big sander is probably the fastest.

27
If the pattern fits well, the completed grating will also fit well — and it does, indeed, here in the interior of a new Hinckley yawl.

28
As with most boatbuilding operations, there are various ways to make good-looking gratings efficiently besides the technique described here. Some gratings have full-depth strips in both directions, double-notched where they cross. Others use a different method of joining the margin pieces. Evaluate the next gratings you see, and try to figure out the sequence of steps used to build the ones you prefer.

Ken Woisard

A Cheap Boat Shelter

by George Cadwalader
Photographs by James Marlinski

The author's bowed-frame temporary boat shed attached to the back of his workshop. The bowed rafters allow the width of the building to be carried higher than that of an A-frame structure.

One winter I set about rebuilding the galley on our boat. She lay at the time at a pier about 200 yards across the pond from my shop, and I thought it would be easy enough to row back and forth from the shop to the boat.

I must have rowed that trip a thousand times. No sooner would I arrive at the boat than I would remember some indispensable tool that I'd left behind and

back I'd go. Templates that fit perfectly produced parts that did not, so it was once again into the skiff, across the pond, tie up the skiff, recut the part, back into the skiff, back across the pond, retie the skiff, climb under the winter cover, and the damn thing still wouldn't fit. Never again, I decided, would I undertake a job of any size unless the boat were right outside the shop.

Some time later I undertook a bigger modification

below, and having learned my lesson, moved the boat into the yard. There I built a frame on deck, covered her with canvas, and spent the rest of that winter performing Houdini-like contortions trying to get in and out from under the frame. After that experience, I resolved to take the time to build a proper shed. The additional cost, I concluded, would be more than repaid by the time I'd save.

In due course another major job presented itself, and I began thinking about the most inexpensive way to build a temporary structure to accommodate a 41-foot-long deep-keeled sloop with a 9½-foot beam and measuring 12 feet from keel to housetop, and still have enough room left over to work all around her. My yard was wide open to winter gales, and my neighbor was acutely sensitive to unsightly alterations to her view, but the biggest problem was that I had only $500 to spend on materials.

While pondering these difficulties I recalled a laminated stem piece I'd once made. I had felt certain that the whole thing would spring straight again as soon as I unclamped it from the mold, but of course it hadn't, since as long as the glue held and the adjoining strips couldn't slide relative to one another, the curve was locked in. Why, I wondered, couldn't the same principle be used to build bowed rafters for my shed? Allowing 18 inches for the trailer the boat would be delivered on, I needed a minimum width of 10 feet at a height of 10 feet to allow clearance for the point of maximum beam. The advantage of bowed rafters was that they would carry the width of the building considerably higher than could straight ones on a structure of the same overall height.

A Design in Progress

As an experiment, I used a couple of 16-foot lengths of 1-inch by 3-inch spruce strapping left over from the winter cover. Lying one of these on edge on a relatively flat part of the lawn, I pounded a stake into the ground about 2 feet from one end to allow for the end

to pull toward the center as the piece bent. At the midpoint and on the opposite side from the first stake, I pounded in a second one. Then proceeding to the opposite end, I began very cautiously to bend the strap against the center stake. When ominous crackling announced that the strap was near the breaking point, I stopped and secured the end with a third stake. The result was a rather pleasant curve.

I bent the second strap to the first one and, after clamping the two together at a number of points, lifted them off the stakes. The curve held fine but the assembly seemed a bit too limber for my purposes. To correct this I cut a 2 by 6 into 8-inch blocks and placed these at intervals between the two straps to form a girder, which added enough rigidity.

Using the first girder as a pattern, I pounded a lot more stakes along the periphery of the curve. To make a second girder required only that I draw another strap up against the stakes, lock it in place, distribute my blocks along the inner face, draw the inner strap up against the blocks, and nail the whole thing together with 6-penny common nails driven into the blocks from both sides. Had I thought of it at the time, I would have done better to space the blocks at 2-foot intervals to provide nailers for the purlins we later nailed across the rafters. And I could have saved later grief had I made the block at the upper end extra long and placed my nails to allow for cutting the angle to the ridge pole.

The width of my driveway dictated that the shed be no wider than 16 feet. The height of the shed was governed by my intention to run the ridgepole under the rakeboards on the gable end of the shop. Doing so would permit a tight seal between the buildings. By butting the two end to end, I'd also avoid having to frame up the back of the shed and would gain direct access from the shop to the shed.

Since the curve of the rafters was dictated by the breaking point of the strapping rather than by mathematics, I wasn't sure I'd get enough width at the required height and still stay under the rakeboards. To find out, I spread the lower ends of my two rafters 16 feet apart, butted the tops together, and shoved the whole works up as high as I could get it under the overhanging roof of the shop. Happily, the random curve gave the width I needed at 10 feet but didn't leave me much height above the side decks at the point of maximum beam. I decided I could live with this in exchange for the convenience of abutting the shop. Obviously, someone putting up a free-standing building using the same technique could end up with any combination of height and width he wanted. The arch achievable from bending 16-foot straps could probably span up to 20 feet at its base and still retain adequate pitch to shed snow.

While the first two rafters were still in position against the shop, it was easy enough to establish the angle to the ridgepole using a level to mark off a vertical line at the point where the top ends butted. The marked rafter became the pattern for the rest, which were cut on the flat. When bending the strapping, the inside piece ended up being longer because of its tighter curve. Rather than cut the bases flush, I left the inner strap long to form a lip gainst the plate.

My driveway slopes away from the shop at an incline of roughly 1 feet in the 48 feet I planned as the length of the shed. The easiest way to build a knee wall of changing height seemed to be to set posts in the ground at 4-foot intervals and then cut them all off level. I wasn't much concerned about these posts rotting in the year or so that the shed would stand, so I decided 6-foot lengths of green scrub oak would do fine and cost nothing if I cut them myself. Before I had the chance to do so, a friend came by with some cresoted timbers salvaged from an old pier, and we used these instead. Another friend produced four doubled-up 16-foot 2 by 4s that had become too chewed up to use for his pump jacks; these did fine as a plate to span the posts. To sheath the knee wall I scrounged bits and pieces of plywood from old concrete forms. None of this cost anything.

At ground level, the shed provides plenty of room for maneuvering, and the 10-foot width at a height of 10 feet allows adequate clearance for the maximum beam of the boat.

My luck ran out when it came to finding more strapping, and this I had to buy. Spacing the bowed rafters at 4-foot intervals required 12 pairs, or a total of 48 16-foot straps. Strapping can be bought by the bundle where I live. Usually only about half of every bundle proved clear enough for bending; we put aside the rest for purlins. I got a lot of 2-inch scraps of various widths from construction jobs and cut these down to make the necessary 2 by 3 blocking.

Erecting the Shelter

Two friends, John McRoberts and David Masch, helped put the building up. Bending, nailing, and cutting the rafters took us one full day. We then spent the better part of two more days getting up the knee walls. The slowest part of this job was digging the post holes.

Our rented power post hole digger proved more effective at whirling the operator around the auger than it did at penetrating the hard-packed gravel in the drive, so we ended up using shovels.

The boat itself seemed like the perfect scaffold from which to raise the rafters. Consequently we waited to finish the job until the boat was delivered by hydraulic trailer to my yard. Then, with John as high man atop the boat and David and me passing rafters from either side, we were able to raise the roof in one afternoon.

I made two mistakes here. One was to use strapping for a ridge pole. Although I was able to stiffen this by capping it with a second piece to form a T, I still wish I'd used something heavier. The second mistake was not taking the time to better match up the pairs of rafters. Using knotty spruce for bending stock

The rafters are made of two pieces of strapping held apart by 2-inch by 3-inch blocking. Inset: The inner straps are left long to form a lip against the plate.

an envelope of double-thickness plastic, sealed around the edges, and inflated with a constantly running blower to form a largely free-standing, surprisingly rigid structure. This system is generally erected over a framework of light steel box girders but could be adapted to a wooden structure such as mine. Its great advantage is that two thicknesses with air between them insulates against heat loss and is less prone to sweating on the inside than a single sheet.

As I write this the temperature outside is -5 degrees F, and the idea of an insulated structure seems mighty appealing. However, it's also blowing a gale from the north, the lights are flickering on and off, and we may be in for yet another power failure. God knows what would happen to a shed with blown-up walls should the electric blower fail in these conditions. Cam tells me that loose plastic will stand up to quite a flogging as long as there are no rough edges for it to tear against, but nonetheless I'd be pretty worried that, with the flimsy framework this type of structure is usually built over, the whole works might collapse if it lost the rigidity provided by the inflated walls.

Still, if you had a backup generator and could be sure you'd always be around to hook it up if needed, an inflated shed is unquestionably more comfortable to work in and easier to erect than the single-sheet type. But remember, if considering this type of structure, that the metal arches are designed for greenhouse use and probably won't give you the height you need for a boat unless you extend the frames with welded pipe or else build higher sidewalls.

These considerations, along with the fact that I couldn't afford it, led me to abandon thoughts of a double-walled shed. As an alternative, Cam suggested a type of covering that consisted of a laminated triple-layered polyethylene, with the middle layer being a rip-stop weave of glass fibers that controlled puncturing and resisted brittleness and shattering in cold. It had been developed by a greenhouseman in the northern plains. I decided to go with that product, which came in 10-foot widths and which could be sewed together

resulted in a fair amount of variation among individual rafters, and I should have stacked the 12 sets on the flat and rearranged them then to minimize wandering. As it was, the purlins, which we nailed up on 2-foot centers, helped to fair things up a bit, but not enough to eliminate all the dips and humps that later caused problems when we tried to pull the wrinkles out of the plastic covering.

The Covering

For advice on the best plastic to use, I turned to Dr. Cam Gifford who runs our local nursery. Glass has pretty well given way to plastic on greenhouses and as a result, nurserymen are apt to be the best sources of local knowledge about covering large structures with plastic sheeting. Our greenhousemen were using

or joined with a special plastic channel and insert strip. (For sources of this type of covering or something similar, check with your local nursery.) '

Under Cam's imperious direction, we raised the plastic by throwing lines over the ridgepole and tying these to bunched-up sections of the cloth, which we had previously laid out flat next to the shed. With three of us pulling on the lines and Cam issuing muffled orders from beneath the cloth where he had stationed himself to prevent snags, the plastic slid smoothly up one side and down the other. We then nailed one edge down under battens and rolled the opposite edge around another batten, which we used to draw it up tight. This operation is best performed on a warm, calm day or else you'll find yourself borne aloft by a 40- by 50-foot spinnaker. Warmth is preferable, since the cloth will contract and tighten as the temperature drops.

I was reluctant to tack down the cloth with battens nailed to the purlins for fear of creating leaks. As an alternative I passed lengths of old fire hose over the ridgepole and nailed these fast to the knee walls after drawing them down as tightly as possible. These have proved reasonably effective in reducing the wave effect that high winds create under the plastic, but there remains more flapping than would exist were the plastic itself nailed down. I may eventually have problems with the panel stitching tearing out, but so far so good.

The shed has withstood a good many days of gale force winds and subzero temperatures. I've had to shore up the knee wall with flying buttresses in places to resist the spreading force created by the downward pressure of the rafters. Guy lines inside the building reduce racking at the expense of hindering mobility.

When the temperature rises above freezing it literally rains inside as the frozen condensation that forms on the plastic begins to melt. This, together with the leaks from along the sewn seams, are my only complaints. However, an occasional shower seems a small price to pay for the convenience of bringing the boat right into the shop.

A Rudder

by Philip Teuscher

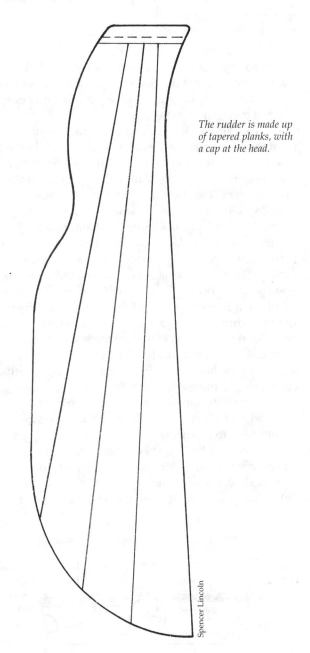

The rudder is made up of tapered planks, with a cap at the head.

Before I purchased my William Atkin-designed cutter, *Statis*, I checked her over as carefully as I could, but detected no rot in her. She was then over 20-years old and had been moored, unused, for eight years or so. I would not have been surprised if I had discovered some punky spots in her upper-works due to exposure to fresh water, but I didn't quite expect what I found later.

As I scraped in a hard-to-reach spot, while wooding the hull and the rudder, my chisel buried itself deep into the rudder. Like a dentist removing decay from around a cavity, I created a hole that grew to depressing proportions. After considering the alternatives, I decided to construct a new rudder using the old one as a pattern.

The first order of business was to find the proper materials for this job. In keeping with *Statis*'s traditional construction, I sought only traditional and time-proven materials. In retrospect, this search proved more time consuming than the actual construction of the rudder.

My search at local boatyards in southern Connecticut proved fruitless; the usual advice volunteered was: "Why not build the rudder of ply and fiber?" My first break came when I spoke with John Jacques of Dutch Wharf Boat Yard in Branford. He turned me on to sources of white oak, wrought iron stock for drifts, and copper rod for rivets. So the last great obstacle had been removed, and there was nothing left to do but begin.

Layout

Obtain rough-sawn, seasoned stock and plane it to the rudder's thickest dimension, at the leading edge. Once you begin planing and dressing the stock, continue the work uninterrupted until the rudder

Spencer Lincoln

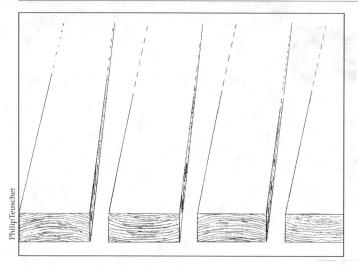

Alternating grain for rudder planks.

is bolted together, because the planks will tend to warp if their freshly dressed surfaces are exposed to changes of humidity and temperature without being bonded together by fastenings.

The rudder planks that will be bolted together to form the full structure should be kept relatively narrow, for the tendency of plain-sawn stock to warp in the tangential (across the plank) plane is exaggerated in wider stock. The optimum width in my case seemed to be from 9 to 11 inches at the widest dimension.

Lay out the planed planks on the floor, starting with the forward-most. Alternate each one so when the planks are edge to edge, in final sequence, the end-grain pattern will alternate: one convex, one concave, one convex, and so on. This will ensure that each plank's tendency to warp will be counteracted by its neighboring plank's desire to go the other way. Number the planks as you place them in sequence.

When building a rudder, the component planks should all be tapered, with the diminishing widths converging at the rudderhead. This accomplishes two functions: all the tapered ends of the planks fit under the rudder cheeks, promoting strength, and the tapered planks tend to warp less.

Using a straightedge, lay out each plank in a taper so the combined tapers will converge under the rudder cheeks. On a bandsaw or a table saw, rough-cut along your taper guidelines. These planks must

be run through a jointer to make both edges perfectly straight. Make sure that the guide on the jointer is set at 90 degrees to the surface of the jointer bed. Be certain you're pushing the stock through the jointer in the proper direction, otherwise the blade will rip and tear the exposed edge-grain. Push the larger end of the tapered plank into the cutters and you won't have any problem.

Lay out the planks in their numerical sequence and clamp them firmly together with bar clamps. Place the old rudder on top of this assembly and nail soft pine battens around the periphery of your rudder pattern, or trace its outline carefully with a carpenter's pencil. Mark on the clamped-up assembly all rivet holes (for cheeks and rudder hardware), the paths, widthwise, the bolts will follow, and the location of the propeller aperture.

Remove the old rudder pattern and with a pencil mark the outline of the rudder by drawing a line along the nailed battens. Mark all the paths that the bolts will take, using a batten or a straightedge as a guide. These paths must avoid all fastenings for cheeks and hardware.

Remove the clamps, and with a bandsaw, cut to the outline of the rudder marked on the individual planks, following the pencil line.

Where the marks (those indicating the bolt paths) meet the edges of each rudder plank, take a carpenter's square and join these lines across the edge of each plank. Mark the center of this line.

Bore for the Bolts

Now you're ready to bore edgewise through each plank for the bolts. Using a normal twist drill or an auger bit of the same diameter as the bolts, bore a 1-inch-deep pilot hole at those center marks on each edge. This is in preparation for boring the final holes with a barefoot auger. A barefoot auger looks just like its regular woodboring cousins, except it has no screw on the end to make it draw — thus, a pilot hole is necessary to get it started. The beauty of this tool is that it bores where you guide it — in other words, it runs straight!

Now, in order to guide the barefoot auger, you must construct and use a drilling jig: two pieces of pine

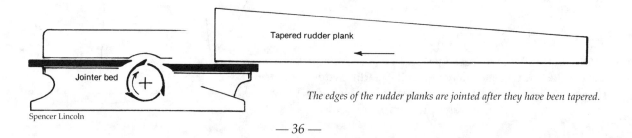

Tapered rudder plank

Jointer bed

The edges of the rudder planks are jointed after they have been tapered.

Spencer Lincoln

¾ inch to 1 inch thick, and approximately 18 inches long, rectangularly shaped with a cutout along one side. These two guides are tacked temporarily in place, one edge of each guide on opposite sides of the plank, following the guidelines for the bolt holes that were just marked on the sides. The jig is designed to allow just enough space for the auger to fit between the two guide pieces when these are tacked securely to the rudder plank, providing a snug lateral guide. To guide the auger longitudinally, sight down the drill jig halves, keeping the auger exactly parallel to these as you stand over your work and bore the holes.

Using a powerful, slow-turning electric drill, bore down into the plank for half its width. After each hole is bored the jig must be moved and set up again for the next hole. When all the holes on one edge have been bored, turn the plank over and repeat the procedure on the opposite edge. The holes will meet, perfectly aligned. Working through wide stock from only one side can be risky for the inexperienced, since the slightest error can cause severe misalignment at the other side.

Clamp all the rudder planks together in their correct position. Use a metal boring bit that is ¹⁄₃₂ inch greater than the diameter of the bolts to ream out the holes through the total width of the rudder. This clears away any chips and aligns the edges of each hole so the bolts will not bind when they are inserted.

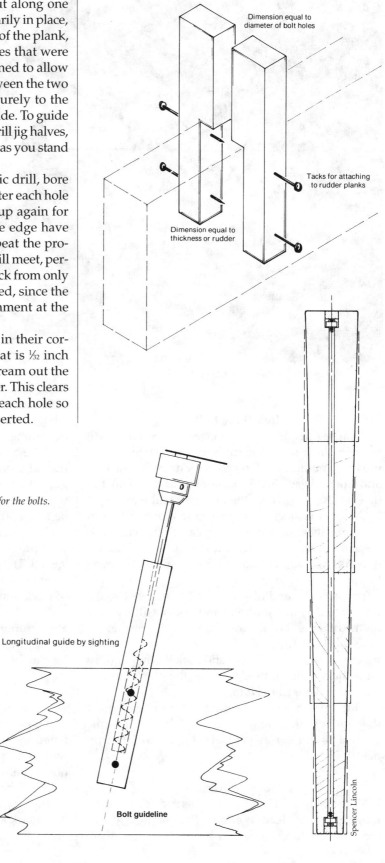

Dimension equal to diameter of bolt holes

Tacks for attaching to rudder planks

Dimension equal to thickness or rudder

Boring for the bolts.

Lateral guide

Longitudinal guide by sighting

Bolt guideline

Rudder plank

Spencer Lincoln

Andrea Darif

The structure complete, the author notches out for the pintle straps.

two ways of accomplishing this task. The rudder can be built up of stock in a consistent thickness, creating the need to cut away a great deal of stock to achieve the taper. Or, after the planks have been aligned and bored through, the planks can be planed (milled) to the proper thickness to achieve the taper. Thus, the plank on the trailing edge of my rudder will be known to taper from 1¼ inches aft to something like 1½ inches forward. That plank can't be thinner than 1½ inches, but very little cutting away will need to be done by hand. The remaining planks step upward in thickness until the plank at the leading edge, the thickness of which is 2¼ inches.

A jointer plane is used. Its long base precludes the tendency toward waviness that a shorter-based smooth plane will create when used over a long surface. Also, the extra weight of this tool helps take some of the drudgery out of the labor by carrying its momentum as you plane across the grain.

Make a line around the entire outside edge of the rudder, along the center of the edge. This will be your guide to use as a reference for determining how much wood has been removed, and how much remains to be taken off.

Using a large metal or wood straightedge to gauge your progress, plane diagonally across the grain, fore and aft. The plane must be kept sharp, and the straightedge must be used continually to check the amount of wood removed and to prevent hollows.

After the rudder has been tapered, round the edges and contour the propeller aperture. A wood rasp and heavy grit sandpaper used with a block are good tools for this job.

Install the Bolts

Because threaded rods with washers and nuts will be used, the leading and trailing edges of the rudder must be counterbored to accommodate the washers and nuts. These counterbores should be 1½ inches deep so the bungs over the nuts will seat well.

Cut the rod stock to the proper length by measuring across the clamped-up rudder assembly. From this measurement, subtract 2 inches to accommodate two nuts and two washers that will be recessed in the bung holes.

Thread each end of each rod 1½ inches. Place a washer and a nut on one end and smear a little grease on the other end of the rod. Tap the rod through its hole until the threaded end appears, then place a washer and nut on this end and sock it down tightly. Note that no glue is used between the planks, as oak does not take well to gluing.

Glue the bungs in the leading and trailing edges of the rudder with waterproof glue. Make sure that the grain of the bungs runs parallel to the grain of the rudder planks.

Taper the Rudder

Now for the difficult part. The rudder must be tapered from the leading edge to the trailing edge (2¼ inches down to 1¼ inches for my rudder). There are

Finishing Off

To prevent fresh water from getting to the end-grain of my new rudder, I fabricated an oak cap that I fastened to the rudderhead. This cap, which is glued with waterproof glue, is fitted over a tenon and runs horizontally across the top of the rudder.

Using the old rudder cheeks as a pattern, lay them on top of the new stock and trace around their outline; mark all the rivet holes. Cut out the new cheeks on a bandsaw and drill the rivet holes.

Clamp one of the rudder cheeks into position on the new rudder, and using it as a pattern, drill out the rivet holes in the rudderhead. Clamp the cheek on the opposite side in preparation for riveting.

The rivets should be measured and cut exactly to length. This length is the combined thickness of the cheeks, rudderpost, and two clinch rings. If the rivets are too long, they will buckle when peened over and force the cheeks away from the rudderhead.

To rivet the cheeks to the head, put a clinch ring on one end of a rivet and drive the rivet through until the other end appears on the opposite side. Place a clinch ring over this end. Using a metal block as a backup (a piece of railroad track is ideal), peen the soft copper into the countersink of the clinch ring. Repeat the process on the opposite side using the metal back-up plate against the side just completed. The soft copper will flow into the countersunk clinch rings, leaving a neat-looking job that is incredibly strong.

With a bevel gauge, transfer the position of the gudgeons from the old rudder pattern to the new rudder. Fasten this hardware with copper rivets, following the same procedure for cutting and peening the rivets as you did for the rudder cheeks.

Cut in the waterline on the new rudder with a backsaw, or a very sharp raise knife using a batten guide tacked to the rudder.

Sand and paint your new creation, stand back, and be proud!

Materials

The following materials are the basic components for a rudder constructed to the builder's plans of *Statis*:
- White oak, selected and cut to specifications.
- Wrought iron rod, galvanized, for drift bolts.
- Copper rod, for rivet stock.
- Brass or bronze plate stock, 3/16 inch thick, for clinch ring stock.

The white oak should be winter cut, when the sap is out of the tree, and seasoned for at least a year by air-drying under cover. The stock must be rift-sawn and clear of knots. For the rudder's leading edge plank, I had the sawyer select a log with grain that curved parallel to the sternpost, thereby insuring that this plank would be of optimum strength.

The wrought iron rod should be ordered galvanized, which will delay delivery somewhat. If you can get around the minimum order policy when buying the copper rod, you will do better than I did, for I had some left over and this is an expensive leftover. Usually, a scrap yard will give you the size copper or bronze plate that you request without quibbling about the small amount.

Clinch rings for the rudder cheek fastening rivets are fabricated in this way: The plate stock is cut into squares, which are then center-drilled. These squares are attached to an arbor and turned on a lathe to the proper outside dimension. One side of the outside dimension is beveled. A hole the same diameter as the rivet stock is reamed and this hole is countersunk on the side of the beveled outside dimension.

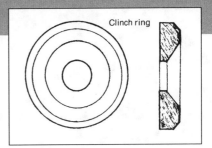

Clinch ring

Patternmaking for Custom Hardware

by Michael Sandor Podmaniczky
Drawings by Samuel F. Manning

*I*f you are a professional or an amateur boatbuilder, in a small or large operation, working on traditional or modern craft, power or sail, wood or even plastic, one thing you always have to consider is the matter of hardware. Chocks, portlight frames, tiller fittings, and even engine parts often can be bought as standard items. Occasionally, standard parts of something more specialized can be adapted (usually cobbled) to do a fair job. For peak efficiency, however, and for the most pleasing appearance, the hardware, like the rest of the boat, should be custom made.

Once the hardware patterns have been made, the cost of the castings made from them will be remarkably low. It is the patternmaking itself that so lopsidedly raises the price of the finished custom hardware. In industries where castings are mass produced, the patterns, even though expensive, can be used over and over again, and have little effect on the unit cost. But for the boatbuilder who needs "one of these" and "four of those," it is another matter. Professional patternmakers are highly skilled woodworkers, and their hourly rate often reflects the extensive and complicated work usually needed in an industrial product. Yet the patterns required for a boat's hardware are usually very basic and straightforward, requiring few of the higher skills of the patternmaker.

Finally, the cost of professionally made patterns is high because there is a great demand for pattern work, and there simply are not many skilled patternmakers around. Let's face it, have you ever actually seen a patternmaker? So why not eliminate him and do the work yourself? With a basic understanding of sand-

casting methods and a few key patternmaking principles, the boatbuilder can produce his own patterns, cut the cost of custom hardware, and provide the boat with a unique touch to set off the finest kind of workmanship in wood.

To start your thinking right, remember that a pattern is not a mold, or a negative shape of what you want. It is a positive form — usually of wood — from which a mold is made. The molder packs green sand (which becomes the mold) around the pattern, and when he removes the pattern, an impression remains that will receive the molten metal. Molds are usually made of a top or "cope" half, and a bottom or "drag" half. If possible, very simple work is cast entirely in the drag, and the cope is merely a top to close off the mold. Often the patternmaker constructs his pattern in two pieces, with each half making an impression in both the cope and the drag respectively.

Another approach to molding involves an interlocked mold. In this method, an uncommon one in most high-production industries, one produces green-sand projections from the cope half of the mold. These projections extend down into impressions in the drag half — a technique requiring much more time and skill on the part of the molder. Marine hardware, often quite organic and sculptural in shape, tends to be best suited to the interlocking-mold technique. This method is called "coping down" and will be discussed later.

While the green sand does not harden during the casting process, it does pack like wet snow due to the clay content (in natural sand), or an oil-base binder (in man-made sand). Green sand will pick up an amazing

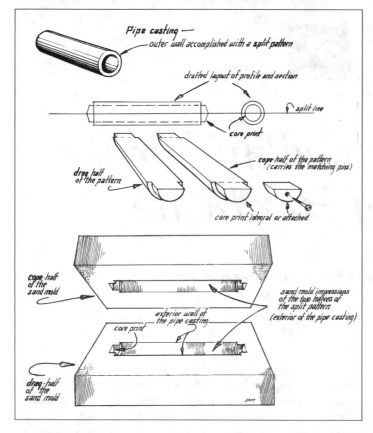

Pipe casting —
— outer wall accomplished with a split pattern

drafted layout of profile and section

split line

core print

drag half of the pattern

cope half of the pattern (carries the matching pins)

core print integral or attached

cope half of the sand mold

exterior wall of the pipe casting

core print

sand mold impressions of the two halves of the split pattern (exterior of the pipe casting)

drag half of the sand mold

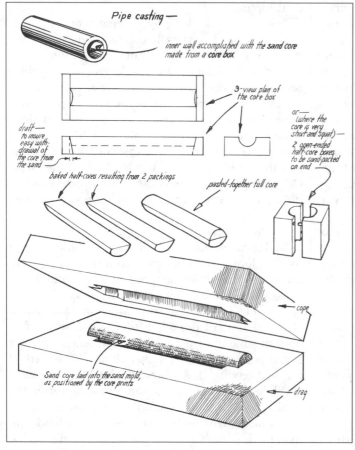

Pipe casting —

inner wall accomplished with the sand core made from a core box

draft — to insure easy withdrawal of the core from the sand

3-view plan of the core box

or — (where the core is very short and squat) — 2 open-ended half-core boxes to be sand-packed on end

baked half-cores resulting from 2 packings

pasted-together full core

cope

drag

Sand core laid into the sand mold, as positioned by the core prints

amount of detail. Packed around the pattern in a flask, it will retain the impression of the pattern even in the cope, which must be inverted over the drag. The rush of hot metal will not disturb a properly made mold, but when cool, the sand easily crumbles away from the casting to be used again.

Flatbacks

To cast an object entirely in the drag as a flatback, the molder places the pattern on a bottom board with the drag flask around it, packing sand around the pattern until the flask is filled. The flask is then inverted, and the pattern withdrawn. If the patternmaker constructed the pattern correctly, it can be removed easily from the sand. This means that all vertical sides of the pattern must be drafted (inclined) away from the surface of the mold from which it will be removed in order to eliminate the drag of sand on wood. Removal can also be facilitated by the use of rapping plates (or draw straps on larger jobs), which the molder taps to loosen the pattern from the sand. Finally, he places a solid cope on top to close off the mold.

If the pattern is complex, it is usually constructed in two halves with flat mating surfaces. The drag half of the pattern is molded as a flatback, but instead of being removed when the flask is inverted, the cope flask is set on top of the drag flask, the cope half of the interlocking pattern is positioned on the drag half, and the cope is packed with sand. (Parting sand dusted on the drag allows the cope to be packed in place yet not stick to the drag sand.) After lifting the cope away from the drag, the pattern halves are removed and the molder makes a gate for the molten metal to run into the resulting impression. Finally, he replaces the cope mold over the drag mold.

Coring

Up to this point, the patternmaker's job is relatively easy. It is one thing to cast a solid object; it is another matter to cast something that is hollow, has openings through it, or has projections that would undercut the sand and prevent the removal of the pattern from the mold. A core will solve this problem.

When coring, the molder rams up the flatback or split pattern as described. When the pattern has been removed but before the two flask halves have been reunited, sand — which will exclude metal from those parts that must be left open or hollow — is put into the impression of the mold. Though it sounds implausible, this procedure is very straightforward.

Take, for example, a section of cast bronze pipe. Though the pipe is hollow, the pattern-maker will construct a solid, split pattern. At either end, he will attach projections that are the same diameter as the inside of the pipe. These additions to the pattern are called core prints, and are not cast. The prints that they leave in the sand locate the position of the core in the mold, and this core will form the inside of the casting. The core is formed in a core box, which is just a wooden mold of a half cylinder. The diameter of the cylinder equals the diameter of the pattern's core prints (which is in turn the diameter of the inside of the pipe). The length of the core equals the length of the pattern plus the core prints.

The core box is packed with core sand, which is scraped off evenly, and the contents are turned out onto a steel oven plate. Two of these halves are baked hard and then pasted together to form the complete core. This is placed in the impression left by the pattern in the drag, fitted snugly into the two prints. When the cope mold is placed on top, its prints locate over the core. The mold will now yield a hollow pipe. (If the core is not too long, two open-ended half-core boxes can be made and located together. The complete core is then rammed up standing on end. When the two halves of the box are pulled away, the entire core is left standing on the oven sheet, and no pasting will be needed.)

Coring can solve another problem. Occasionally a pattern with protruding parts cannot be withdrawn from the mold without the addition of a core print, which creates a void between the protrusion and the sand surface. After the pattern is taken from the mold, a core is inserted into the print, eliminating the unwanted void.

Coping Down

One can often resort to the "coping down" method of casting for most projections and surfaces that would otherwise undercut the sand in the mold. Coping down simplifies the patternmaker's job, but requires slightly more work for the molder. Instead of adding a core print, the projection is left as is and the pattern (or drag half pattern) is rammed up.

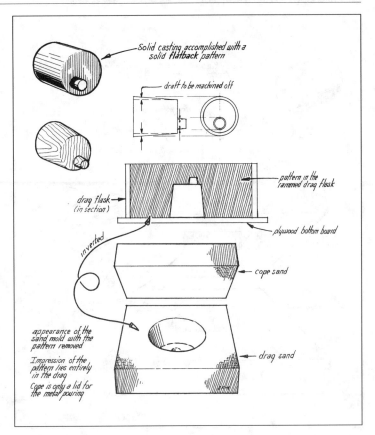

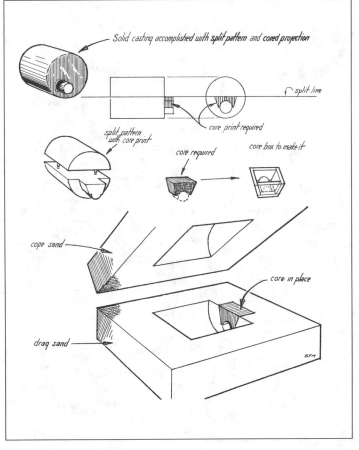

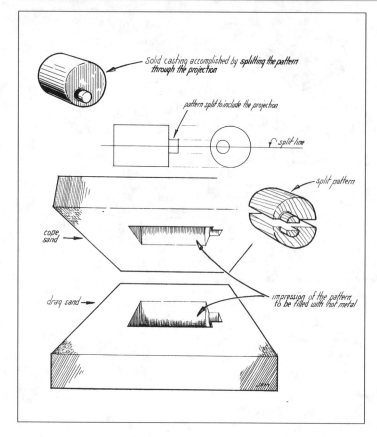

Solid casting accomplished by **splitting the pattern** *through the projection*

pattern split to include the projection

split line

split pattern

cope sand

drag sand

impression of the pattern to be filled with hot metal

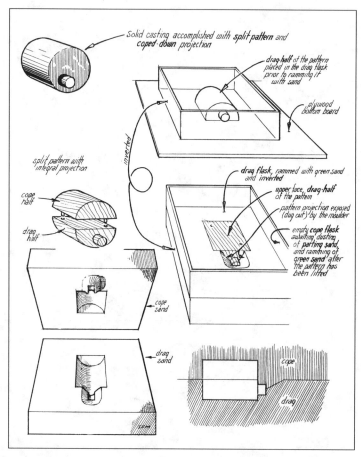

Solid casting accomplished with **split pattern** and **coped-down** projection

drag-half of the pattern placed in the drag flask prior to ramming it with sand

plywood bottom board

split pattern with integral projection

inverted

cope half

drag half

drag flask, rammed with green sand and inverted

upper face, **drag-half** of the pattern

pattern projection exposed (dug cut) by the moulder

empty **cope flask** awaiting dusting of **parting sand**, and ramming of green sand after the pattern has been lifted

cope sand

drag sand

cope

drag

When the mold is inverted, the molder digs down to the undercut, exposing the offending part or surface, and slopes the sand away from its edges in all directions. When the cope half is rammed up, sand will pack down into the depression and take the shape of the exposed area. The sand comes out with the cope when it is removed, and since the undercut is now exposed, the pattern can be withdrawn. Back in place, the cope extends down into and defines part of the shape of the casting in the drag.

Planning a Pattern

It is critical to understand the concepts and practices of coring and coping down. At the design stage the boatbuilder can alert himself to what is or is not possible, and how to correct a problem. This is simply done by picturing the pattern in the mold, and imagining what steps the molder would take to remove it. The form of the pattern will almost always follow naturally.

As an exercise, pick out a few cast objects around you: a tool, a tiller-head fitting, a through-hull fitting, or a machine part. Try to imagine how the patterns, core prints, cores, and core boxes must look. Where are the prints located on the pattern? Was the pattern a flatback or split, and if split, where? Is there a projection or surface that needed to be cored? Often split lines are not completely ground off castings; they provide clues to the method used to mold the piece.

To construct the pattern, begin with a full-size, three-view layout of the piece, similar to a lofting. Since metal shrinks when it cools, the pattern must be made slightly larger than the casting. To account for the shrinkage, lay out the drawing with a so-called shrink rule (available from a pattern supply house), whose increments include the shrinkage factor of the particular metal used.

Shrinkage is expressed as a fraction of an inch per foot. Manganese bronze, for example, has a shrinkage factor of $3/16$ inch to $1/4$ inch per foot. In the absence of a shrink rule, rough calculations may be used. It is always prudent to check with the foundry for the expected shrinkage factor.

Building a Pattern

Next, decide if the piece can be a flatback, has to be coped down, or must be split. Since there are often a number of ways a pattern can be split or oriented in the mold, it is also wise for the amateur to discuss this with the foundry. If the pattern is to be split, the split line must be established on the layout. Draft is added rather than subtracted, so one ends up with a little extra metal that can be machined off if necessary.

"Finish" (extra metal) must be added to the layout on all surfaces that will be bored, turned, sanded, or otherwise machined. An allowance of 1/16 inch to 1/4 inch (in the case of very large castings) is usually plenty. This extra finish as well as the draft is often drawn on the layout with colored pencils to prevent confusion.

Finally, if the pattern is cored, the core prints are laid out. Usually the drawing is a superposition of the inside and the outside of the casting, which translates into the core box and the pattern respectively. Core prints then are drawn with the same line for both the core box and the pattern. Remember, the core should fit exactly into the prints of the pattern.

To ensure dimensional stability and workability, only certain kinds of lumber should be used for making a pattern. Clear white pine, white cedar, Spanish cedar, whitewood, or cypress are excellent choices. When a very tough wood is needed, cherry is best because it is quite stable, but maple or birch may be used for small patterns. Honduras mahogany is the very best all-around pattern lumber, a fact that should warm the heart of the boatbuilder-turned-patternmaker.

The simplest pattern to make is a flatback or coped-down pattern with no coring. For a small casting, such as a chock for example, a block of lumber (glued up if necessary) is gotten out, and carved or machined to the desired shape. It is helpful to profile the finished shape on the block and alternately work in from each plane as was done with the bow chock patterns in Photo 1. Sometimes templates are useful on a very shapely piece. A patternmaker usually works out from the centerlines, since running dimensions from one edge to another are difficult to keep track of on an odd shape, or when various planes are drafted. If the pattern is complicated, make up parts of it separately and fasten them together. Don't forget the draft. A larger pattern that would use a great deal of lumber or would move too much with humidity changes can be built up skin-on-frame.

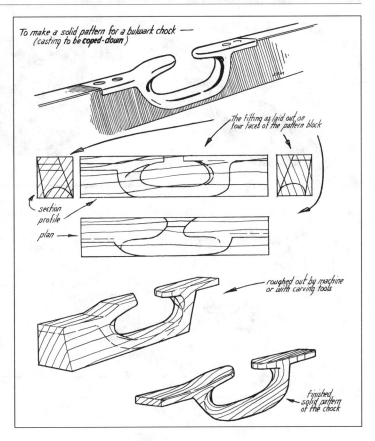

To make a solid pattern for a bulwark chock — (casting to be **coped-down**)

The fitting as laid out on four faces of the pattern block

section profile

plan

roughed out by machine or with carving tools

finished solid pattern of the chock

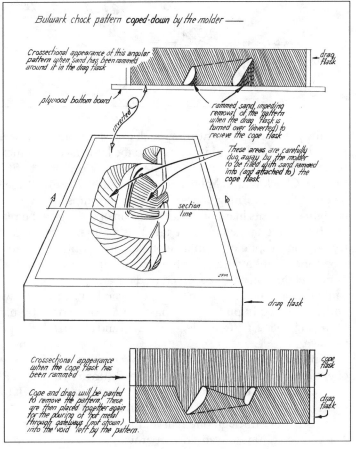

Bulwark chock pattern **coped-down** by the molder —

Crossectional appearance of this angular pattern when sand has been rammed around it in the drag flask

drag flask

plywood bottom board

rammed sand impeding removal of the pattern when the drag flask is turned over (inverted) to recieve the cope flask

These areas are carefully dug away by the molder to be filled with sand rammed into (and **attached to**) the cope flask

inverted

section line

A   B

drag flask

Crossectional appearance when the cope flask has been rammed

cope flask

Cope and drag will be parted to remove the pattern. These are then placed together again for the pouring of hot metal through gateways (not shown) into the void left by the pattern.

drag flask

1

2

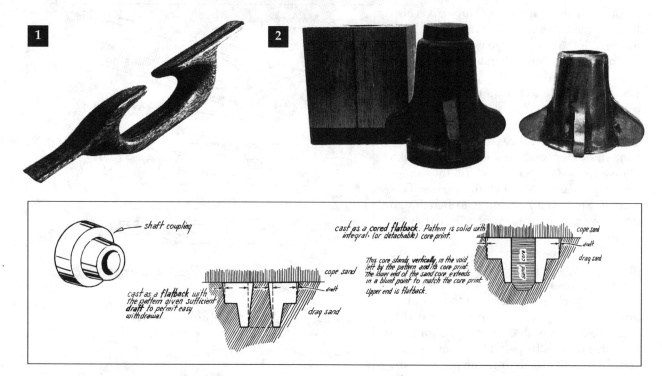

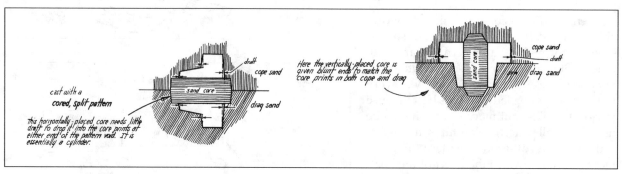

If the pattern can be a turning, such as a shaft coupling, the block of wood is screwed to the lathe faceplate and worked down to shape like any other turning. Check with calipers and a rule to match the layout. Often a turning is best glued up in four, six, or eight segments like a pie, with the grain of the segments running tangent to the edge. This maintains a true round in spite of shrinkage or expansion of the wood and also allows easier cutting on the lathe. Arms or projections can be glued or screwed on, and pieces can be cut in and shaped in place, or even built up with wax or body putty. The tangs on the bowsprit fitting in Photo 2, for example, were cut in and shaped in place.

A split pattern is worked in the same way as a solid one, but the initial block of material is made up in two separate pieces. These are temporarily screwed together, and two or three ¼ inch or 5⁄16 inch holes are bored squarely through one half and into the other. The pieces are unscrewed and separated, and short dowels are glued into the holes of one half with about ¼ inch to 3⁄8 inch protruding. Sanded slightly smaller to fit easily into the matching holes of the other half, these locate the two pattern halves together. The half without the pins will be the drag half, since it must be placed flat on its mating surface for the first stage of ramming up.

For a longer-lasting pattern, male and female brass dowel pins can be obtained from a pattern supply house. Once the pins are in and the two halves are screwed back together again, the block is squared, and by using the split line as the centerline of the piece, the pattern is cut out and worked down. When finished, the screws are removed, their holes filled or bunged, and a perfectly aligned, split pattern results (see Photo 5).

If the pattern requires additional pieces, attach them the same way as to a flatback. However, if the addition falls on the parting line, you must also split the added piece. To do this, two matching shapes are

made, each one-half the desired thickness of the whole. Working on a flat surface, the drag half pattern and additional piece are laid down and slid together, positioned, or cut in together correctly, and fastened. The cope half pattern is then aligned with the drag half, and using the added piece on the drag half as a guide, the cope half of the added piece is fastened in place (only to the cope) exactly flush and aligned with the drag half. Thus, the parting line of the pattern is continued through the added portion (see Photo 3).

If the split pattern is symmetrical, it can be turned before added pieces are attached. The two halves are temporarily screwed together, the parting line is located between the centers of the lathe, the piece is turned, and the resulting pattern splits right down the middle. Sometimes it is possible to locate the screws in waste wood at either end of the piece, so when the waste is cut off after turning, there will be no need to fill screw holes in the pattern. Turned and split added pieces are also made this way before they are positioned and fastened to their respective pattern halves.

Cored patterns require slightly more work. If a pattern is to be cored, hollow or pierced, the split pattern is made as before but with core prints added. Sometimes the pattern is made and separate pieces are added to it to form core prints. Often it works out that the prints are cut or turned from the same piece of wood (see Photo 3). A core box is then made to correspond to the inside of the casting plus the core prints on the pattern. In this type of work, the cores that are most often encountered are straight or tapered cylinders (see Photo 4). If short and squat, the core boxes may be glued in segments, screwed to the faceplate, and inside turned. If long and narrow, they must be carved out, a job facilitated by a patternmaker's core plane (unfortunately, a rare item).

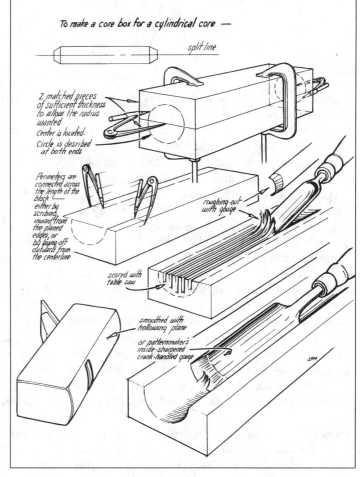

To make a core box for a cylindrical core —

split line

2 matched pieces of sufficient thickness to allow the radius wanted

Center is located. Circle is desribed at both ends

Perimeters are connected across the length of the block — either by scribing inward from the planed edges, or by laying off outward from the centerline

roughing-out with gouge

scored with table saw

smoothed with hollowing plane

or patternmaker's inside-sharpened crank-handled gouge

SFM

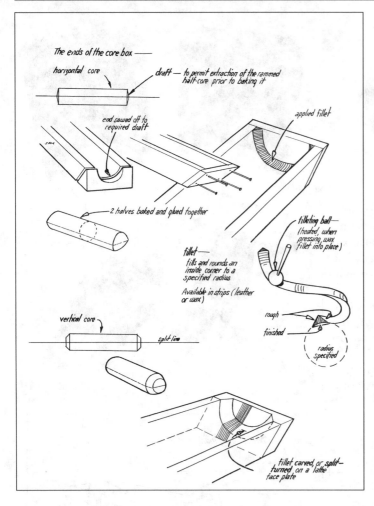

the hot casting cools (and shrinks) in the mold. Castings can crack along sharp concave corners when shrinking; a generous fillet prevents this, as well as provides for neat, strong hardware. Corners are filled with either wood, leather, or wax fillets.

In section, a fillet appears three-sided; two sides are straight and the third is concave at a specific radius and tangent to the other two sides. Generally, large fillets of one inch or more are made of wood and glued in place. Smaller ones can be made of leather, which is soaked in water to allow it to conform better to the curves of a pattern, glued, and then rubbed into place with the corresponding filleting ball. Pre-formed wax fillets are available from pattern supply houses, but beeswax, softened with a little heat and rolled into strings, can be worked into corners with a heated filleting ball. In many cases fillets can be carved right into the wood itself, or turned in place when lathe work is required. Fillets from ⅛ inch to ½ inch are as big as we need for the patterns discussed here.

The completed pattern and boxes are painted to seal the wood and to provide extra durability to the surfaces. Paint the core prints a contrasting color to alert the molder to the presence of a pattern that will require cores. Also, the shape of the core is painted in a contrasting color on the mating surface of the drag half pattern, so the molder knows which is to be used and in which way (see Photo 3). Though you can use a lacquer-base paint to finish the pattern, a more beautiful and traditional finish is clear orange shellac. (Add lampblack to the shellac for the contrasting color.) The quick-drying properties as well as the hard finish of the shellac make it ideal for pattern work.

As mentioned before, sometimes it is possible and desirable to make two open-ended half boxes so the core can be rammed up on end in one piece (see Photo 4). To make a box like this, two blocks are located together with dowel pins in the manner of a split pattern, squared, and marked out. The halves are separated and work proceeds as above.

Variations in a finished casting are not terribly important. The integral tolerance as far as a patternmaker is concerned is the relationship between the core box and the pattern core prints. A large pattern and core box may shrink or expand substantially, and corresponding parts should match closely. If the grain in the pattern runs longitudinally, the grain in the core box should also run that way in order for both pieces to shrink and swell in the same manner.

Patterns are fastened together with screws, nails, and glue (either hot or white), but remember that you may have to undo your work some day because of a design change; use fastenings and adhesives judiciously!

Usually both convex and concave corners on a pattern are rounded to specific radii. This not only makes a stronger casting but also helps stop cracking when

Tools

Most boatbuilders have in their kit a complete selection of tools that would enable them to practice pattern work. However, there are a few that have been developed specifically as patternmaking tools.

Crank-handled chisel and gouges, inside-sharpened, are used for paring and working flat in the center of a large area. Crank-handled inside-sharpened gouges also permit the occasional carving of fillets directly on the pattern. Being inside sharpened, their dimensioned radius is outside, producing the specified fillet. Once you have used one of these patternmaker's gouges, you will wonder how you have ever lived without a complete set of them. They will do anything a straight-handled gouge will do and much more. The only thing you can't do is hammer on them. (As an old English modelmaker I worked with used to say: "Only bad boys strike their bent chisels.")

A pattern hammer has a narrow head somewhat like an upholsterer's hammer (a good substitute) and is useful for driving brads in difficult spots. The filleting tools already mentioned have a thin shaft for a handle, with a steel ball on the end that corresponds to a given fillet radius. (I have used the ball on the end of a caliper's screw adjuster in a pinch.) Boatbuilders usually have a full set of cove and barrel planes and will have no problem in that department.

Finishing the Casting

With your pattern and core boxes completed, deliver them to the foundryman, who will take it from there. The finished casting will have a rough texture from the sand mold. It can either be brought up to polish at the foundry or by yourself. Grinding and sanding heads of various grits can be obtained through the foundry and used on a bench grinder to bring the surface up to the texture where a buffing wheel and rouge will finish the job. Stop short of this if the casting is to have a matte or brushed finish, or is to be painted.

Finding a Foundry

You should be aware that most foundries specialize in either ferrous or nonferrous metals. The one most suited for your purposes will be a small, one- to ten-man operation that does not mind the small or one-off job. This type of foundry is usually more skilled at difficult molding work and will be more helpful with hints on coring and pattern construction. The best place to track down this type of operation is at a local machine shop, since they will have dealt with most of the foundries in the area. Unless you have your own facilities for metalworking, this shop will do any necessary machining for you.

Special thanks to master patternmaker Roland Boucher.

Glossary

Back draft—Reverse draft that will lock a pattern in the sand mold.

Bottom board—Large board, usually plywood, on which drag flasks are rammed up.

Chaplet—Thin metal strip bent into an upright Z. It is placed in a mold to hold up a core or part of a core when there is no core print. It becomes part of the casting, which usually is no problem.

Cope—The top half of a pattern, core box, or mold.

Core—The hard-baked sand that is used to form the inside of a hollow or undercut pattern.

Core box—The mold in which the core is made.

Core print—Projection on a pattern that makes a void (also called a core print) that will cradle the core in the mold.

Core sand—Sand with a special binder that permits the sand to be baked hard.

Draft—Taper on all vertical sides of a pattern or core box.

Dowel pins—Pins that consist of a male and female half, each threaded on one end. These are screwed into corresponding holes in both halves of the pattern for locating one half to the other.

Drag—Bottom half of a pattern, core box, or mold.

Flask—Four-sided box, metal or wood, in which the pattern is rammed up. It consists of interlocking cope and drag halves.

Gate—Opening through which metal is poured in a mold.

Green sand—Sand in which a pattern is rammed up to form a mold.

Ram, ram up—To pack sand into a core box or flask, and around a pattern.

Rapping plate—Metal plate let into the flat of a pattern and screwed in place. It is rapped by the molder to loosen the pattern in the mold and has a threaded hole which can be hooked to help withdraw the pattern from the sand (available from a pattern supply house).

Pattern Supply Houses
The Kindt-Collins Company
12651 Elmwood Ave.
Cleveland, OH 44111
413–739–9666

Freeman Manufacturing Company
1246 West 70th St.
Cleveland, OH 44102
216–961–4200

A Simple Wooden Plane

by David C. "Bud" McIntosh
Drawings by Samuel F. Manning

Billy Simms

Although most professional boatbuilders use wooden planes to a great extent, probably most amateurs use them almost not at all. This fact is sometimes taken as a sign that the pro is eccentric, parsimonious, and of a weak mind, which he probably is — but his use of wooden planes is not the best evidence you can present. In fact, wooden planes in boat work have a lot of advantages over metal ones. This is particularly true on the biggest planing job of all — smoothing the hull. And if you have a grinder and another plane, you can shape the blade and the bottom to fit any surface on the boat. Of course, the thing to do is to collect half a dozen wooden planes or more, of various lengths, weights, widths, and curvatures. But the best way to get them is to make them, which is fairly easy to do in the simplified form I will describe here.

The traditional type of wooden plane, as you probably know, is made from a solid block of hardwood. The cutter is held in place with a wedge, which fits into tapered channels cut into the wood of the sides. The blade may or may not have a chip breaker (it's known as a "double iron" if it has one) and is at least twice as thick at the cutting end as the blade in your iron plane. The smoother plane usually has no handle. If the workmanship is perfect — if the wedge and the passageway for the chips is shaped exactly right, smoothed to a high polish — then this plane is a good one, not subject to the usual amateur criticism that you have to spend half the time setting the blade to the right depth and the rest of the time trying to dig out the jammed shavings.

I have seen planes of this type that are works of art, and I have even made some myself that were

Smoother (with handle)

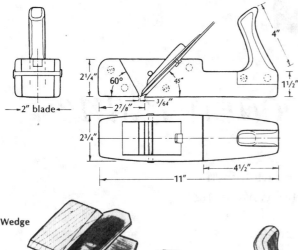

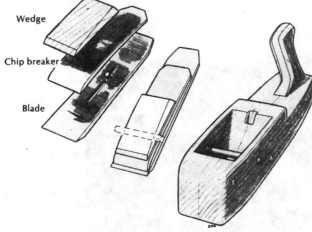

Wedge

Chip breaker

Blade

Round-bottomed hollowing plane

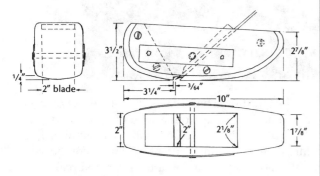

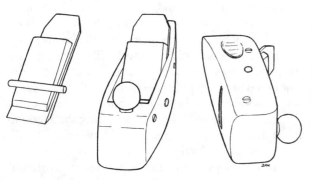

satisfactory, but the job of making one requires too much time and patience to suit me. The type I have developed for my own use (and for which I claim no originality, by the way) is very easy to make, and so far as I can see has all the virtues and none of the faults of the usual type.

Materials

Almost any hard, dense, tough, and heavy wood can be used for the plane. The old boatbuilders like to use a block of lignum vitae, rosewood, ebony, or other rare and costly tropical wood for their pet plane, but beech, hard maple, locust, live oak, dense white oak, walnut, and elm do very well. The harder the wood the less it wears away and the easier it slides, but excellence of material is not so important in a plane that you can make in just a couple of hours.

The cutter is more of a problem. Years ago, every hardware store, particularly in shipbuilding districts, had an assortment of single and double "irons" on hand especially made for wooden planes. For some reason unknown, the shops that made these blades were always run by brothers, and for some other reason the blades were better than any you can get nowadays except from the same makers — and any who have survived are now probably making power lawn mowers. Try the oldest hardware store in town; ask them to show you Buck Brothers' catalog. Junk shops are another possibility; but beware of a used blade unless you test it for hardness, as someone may have burned the temper out in grinding it.

Most boatbuilders prefer a double iron for all-around use in a smoother. The chip breaker, set as close as possible to the cutting edge, is especially valuable on irregular grain and absolutely necessary on such wood as dark-figured Philippine mahogany, because it (in combination with a very small throat opening, of which more later) prevents the contrary grain from picking up. A single iron cuts somewhat more easily, however, and is the type to use in a rounded hollowing plane.

As for size: a blade width of 1¾ or 2 inches is most common for a smoother or a hollowing plane. It's worth remembering that a narrow, round-bottomed plane with a fairly low-angled blade and large throat opening, used across the grain, is almost as good as an adze for removing a lot of excess wood quickly and easily — tapering an oak rudder, working down deck blocking, and fitting the ends of floor timbers, for instance.

The only other materials required are a few wood screws and a piece of rod — brass, iron, or what have you — as long as the plane is wide. You'll need a sharp, preferably fine-toothed, crosscut saw, ½- and ¾-inch (or larger) chisels, an adjustable trisquare, a rasp, and a flat file, and a good plane, sharp enough to shave with. I confess with embarrassment that I always use one of Mr. Stanley's excellent steel jointers in plane-making, as in most other benchwork.

Making the Body

This style of wooden plane is made in two pieces, to simplify cutting the opening for the blade and the wedge. The first step, then, is to get out a piece of stock twice as long and half as wide as the finished plane. The plane shown in the drawings is made from a piece of 1⅜-inch by 2¼-inch by 22-inch stock.

Cut the piece in two, joint off and square the inside and bottom surfaces, and mark for the cuts on the inside of one half. This must be done with some care. With your trisquare at a 45-degree angle from the bottom of the piece, mark for the back of the blade. Place the blade on edge against this line, and mark the intersection of the forward face of the blade with the line of the bottom. From this point, mark the forward end of the opening — at an angle of about 30 degrees with the vertical. These marks allow for no throat opening. Now square across on the top and the bottom, and mark lengthwise for the depth of cut — 1 inch from the centerline for a 2-inch iron, of course.

Before cutting, clamp the other half to the marked piece, and extend the top and bottom marks to it. Take the pieces apart again, and proceed to cut the two notches with your saw. Be very careful to cut exactly square on the end marks, especially on the bottom of the plane, and still allowing for no throat opening. It is safer to file this opening after the assembled plane has been trued up and otherwise completed, including the wedging. Now make two or three more saw cuts to the correct depth between the end cuts, and split out the pieces with your chisels.

The next step is to fasten the halves together. You can use through-dowels and resin glue, blind dowels with fox-wedges, copper rivets, or plain flathead wood screws. (I prefer the screws.) For the plane shown in the drawing, use 2-inch No. 12 steel or bronze screws, with the heads set in ⅜ inch, located as shown — two driven from each side. True up the sides of the opening so the blade is a close fit at the bottom and can swing about 1⁄16 inch each way at the top, and the plane is ready for the fitting of the wedge and the handle.

It is probably best to make the wedge before boring for the through-bar that holds it against the blade. The wedge will, of course, be the same width as the blade and is usually made from the same type of wood as the rest of the plane. Shape it with a very slight

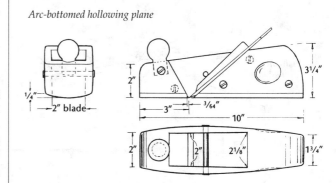

Arc-bottomed hollowing plane

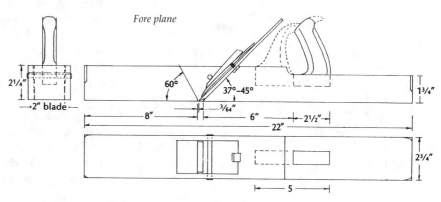

Fore plane

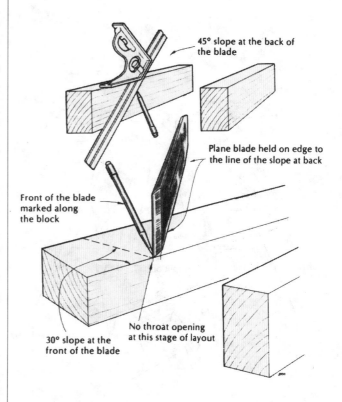

45° slope at the back of the blade

Plane blade held on edge to the line of the slope at back

Front of the blade marked along the block

30° slope at the front of the blade

No throat opening at this stage of layout

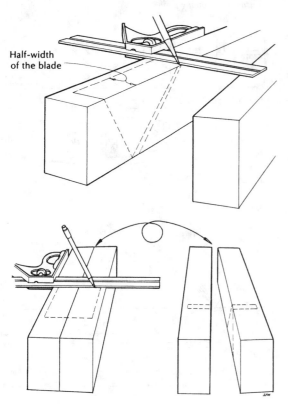

Half-width
of the blade

Marks squared across to the other block

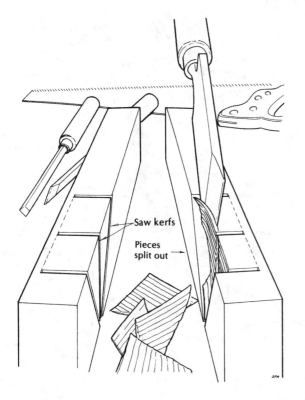

Saw kerfs

Pieces
split out

hollow (lengthwise) on the under surface. The angle should be about 8 degrees.

Lay the blade in place, hold the wedge in position, and mark where the upper surface fits against the sides of the plane. The wedge should be about 5/16 inch thick where it hits the bar. You will probably have to cut off the point to get it down to the proper position.

Now locate and bore the 5/16-inch hole for the bar. Insert a piece of rod of the same size, cut it so the ends are flush with the outside of the plane, and spread the ends with a ball-peen hammer just enough to hold it in place.

Finish off the bottom of the plane fair, flat, and smooth. The final finishing can be done by rubbing the plane over a piece of sandpaper laid on a true surface, such as a machined saw table.

The size of the throat opening, which is adjusted next, is important. If the opening is too large, the plane will tear up the surface of the wood you are working on. If it is too small, it will not allow fast work on soft wood. File or pare the wood with a very sharp chisel to provide a plumb face about 3/64 inch ahead of the cutting edge. An opening of this size ought to give good all-around performance. While you have your hand in, though, it would be a good idea to make another plane to take the same iron but with a throat opening of half the size — and then enlarge the first one to 1/16 inch or even more, for rough work.

If you want to do without the handle, the plane is now ready for use except for tapering the ends slightly and adding another pair of screws in the after end. But unless you are used to this simple block form, you will probably find the handle a worthwhile addition. The drawing gives dimensions for cutting off the top of the block behind the blade. Cut a slot 7/8 inch wide, 2 1/2 inches long, at the back end. Make the handle with the grain running lengthwise, fit it to the slot, and through-fasten from side to side with 2 1/4-inch screws or copper rivets. Let the heads in, of course. Shape and smooth the handle to suit, and chamfer or round off all the corners.

A nice touch is to simmer the plane body for an hour or so in paraffin carefully heated slightly above the boiling point of water. This will effectively get rid of all moisture in the wood, and give it a built-in lubricating system.

Once you get used to it, adjusting the blade in a wooden plane is as easy, quick, and accurate as in any other. It's all done by tapping — with a light hammer or a mallet — and doing it gently. Hold the plane upside down, front toward your eye, and sight along the bottom to see where the cutting edge is. Tap down on the nose to retract the blade or to remove the blade and wedge. Tap on the front end, low down, or on the upper end of the blade, to get a thicker shaving. And,

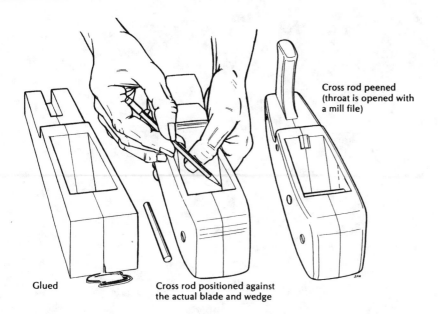

Cross rod peened (throat is opened with a mill file)

Glued

Cross rod positioned against the actual blade and wedge

of course, tap the wedge in, but not hard, to keep the blade where you want it.

Use a fine carborundum stone, with kerosene on it, for sharpening the iron. It will seldom need grinding, but when it does, keep the iron cool, and keep it square across. Whet the corners back a bit for planing across the grain on such woods as oak and hard pine. And keep it sharp, even as does the pro, who never begrudges the time it takes to sharpen up, even when he's working for himself.

Making Planes

by James Curry

Whether we work with tools for the joy of creating or simply for the pleasure of handling them is a moot point. I have yet to meet anyone who uses tools well and does not have an interest in and a great respect for fine ones. I've spent many an hour browsing through hardware stores and tool catalogs, wondering when I would be able to afford this tool or that. The process of acquiring new tools never seems to end, but we have been conditioned to buy our tools rather than make them. If one needs this chisel or that screwdriver, the most natural course is to go out and buy it. This attitude is not entirely unreasonable since mass production once did make fine hand tools available at prices many could afford. This is not so any longer, for the introduction of cheap power tools has taken its toll, along with the decline of the woodworking trades. Toolmakers have dropped all but the high volume items from their lines, so the general handyman, and not the skilled craftsman, dictates what tools a manufacturer will produce. Mass production, which once brought us an abundance of quality hand tools, is steadily weeding out the quality and substituting plastic-wrapped junk in its place. Most of us may not be ready to forge our own steel, but making simple hand tools is beginning to look worthwhile.

One of the less obvious differences between the turn-of-the-century boatbuilder and come-latelys like

The author's homemade boatbuilder's plane (right), designed for use on curved surfaces, and a store-bought German-made Ulmia. Both planes use a 1¼-inch iron.

myself is that the old-timer made many of his own tools out of sheer necessity. Then as now, boatbuilding required a wide range of specialty tools, particularly hand planes, which no manufacturer could hope to cover. Obviously the great variety of boatbuilder's planes — smoothing, jack, joiner, spar, grub, rabbet, and rocker planes — had to be made by the men who used them. To be sure, a boatbuilder of yesteryear had a flourishing industry to grow in and probably had better materials to work with than those taking up wooden boat building today, but the most vital difference is that he actually made many of his tools with his own hands. It seems to me that the man who makes his own tools must be closer to the creative process

The cap iron must be ground to fit snugly against the blade, so that no chips can lodge between the two. Such obstacles will cause the plane to chatter and stall.

Below: The cap should be set close to the edge so the plane will pick up thin, uniform shavings, not slivers.

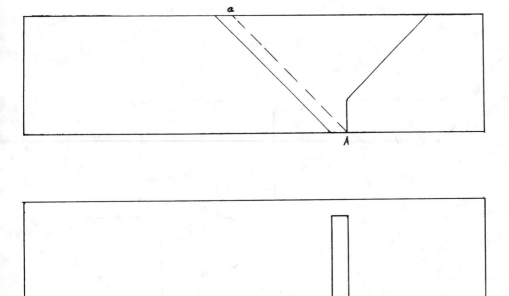

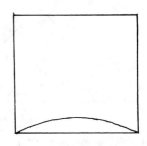

Spar Plane Layout 1: *Lay out the three views as if you were about to make a smooth plane. The body cavity is shown with a 45-degree iron angle (minus the iron and the chip). Draw the arc that will be the shape of the plane sole. Now, since the throat will move up and to the rear as the sole is shaped, project line A-a parallel to the slope of the iron. This is what the plane layout should look like for a spar plane. If you were making a grub plane, the process should be reversed to project a convex instead of a concave throat.*

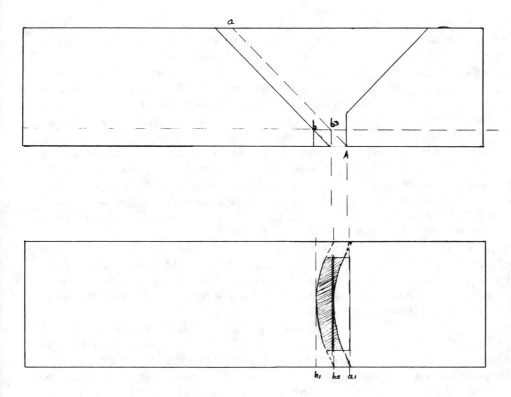

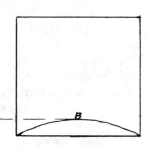

Spar Plane Layout 2: *Project line B-b. This is the top of the plane sole arc. Drop a perpendicular from b to b1. This determines the rear edge of the throat at the centerline of the sole. Perpendicular b3-b2 indicates where the rear edge of the throat intersects with the side of the plane. Actually, both front and rear edges of the throat are ellipses, but an arc drawn tangent to b-b1 and intersecting a b3-b2 is accurate enough to define the rear edge of the throat. The throat's front edge is defined by drawing an ellipse tangent to b3-b2 and intersecting the side of the plane at line A-a1. The two ellipses should be parallel. The side of the throat can be drawn in according to the iron width and will produce the shape defined by the shaded area on the drawing. This is what the throat should look like before you do any cutting.*

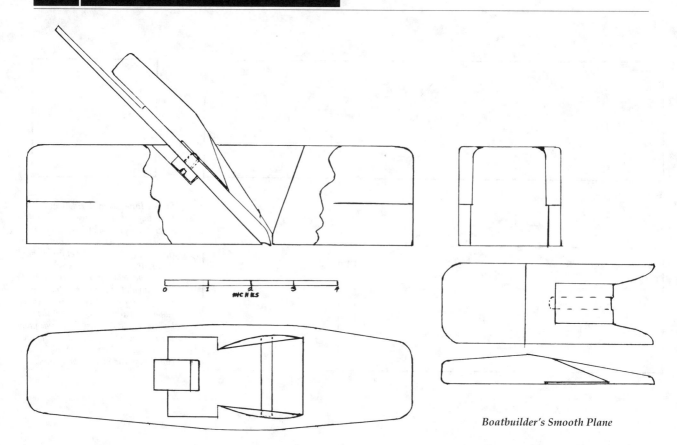

Boatbuilder's Smooth Plane

than one who orders by figure number from a catalog. Why this is so I just can't say, unless there is a confidence and sureness developed by making the very first link in the creative chain, the tool itself.

Why make wooden planes? For most of us there is no other way to come by those tools required in boatbuilding, and it is an experience worth enjoying for its own sake.

Ordinary carpenters' iron planes and their wooden counterparts are fine for bench work but practically worthless for fairing concave planking or any surface with the slightest reverse curve. The characteristic coffin shape of the boatbuilder's smoothing plane allows it to work into curves where the larger and more awkward carpenter's plane will not. I can well remember knocking myself out planing overhead on boat bottoms with a heavy iron plane and how much easier the job became with the proper tool. A smoothing plane is a basic boatbuilder's tool so I chose it for my first plane-making project.

Wood and Iron

The types of wood used in planemaking vary from the harder domestic types, such as beech (the most common wood in mass-produced planes), rock or sugar maple, and apple, to exotic hardwoods such as cocobolo, mesquite, lignum vitae, and rosewood. Live

oak is a desirable domestic wood for planemaking, but it is difficult to obtain as it is now protected by law in the states where it grows.

Generally, desirable woods are hard, dense, resistant to splitting and checking, and capable of being easily worked and taking a fine finish. Soft woods won't wear well and are too light in weight to make a good plane. To make a plane I used a piece of the worm shoe from an old catboat I was working on, because it was a very hard, dense wood. It had to be glued up so that the plane body could be finished to 9 inches long, 2¼ inches wide (tapered to 1¾ inches at the ends), and 2⅛ inches deep. This piece of wood, which may be greenheart, turned out to be a bad choice, since it is extremely brittle, is difficult to work, and checks quite badly. Even so, when sharp, this tool leaves a polished surface and pushes freely since the wood is oily, but I would not use this wood again.

A wooden plane should last a lifetime, and enough time goes into the making of one to warrant care in selection of the stock to be used. The local lumberyard probably won't have anything suitable for plane making, but small sawmills or lumber importers should be able to help.

Old planes had single irons; that is, irons without caps. ("Iron" is the traditional name for a plane blade.)

The cap is an improvement made in the last century and stabilizes the iron to prevent chatter and reduce gouging of the surface being planed. A double, or capped, iron should be used and can be obtained from mail-order specialty tool companies.

Plane sizes for boatbuilding were standardized a long time ago. Smoothing planes run about 8 or 9 inches long and use an iron of 1½ or 1¾ inches wide. Jack planes were 12 to 18 inches long and used a 1¾-inch or 2-inch iron. Joiner planes were as long as 24 inches.

Layout

With the wood and iron selected, the next step is layout of the plane body cavity, starting with the angle of the plane iron. An angle of 45 degrees is common for general use, with as much as 60 degrees used in a plane intended for smoothing very hard or curly grained wood. The wedge, or chip, which secures the iron in the plane body, usually has an angle of 10 degrees, since less angle would make it difficult to loosen, and more angle would allow it to loosen too easily. The throat must allow shavings to clear the cap without jamming.

The layout of the body should be done with the actual iron and cap to be used with the plane. The mouth (slot in the bottom or sole) is located about 40 percent of the length from the front of the plane, allowing room for the hands at each end. The plane body is at least ½ inch wider than the iron and usually 2 to 2¼ inches thick in the case of the average smooth plane. Once the profile is drawn in, the top and mouth can be squared across and drawn in.

Laying out a spar or a grub plane is different in that the mouth is an arc, not a straight line, until the plane sole is shaped: a spar plane is hollowed and a grub plane is rounded. The shape of the arc is found by projecting the depth of the hollow (or round) to the angle of the iron, then dropping to the sole and squaring across. A little study of the drawing shows how it is done. Do not try to convert a smooth plane to a spar or grub plane; it will only result in an incorrectly shaped mouth that will have to be shimmed.

The layout of the top of the plane is straightforward. Leave about ¼ inch on each side to act as a stop for the chip. The chip puts considerable pressure on this area, so poor wood selection, sloppy layout, or careless workmanship can result in a plane body that distorts or splits in a very short time.

Making the Plane

Once the layout is complete, the body cavity can be roughed out. Plane making requires precision workmanship from start to finish if the end result is to be a fine tool that will have many years of use. Anyone who starts making his first wooden plane in the

Plane bodies showing (front to rear) the body cavity laid out, the body cavity roughed out, and the finished body cavity.

Laying out the angle of the plane iron on the blank. The wooden plane body in background has a split at body cavity and has been repaired by riveting.

Plane layout in profile, top of body being laid out.

Roughing out the body cavity with a drill and a jig.

The body cavity begins to take shape.

A pad saw or a hacksaw blade is used to cut the slot for the iron.

A file is used to square the corners.

morning with the idea of using it that afternoon is going to be working too fast for accuracy. Begin by cutting in the mouth to a depth of about ¼ inch. The rough cut should be undersized; this is to prevent the sole from being broken out when cutting through from the top. The mouth can be enlarged to its final size later. Probably the most common mistake is to allow the mouth to become enlarged, although this can be repaired by gluing in a shim.

One of the easiest ways to rough out the body is to drill out the excess wood. A jig (or a good eye and a steady hand) and brad point or auger bits should be used here; twist drills tend to skid when started at an angle in wood. A jig should have an index mark to avoid drilling on the wrong side of the layout line (as I did — sharp-eyed readers will spot the hole drilled by mistake at the front of the body cavity). Different size chisels, saws, and files are used to finish shaping the inside of the body.

In finishing the body cavity it is most important to make all surfaces straight and all corners square, or the iron and chip will not seat properly. This is slow, painstaking work and requires the use of a small pad saw or hacksaw blades and a lot of file work in the corners. So much time goes into a wooden plane that it is simply not worth doing badly. The iron should be tried for fit from time to time, to make sure that it lies flat against the plane body.

Final exterior shaping is quickly done with chisel and plane. The notches at the corners are traditional and seem to have no function except to begin the rounding of the top corners for hand comfort. Jack and joiner planes usually had the body cut down in height behind the iron, affording easier control, and had a saw type hand grip mortised in place.

The only thing lacking at this point is the chip, which is made from the same wood as the body and shaped to fit snugly in the angled slot. It is relieved over the middle of the iron to allow shavings to clear and projects a convenient distance above the top of the plane body. I found that the wood I had used is so slippery that the iron would slide with the chip firmly in place until I scored the underside of the chip.

If the iron and chip fit, the plane is ready for use, although an overnight soaking in linseed oil is good protection for the wood. After final assembly, check to see if anything will obstruct the flow of shavings through the body cavity. It doesn't take much: protruding corners of the chip, for example, will stop a few shavings so that others will jam up behind them. A little extra time taken now will save a lot later on.

One useful accessory to the wooden plane is a plane hammer, used for adjustment and disassembly. Authentic plane hammers are rare these days, but a reasonable substitute can be made from a small ball-

or cross-peen hammer. I made one by grinding an 8-ounce ball-peen down to a screwdriver tip to fit the cap screw.

Adjustment

The adjustment of wooden planes is a little difficult to get used to, but comes with practice. There seem to be two schools of thought on the matter. One method involves tapping the front of the plane to set the iron deeper and tapping the back of the plane to back the iron out. The other method is to strike the end of the iron to set it deeper. Some wooden planes have metal or hardwood striking buttons set in the ends of the plane body. Any striking of the iron or plane body should be done with care; it is a good idea to shorten up on the hammer handle to reduce the impact. Once the iron has been set to the proper depth, a tap on the chip will wedge it in place. The chip can be loosened by twisting it sideways in the slot.

The iron should be hollow ground to an angle of 25 degrees or a little less and honed on a fine stone. The cap must be a perfect fit to the iron (which it rarely is without grinding), with the end $\frac{1}{32}$ inch or less from the cutting edge. A properly sharpened plane iron will take off transparent shavings and leave a smooth surface on the most ornery cross-grained wood.

Wooden planes are without limit as to size, shape, and use. As long as irons are available, they can be ground to any conceivable shape and a body made to suit. So, take out that choice piece of hardwood that was hidden away for a special project and start your own plane factory. If you can make your own tools, you've achieved an enviable level of resourcefulness.

The author's plane disassembled, showing the iron (with cap), the chip, and a plane hammer.

The plane hammer, made from an 8-ounce ball-peen, used to tighten cap screw.

A Locker for the Main Cabin

— by Aldren Watson —

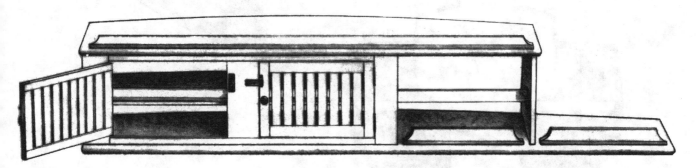

*B*ecause paper and pencil have always been two of my most indispensable woodworking tools, I used to harangue my son on the wisdom of using them before starting to cut up good lumber. He would listen attentively, never say much, and shortly depart for the shop. Then, remarkably, in less time than anyone could possibly scratch even a crude diagram on a scrap of wood, you'd hear the unmistakable sounds of sawdust and shavings in the making. Eventually, it dawned on me that it was his instinct for structural visualization that enabled him to launch into a project immediately at the workbench, without a preliminary stint at the drawing board.

All well and good. But regardless of your special endowments, when you entertain the idea of building a locker to go into a boat, it is essential to see ahead of time — and know that you see — what has to be done, and plan how to proceed to get it right. At first glance, a carpenter might think that a boat's cabin is nothing more or less than an arrangement of aberrant curves and slopes, with a roof that doesn't look right; a place where, in spite of its comfortable symmetry, a square and a straightedge would be of little use.

Not so, however. As a matter of fact, building a locker in a boat is probably an easier task than putting kitchen cabinets into an old house where everything has sagged and shifted out of level, plumb, and square.

Essentially, this port-side locker is a long, narrow box fitted to the hull and installed over the bunk. While it's only reasonable that anyone would be building a pair of lockers, these directions concern only a single locker. Further, it is doubtful that your requirements would be the same as those in our hypothetical example, a Concordia yawl. The principles of layout, fitting, design, and installation, however, can be applied to a wide variety of situations.

The locker's inboard face is straight and runs parallel with the boat's fore-and-aft centerline, while its outboard side is against the hull ceiling, which forms the back of the locker. Seen broadside, the top of the locker is parallel with the bottom rather than following the boat's sheer, and the whole locker is parallel with the boat's waterline and bunk tops.

Except for a few small parts, the locker is built entirely of ¾-inch pine. It has two compartments closed with slatted doors, an open bookcase section, and an open shelf with no top at the extreme forward end, as well as molded fiddles, top and bottom. For this type of work I like brass fastenings and a hardwood such as mahogany, cherry, or walnut for the doorknobs,

1 *looking aft*

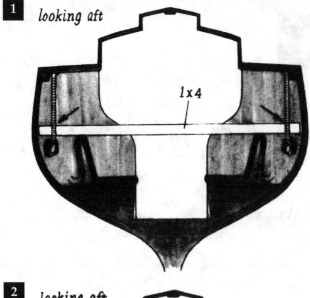

1 x 4

2 *looking aft*

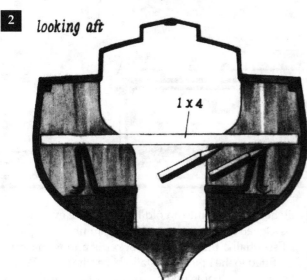

1 x 4

3 *looking aft*

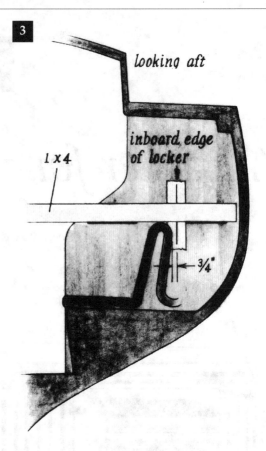

inboard edge of locker

1 x 4

3/4"

4 aft bulkhead

inboard edge of locker

1 x 4

turnbuttons, cleats, and possibly the fiddles. These woods stand up a little better here than pine, and they provide a nice color contrast to the brass and the rest of the woodwork.

The locker is fastened in place with integral cleats at its ends, through which screws are driven into the adjoining bulkheads, making removal a simple matter.

Basic Measurements: Aft

The first job is to take three basic measurements: to locate the level of the locker in relation to the top of the bunk; to find the position of the inboard edge of the locker; and to determine the height of the locker from top to bottom.

Lay a straight-edged 1 by 4 on edge across the bunk tops, flat against the aft bulkhead — which in this case is the end of the cabin having the least clearance under the sheer clamp and the deck beams (see Figure 1). Check the level of the straightedge athwartships by

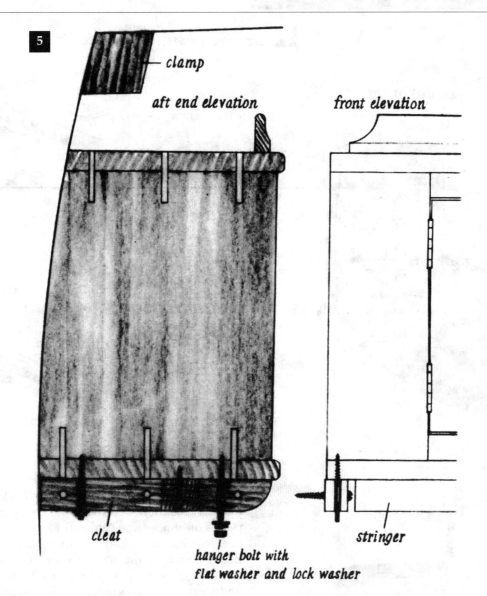

5

clamp

aft end elevation　　　*front elevation*

cleat　　　　　　　　　　　　　stringer

hanger bolt with
flat washer and lock washer

measuring from its top edge up to the deck beams on both the starboard and port sides. If the measurements are not identical, shim up the 1 by 4 until they are, then draw a pair of marks under it on the bulkhead (see Figure 2). These marks define the lower edge of the locker's bottom board.

Then locate the position of the locker's inboard edge (see Figure 3). Stick a piece of tape to the bulkhead, and draw a mark on it at a point ¾ inch outboard from the bunk top to allow some clearance.

The overall height of the locker will naturally be limited by the overhead construction of the particular boat. If there are air strakes, measure from the lower edge of the 1 by 4 to the air strake, and then deduct 1 inch (see Figure 4). This leaves part of the first ceiling plank as a lip above the locker to prevent losing small items into the frame bays. If there are no air strakes, lay out a full-sized diagram on paper to make your calculations. But note that for the locker described

here, the method of its installation on the cleats requires a minimum clearance of 2¼ inches from its top to the sheer clamp (see Figure 5).

Basic Measurements: Forward

Lay another 1 by 4, on edge across the bunks, this time against the forward bulkhead. Check its level by sighting it to over the tops of the aft 1 by 4, as well as by measuring up to the deck beams. It is also useful to sight on other fixed horizontals, such as the paneling of the bulkhead door. If the boat has been leveled athwartships, existing horizontals can be checked with a carpenter's level and compared with the 1 by 4s. Averaging all these checks may not be ideal, but it's important: the installed locker should look level even though the measurements and the instruments do not quite agree. Then use the same procedure as before to mark the level of the locker and its inboard edge. Remove the 1 by 4s.

8 *scribing square, approximate dimensions*

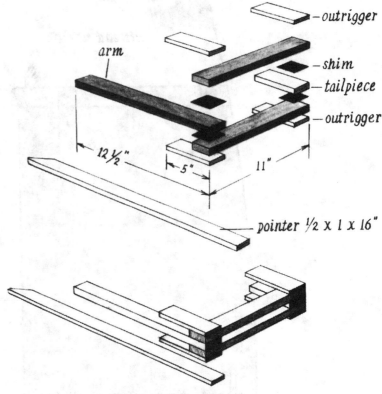

6

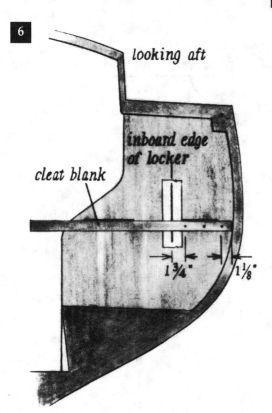

looking aft

inboard edge of locker

cleat blank

1¾"   1⅛"

arm

12½"   5"   11"

outrigger

shim
tailpiece

outrigger

pointer ½ x 1 x 16"

7

looking aft

inboard edge of locker

deadman

Clear Out the Cabin

You'll be making quite a few trips back and forth between the cabin and the workshop, lugging long pieces of lumber and other sticks in and out of the boat for trimming, trying, and fitting. To minimize the risk of damaging the interior woodwork and to have as much space as possible in which to move around and work, it is a good idea to take the swing-down bunks, stove, and table — anything that's conveniently removable and potentially in the way — out of the boat.

Cleat Blanks

After that, make a pair of hardwood blanks for the end cleats from 1-inch by 1¼-inch stock, long enough to reach inboard from the hull to a point a bit over the cabin sole. For now, all that's necessary is to joint their four sides, as they will be trimmed to length, their ends and corners rounded, and fastened to the bulkheads later on.

Clamp or have someone hold one of the blanks against the aft bulkhead, pushed out against the hull and aligned exactly under the pencil reference marks (see Figure 6). Hold it firmly so it cannot slip while you drill a ³⁄₃₂-inch pilot hole in the cleat blank 1⅛ inches in from the hull, another hole 1¾ inches outboard from the edge-of-locker mark, and a third hole halfway

principal parts of locker

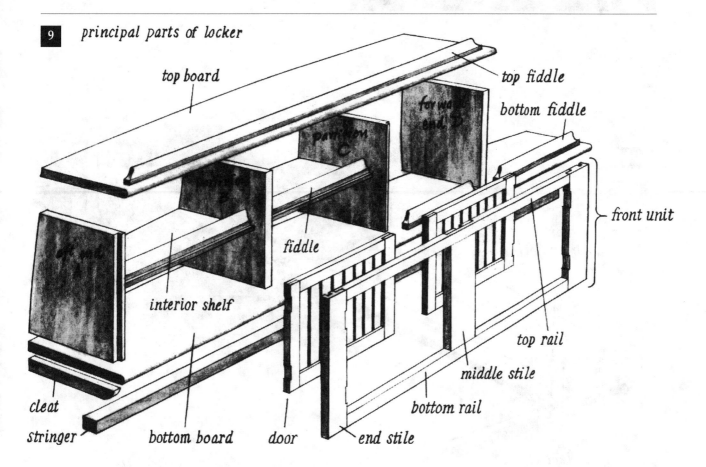

top board

top fiddle

bottom fiddle

forward end D

partition C

fiddle

front unit

interior shelf

top rail

middle stile

bottom rail

cleat

stringer

bottom board

door

end stile

between the two. Drill clear through the cleat blank and about ½ inch into the bulkhead. Locate these pilot holes carefully, as they will be used for final installation of the locker. Refer to Figure 5 for the location of these holes in relation to those for the hanger bolts that secure the locker to the cleats.

Remove the cleat blank and use a ³⁄₁₆-inch drill to enlarge the pilot holes (in the cleat blank only) to take 1½-inch No. 8 round-headed screws. Do not enlarge the holes in the bulkhead. Prepare the other cleat blank for the forward bulkhead the same way.

Then fasten the cleat blanks to the bulkheads with 1¼-inch No. 7 round-headed screws — two only in each blank. These smaller screws leave some untouched wood for the 1½-inch screws that will be used for the final installation.

At this point, it is important to mark the inboard edge of the locker on both cleat blanks for future reference. Leave the tapes on the bulkheads for now, however. Shore up each cleat blank with a 1-inch by 2-inch deadman resting on the sole and fastened at the top end with a single screw (see Figure 7). This stiffens the blanks and creates a solid fence on which all the subsequent work or measuring, scribing, fitting, and installation is carried out — a system that also eliminates much repetitive measuring and the chance of error.

Scribing Square

A scribing square (see Figure 8), which can be put together in a couple of hours, makes it possible, and even easy, to accurately pick up the line of the hull's curvature and transfer it directly to the work piece without using a batten or any intermediate steps. The device illustrated here was glued up (no metal fastenings) from scraps of 1-inch by 2-inch pine for the main parts, and ³⁄₈-inch stuff for the thin outriggers that let it hang under a board for underneath scribing. The dimensions given here are only approximate and can be changed to fit the particular situation.

Obviously, for this device to be worth the making, its main parts (dark-shaded in the illustration) must be edge-jointed and glued together absolutely square. The paper shims, cut from filing card stock, simply provide a little extra clearance for the square to slide easily. Note that this square will work only on ¾-inch lumber. If thicker stuff is used for the top and bottom boards of the locker, the arm and tailpiece will naturally have to be made of material of that same thickness.

Making the Bottom Board

The actual construction begins with the locker's bottom board (see Figure 9). Since this board will be handled a lot in the course of scribing, beveling, and fitting, not to mention carrying it in and out of the

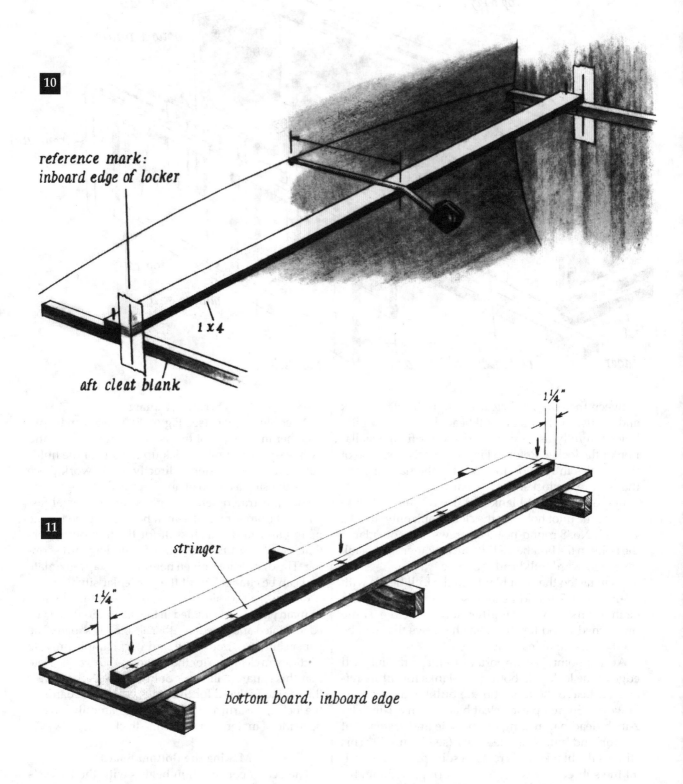

10

reference mark:
inboard edge of locker

1 X 4

aft cleat blank

11

1¼"

stringer

1¼"

bottom board, inboard edge

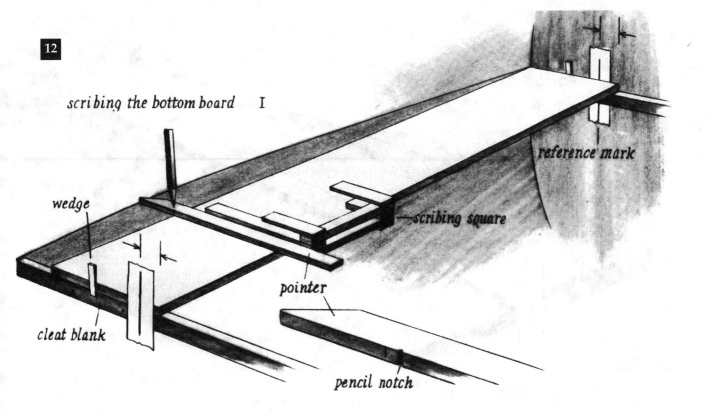

scribing the bottom board   I

reference mark

wedge

scribing square

pointer

cleat blank

pencil notch

---

boat to do all this, its flat surfaces are better left unfinished until later.

Cut a 1 by 4 that will fit loosely from bulkhead to bulkhead. Lay it up flat on the cleat blanks with its inboard edge aligned at both ends with the reference marks (see Figure 10). Tack it in place.

To find the width of the lumber needed for the bottom board, locate the widest gap between the hull and the 1 by 4. At that point measure from the hull to the inboard edge of the 1 by 4, and add 1½ inches or more to allow for scribing and fitting.

To determine the length of the board, measure along the 1 by 4 from bulkhead to bulkhead, and deduct ¼ inch for end clearance (⅛ inch at each end). At the same time, lay a square on the 1 by 4 against the bulkheads to see if they are parallel to one another. If not, measure the angle with a T-bevel, and lay off the saw cuts accordingly.

Then select a piece of clear lumber and sight it from both ends to make sure it is flat and straight. Cut it to length, and plane both ends smooth after laying it in place on the cleat blanks to check the end clearance. Joint one edge to go inboard.

Attaching the Stringer

The stringer is now fitted and attached temporarily to the underside of the bottom board to hold it stiff

and flat for accurate scribing. Select a piece of dry, straight-grained oak or ash, and sight it to see that it has no bow or twist. Mill it to 1¼ inches by 1½ inches, and joint all four sides. Then cut it to length — 2½ inches shorter than the bottom board, to fit between the end cleats with ¼ inch clearance at both ends (see Figure 5). On the 1½-inch side of the stringer, lay off center marks for five pilot holes, one about 2 inches from each end and three more spaced evenly between them (see Figure 11). Drill and countersink ¹³⁄₆₄-inch pilot holes on each mark. Turn the stringer over and give the countersink two or three turns in each exit hole to clean off any wood burrs.

Lay the bottom board face down on three or four skids with the stringer on top. Sight the board's edge from both ends. Because the same holes will be used later to fasten the stringer permanently, the bottom board must be flat. Then clamp the stringer in place about as shown (see Figure 11) — a bit inboard of center. Check to see that it is parallel with the board's inboard edge, and centered end to end. Tighten the clamps and sight along the board again.

Drive 1¾-inch No. 10 flathead screws into the end and center holes only. The stringer will be removed later to facilitate construction, and at a later stage will be fastened permanently with glue and all five screws.

13

scribing the bottom board   II

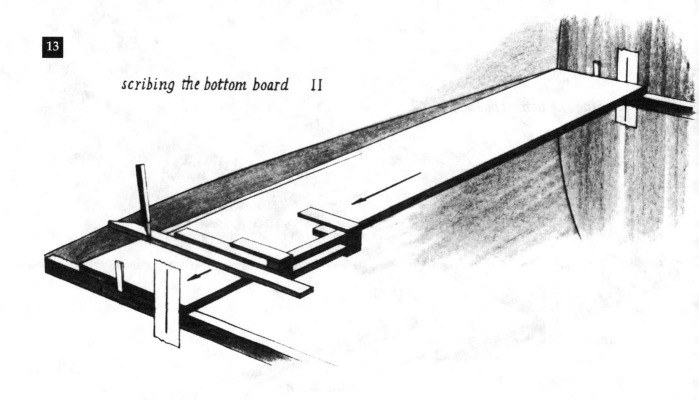

14

scribing the bottom board   III

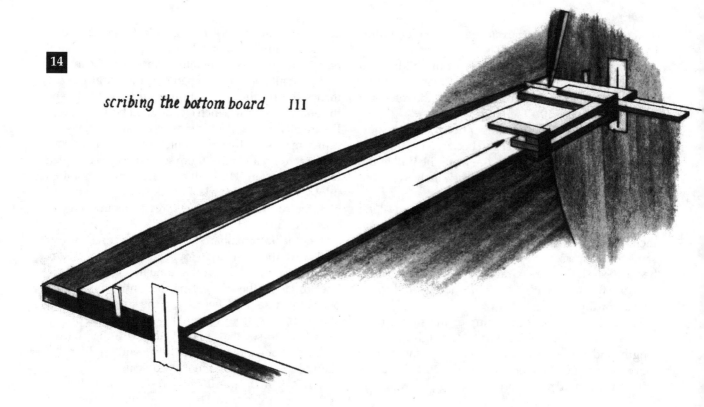

Scribing the Bottom Board

Lay the bottom board on the cleat blanks with its good edge inboard (see Figure 12). Then slide it in to touch the hull, and adjust it so its inboard edge is the same distance inboard from the reference marks on both bulkheads. Lock the board tightly by tapping in a sliver wedge at each end. Check the measurements again, and it's ready for scribing.

Set the scribing square over the edge of the board and lay the pointer alongside its arm (see Figure 12). Slide the square along, with the pointer touching the hull, to find the widest gap in the hull and the board's outboard edge. At that spot, draw a mark on the pointer. Then file a pencil notch about ½-inch inboard from the mark. This avoids attempting to scribe right to the edge of the board, and allows sawing an uninterrupted curve. Replace the pointer, and slide the square along to about the middle of the board (see Figure 13). With the pointer always pushed out and riding against the hull, and a pencil held in the notch, slide the whole works along aft, drawing a smooth line in duplication of the hull curvature. Then flop the square the other way and — again from the middle of the board — scribe to its forward end (see Figure 14). While this can actually be managed by one person working alone, it is certainly faster and easier when a third hand holds the pencil in the notch while you do all the rest. This little machine works best when the square and the pointer are pushed against the pressure of an incoming curve, when it picks up every bump and hollow.

If the hull has much outward flare (which it does not have in the example), it may be worthwhile at this stage to determine the bevel of the board's outboard edge. Do this with a small T-bevel placed to measure the angle between the face of the board and the hull ceiling.

After it has been scribed, take the board out of the boat, unscrew the stringer, and set it aside for the time being.

Sawing and Fitting

Saw to the scribed line but without obliterating it (with the cut angled if appropriate, to approximate the necessary edge bevel). Then smooth off the edge with a couple of nonstop strokes with a sharp plane set very fine.

Wedge the board in place again, and mark whatever spots need to be shaved in order to get a good fit against the hull. Depending on how closely the board's edge matches the flare of the hull, there may be a sliver of a crack showing (see Figure 15), in which case that section of the edge can be more precisely fitted by planing (see Figure 16). There's no harm in exaggerating the bevel, as the underside of the locker will not be visible.

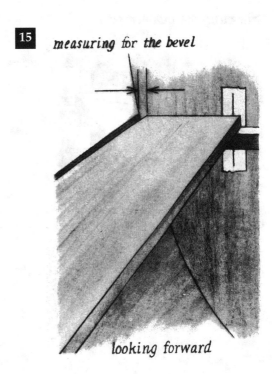

15 *measuring for the bevel*

looking forward

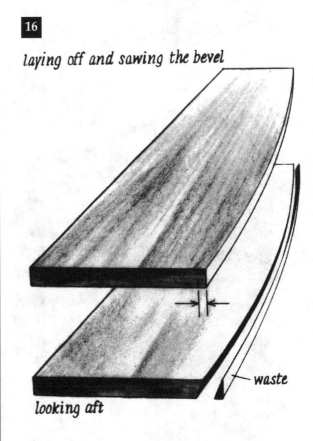

16

laying off and sawing the bevel

waste

looking aft

17

trimming the inboard edge

reference mark

With the bottom board wedged in place, mark its inboard edge for trimming. Transfer the inboard-edge-of-locker marks from the tapes to both ends of the bottom board (see Figure 17). Then lay a straightedge to the marks, and connect them with a line drawn along its edge. I'd saw this line freehand instead of using the saw's fence, since one end may lose more wood than the other. Then joint the edge.

Building the Front Unit

Next build the front unit, calculating its finished height from the measurements taken on the aft bulkhead. This unit covers the two compartments to be fitted with doors (see Figure 18). Its five pieces are assembled with halved joints fastened with glue and screws.

Cut, joint, and surface-plane all the pieces, and shoot grooves in the three stiles (see Figure 19). Work the halved joints — there are six of them — and drill and countersink the screw holes. Finally, cut inlets in both end stiles for ¾-inch by 2-inch brass butt hinges (see Figure 20).

19

front unit, inside view: tongue and groove and halved joints

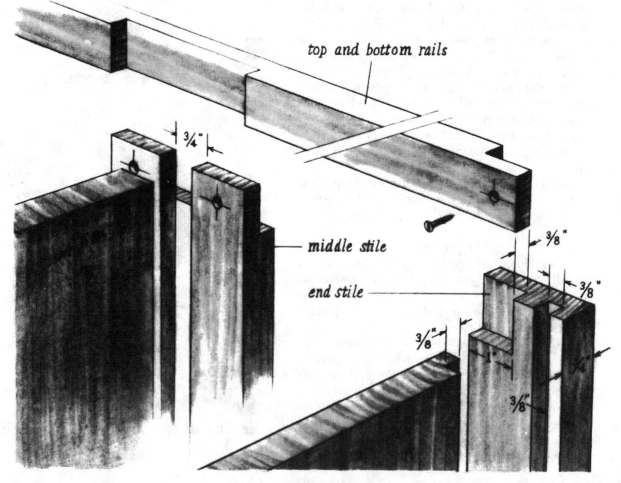

top and bottom rails

¾"

middle stile

end stile

⅜"

⅜"

⅜"

1"

⅜"

¼"

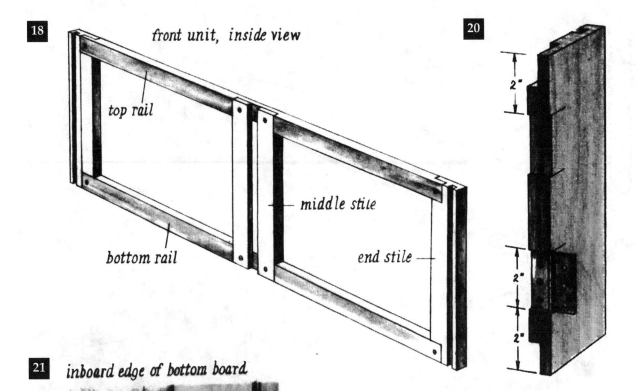

18 front unit, inside view

top rail

middle stile

bottom rail

end stile

20

2"

2"

2"

21 inboard edge of bottom board

To ensure square corners, assemble the unit face-down, flat on a heavy sheet of plywood. This way, the stiles and rails can be glued, laid together and squared, and clamped securely while the screws are driven. I've found that gluing and fastening the joints one by one — with complete drying in between — gives me the unhurried time to square and check them before the glue begins to set up.

Finishing the Bottom Board

At this point, both surfaces of the bottom board can be smoothed with a freshly sharpened plane set extremely fine, primarily to remove the chatter marks left by the machine planer. Both sides are also finish-sanded.

Exactly how the board's inboard edge is finished is largely a matter of taste, although the sharp edges should be knocked off in some fashion, as paint and varnish don't last long on such corners, and they are hazardous things to fall against. I'd prefer narrow chamfers here rather than a full rounded edge (see Figure 21). They accentuate the horizontal, at the same time giving the illusion of greater thickness and an apparent heft that visually supports the weight of the locker. And I probably would not sand them, as that often destroys their crisp, clean lines. From here on, it is important to handle this board carefully to avoid damaging it.

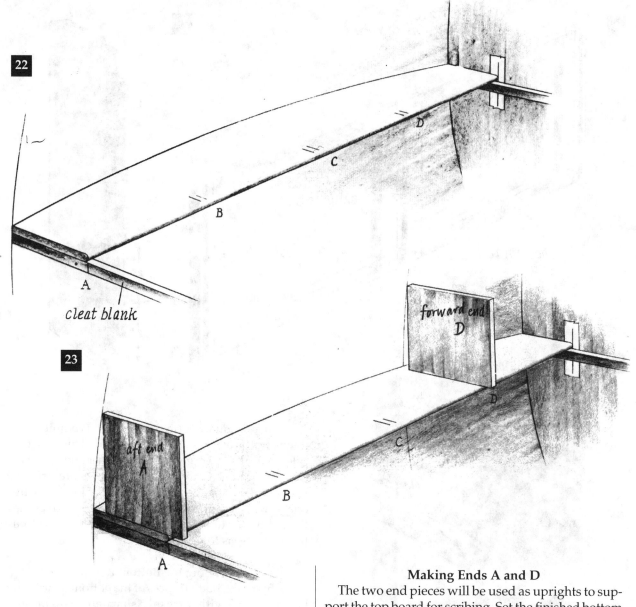

22

cleat blank

23

aft end
A

A

forward end
D

D

C

B

24

aft end
A

level

cleat blank

bottom board

Making Ends A and D

The two end pieces will be used as uprights to support the top board for scribing. Set the finished bottom board in place on the cleat blanks, and with light tick marks locate the position of partitions B and C, and forward end D, using measurements taken directly from the finished front unit (see Figure 22). There is no need to mark the position of end A — it goes right against the aft bulkhead.

Cut the pieces for A and D to exact height, but with an extra inch or more on the width to allow for scribing. Plane their end-grains square. Have someone hold them in place on the bottom board (see Figure 23) while you scribe their outboard edges to the hull (see Figure 24). Then saw and finish the scribed edges and stand the boards in position, pushed out against the hull. End A should stand without help, but end D must be steadied between a pair of hand screws over the edge of the bottom board (see Figure 25).

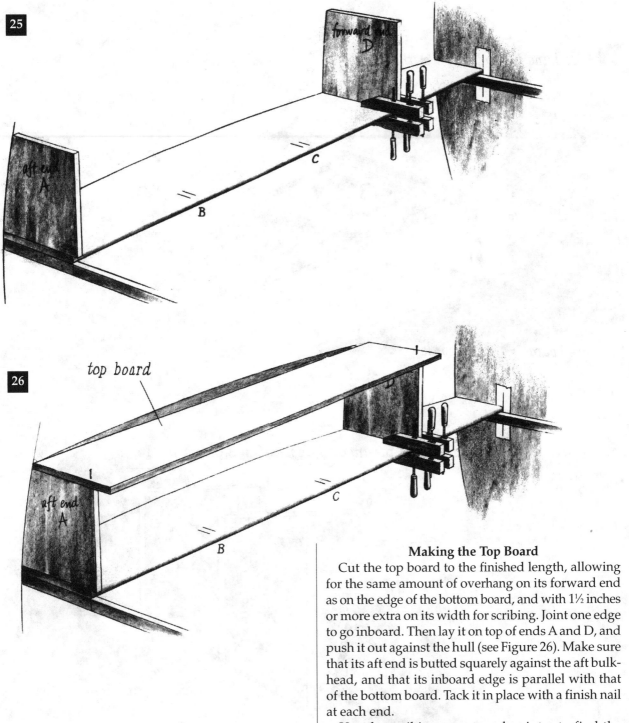

forward end
D

aft end
A

C

B

26

top board

aft end
A

C

B

Making the Top Board

Cut the top board to the finished length, allowing for the same amount of overhang on its forward end as on the edge of the bottom board, and with 1½ inches or more extra on its width for scribing. Joint one edge to go inboard. Then lay it on top of ends A and D, and push it out against the hull (see Figure 26). Make sure that its aft end is butted squarely against the aft bulkhead, and that its inboard edge is parallel with that of the bottom board. Tack it in place with a finish nail at each end.

Use the scribing square and pointer to find the widest gap as before, and file a new notch in the pointer — the old one won't work here. Now get some help, as it may be pretty cramped scribing up under the deckbeams. You may have to scribe slowly for a couple of inches, then move the square along and scribe a little more; or you may have to do part of the scribing on the underside of the board (see Figure 27).

27 *scribing the underside of the top board*

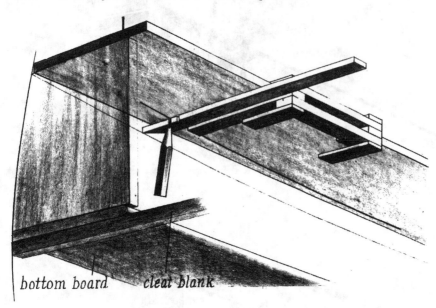

bottom board   cleat blank

28 *trimming the inboard edges of A, B,C, and D   I*

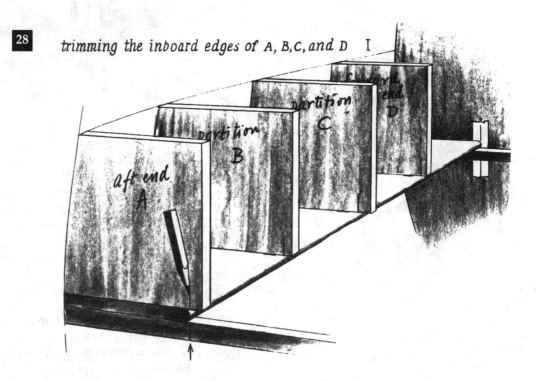

aft end
A

partition
B

partition
C

forth
end
D

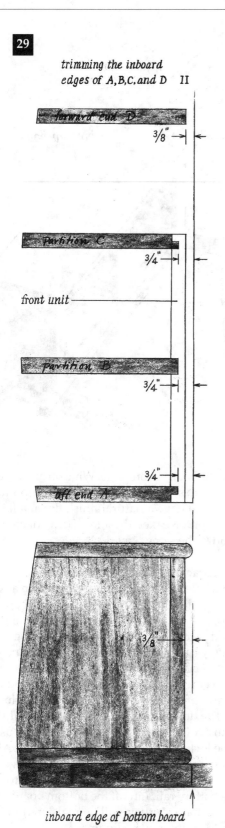

29

trimming the inboard edges of A, B, C, and D   II

forward end D

3/8"

partition C

3/4"

front unit

partition B

3/4"

3/4"

aft end A

3/8"

inboard edge of bottom board

30

Then take out the top board, saw and plane the scribed edge, and shave it to fit while ends A and D are still in place as supports. Leave the bottom board in place.

Making Partitions B and C

Cut pieces for partitions B and C to exact height, but with some extra width, and plane their end-grains square. Have your helper hold them on the bottom board aligned with their respective tick marks while you scribe them to the hull.

To finish the partitions and the ends as well, all of which presumably are the same height and fitted to the hull, you must now trim and mill their inboard edges to fit the grooves in the front unit's stiles. First, set each one in position on the bottom board, aligned with the tick marks and pushed out against the hull. Mark its lower corner even with the inboard edge of the bottom board (see Figure 28). Then refer to Figure 29 and to the front unit itself to trim and shoot tongues on A and C, and to trim B and D (without tongues) to their finished width. The sharp edges of the tongues should be knocked off with a stroke or two of the plane so the joints will close more easily.

Assembling A, B, C, and Front Unit

Lay the front unit face-down on skids (see Figure 30). Attach end A first. With a stiff, narrow brush, spread a thin coat of glue on the tongue, and even less into the groove of the stile. Set end A into the groove, check to see that it is flush with the top and bottom of the stile, then force it down tightly. Put on a pair of clamps, using pads or blocking to protect the work. Then tighten the clamps alternately to draw the joint together evenly. Don't use too much pressure, or it

31

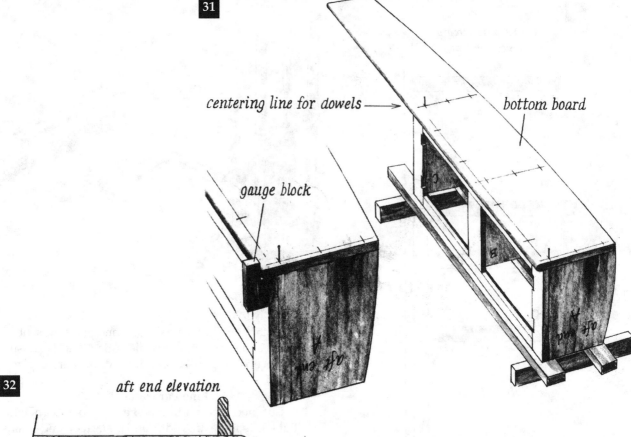

centering line for dowels →

bottom board

gauge block

32

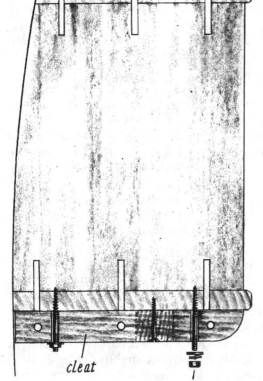

aft end elevation

cleat

**hanger bolt with
flat washer and lock washer**

may buckle the board to one side. Wipe off any excess glue with a damp sponge; this is especially important if the locker is to have a natural finish. Even a fairly wet sponge won't weaken the joint. Then attach partitions B and C the same way.

Attaching the Bottom Board

Turn the whole assembly bottom-side up on a pair of 2 by 4s on skids (see Figure 31). Lay the bottom board on top, adjusting it flush at the aft end and at the outboard (back) edge. Use a quickly made gauge block to ensure a uniform overhang along the inboard edge. Tack the board in place with a couple of finish nails. Draw centering lines over A, B, and C, and lay off three marks on each line for holes to receive glued-in dowels. The dowel holes over aft end A should be staggered to avoid the hanger bolts that will be used to fasten the locker to the cleats (see Figure 32). Also draw a line parallel with the board's inboard edge on which to locate screws to be driven through into the front unit's bottom rail. Lift off the bottom board, but don't pull the nails — they will be registered in the same holes to maintain the alignment.

Get everything ready. You'll need half a dozen bar clamps, a pair of pony clamps, a few pieces of blocking, a ¼-inch drill, 10 dowels ¼ inch by 2¼ inches (one is a spare), and the glue bottle. Sand one end of all the

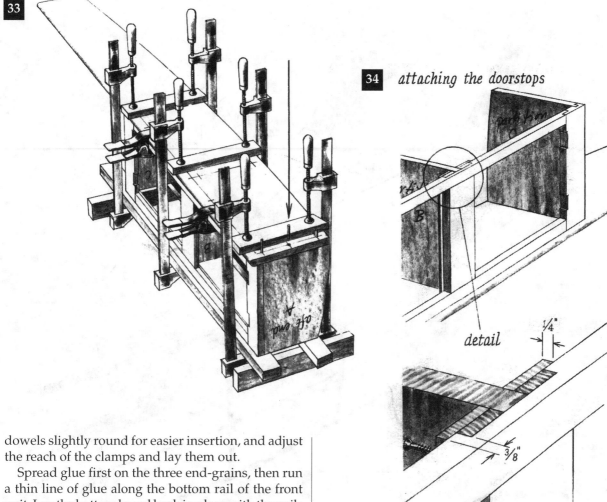

33

34 *attaching the doorstops*

detail

¼"

⅜"

dowels slightly round for easier insertion, and adjust the reach of the clamps and lay them out.

Spread glue first on the three end-grains, then run a thin line of glue along the bottom rail of the front unit. Lay the bottom board back in place with the nails piloted into the original holes. Press down on the board, then lift it off and turn it over. Leave the nails in place. String a bit more glue along the picked-up glue lines, and smooth them into narrow bands. Add a bit more glue to the end-grains. Replace the bottom board on the assembly, using the same nail holes, and give the nails a good tap to seat them. Set up the blocking and the clamps (see Figure 33), tightening them all around in sequence with good pressure. Squeeze a pony clamp over the middle of each door opening. Remove the nails.

Now complete these joints — with the clamps on — by drilling three dowel holes ¼ inch by 2 inches deep on the marks on each centering line (over A, B, and C). If ever it was important to drill straight, this is the place. Quickly clean out the holes by twirling a glue-wet matchstick into them to pick up the drill shavings. Wipe glue around the entering end of a dowel, and twirl a bit into the hole; then drive the dowel home and clean up any squeezed-out glue. Drive the other dowels the same way.

Then drill and countersink pilot holes — two over

each door opening — and drive 1¼-inch No. 7 flathead screws through the bottom board into the front unit's bottom rail. To ensure thorough curing of the glue and fast joints, leave everything as is for at least 12 hours. Then remove the clamps, and trim the dowels off flush.

Attaching the Doorstops

At this stage, before the top of the locker is closed in, make up a pair of doorstops from ¼-inch stock (see Figure 34). Drill and countersink two pilot holes in each for ⅝-inch No. 6 flathead screws. Fasten the stops to the inside of the middle stile of the front unit, butted against partition B. Fasten the stops dry — without glue.

35

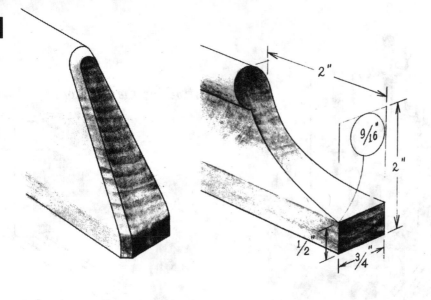

36

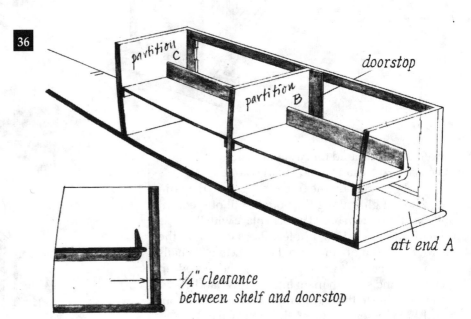

partition C

partition B

doorstop

aft end A

¼" clearance
between shelf and doorstop

37

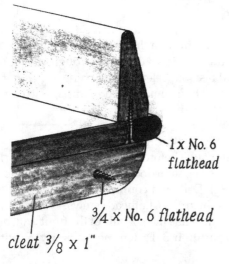

1 x No. 6
flathead

¾ x No. 6 flathead

cleat ⅜ x 1"

Making Fiddle Moldings

The fiddle moldings — for this locker, one size ¾ inch by 1½ inches high and the other ¾ inch by 2 inches — can be as plain or as fancy as you like (see Figure 35), depending on the style of the boat's interior and on the tools and machines available. The 2-inch moldings run along the edges of the interior shelves and the open forward section of the bottom board, while the narrow fiddle goes on the top board. Since only about 8 linear feet of each size are needed, I'd probably elect to cut them with hand tools, settling on a simple design that could be worked with planes, spokeshave, gouges, files, and sandpaper held over specially shaped blocks.

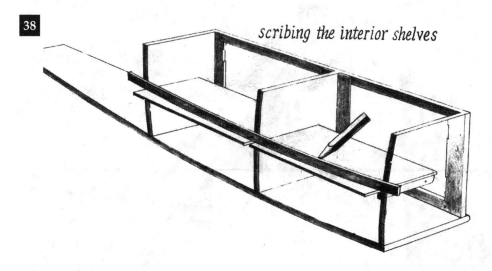

38 scribing the interior shelves

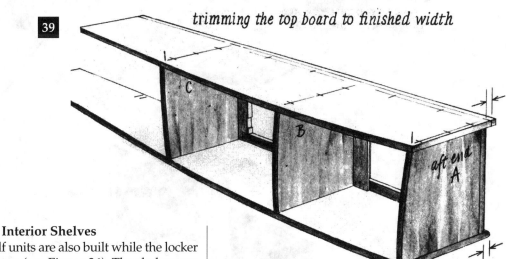

39 trimming the top board to finished width

Interior Shelves

The interior shelf units are also built while the locker is still open at the top (see Figure 36). The shelves are made of ½-inch stock and are supported by glued-on cleats (no metal fastenings) through which screws are driven into end A and partitions B and C (see Figure 37). In determining the level of the shelves, allow adequate space above the fiddles for easy reach-in access. Note also that there is ¼-inch clearance between the doorstops and the inboard edges of the shelves. Their outboard edges are fitted to the hull; this is easily done by tracing a line against a thin batten tacked across the locker at shelf level (see Figure 38). The fiddles for these interior shelves run their full length, and are glued and fastened with 1-inch No. 6 flathead screws driven up through the shelves. Fasten the shelf units in place, then remove them. They are finally installed, using the same screw holes, after the finish has been applied to the inside of the locker.

Finishing the Top Board

To trim the top board to the finished width, lay it on top of the locker assembly, aligned flush with the outboard corners of A, B, and C (see Figure 39). Tack it in place with two finish nails. Then, at its aft end and also over partition C, mark its inboard edge for the same overhang as on the bottom board. Lay a straightedge to the marks, and draw a line connecting them.

Draw centering lines over A, B, and C, and lay off three marks on each line for the dowel holes. Also draw a line parallel with the board's inboard edge on which to locate screws to be driven through into the front unit's top rail.

Remove the board and pull the nails. Then saw the inboard edge to the line, and joint and finish the edge to match the bottom board. At this point, the inside surface of the board should be finish-sanded, after which the finish nails are replaced in the same holes.

Attaching the Top Board

Attach the top board to the assembly with dowels glued into aft end A and partitions B and C, by the

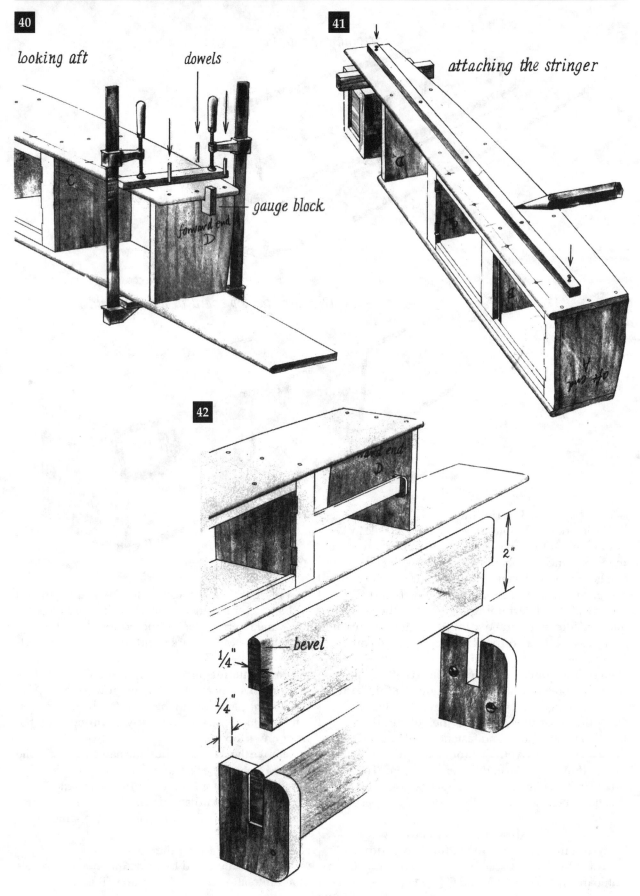

40

looking aft   dowels

gauge block

forward end
D

41

attaching the stringer

C

B

aft end
A

42

forward end
D

2"

bevel

¼"

¼"

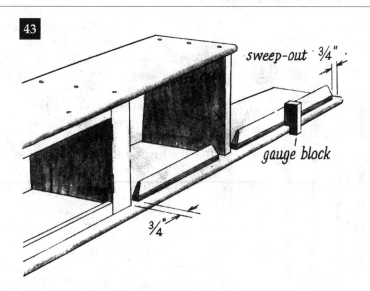

sweep-out ³/₄"

gauge block

³/₄"

same procedure used for the bottom board (see Figure 33). Then drill and countersink pilot holes for 1½-inch No. 7 flathead screws — two over each door opening as before — and drive them through into the front unit's top rail. Again, leave the work in clamps for at least 12 hours. Trim the dowels off flush.

Attaching Forward End D

Stand forward end D in place, sandwiched between the top and bottom boards and held in place with clamps, if necessary (see Figure 40). Check the end overhang with the gauge block, and make sure that everything will align properly. Then remove the board, glue up both end-grains of end D, and complete the dowel joints as before, first through the top board, and then — with the locker turned over — through the bottom board. Leave the work in clamps for another 12 hours, after which the dowels can be trimmed off flush and the top surface of the top board finish-sanded.

Attaching the Stringer

With the basic structure completed, the stringer is now fastened permanently to the underside of the locker. Turn it bottom-side up, with its forward end blocked up level (see Figure 41); sight along the bottom board to make sure it is. Find the stringer and start a 1¾-inch No. 10 flathead screw into each of the end holes. Then lay it on the locker and drive the screws partway into the original holes. Draw pencil lines on the bottom of the locker along the sides of the stringer, to assist in applying the glue. Then back the screws out flush and turn the stringer over. Spread a thin coat of glue on both the stringer and the bottom of the locker, and replace the stringer, using the same screw holes. Then drive the screws, and drive the other three as well. Leave the work to dry thoroughly.

Bookshelf Bar and Brackets

To fit up the open compartment as a bookshelf, install a simple retainer bar and a pair of brackets (see Figure 42). Trim the bar a bit short to give it some end play, and sand slight bevels on its ends so it will drop easily into the bracket slots. Like the interior shelf units, these brackets are first screwed in place and then removed, to be finally installed after the finish has been applied to the inside of the locker.

Attaching the Bottom Fiddles

Cut and finish the ends of two pieces of the 2-inch molding, one to run between C and D, and the other from D to the forward end of the locker. Allow for ¾-inch sweep-outs at the ends (see Figure 43). To fasten the fiddles, clamp them in place aligned with the inboard face of the front unit. Turn the locker bottom up, and lay off a screw line. Drill and countersink pilot holes in the bottom board for 1¼-inch No. 7 flathead screws — two for each piece of molding. Drive the screws just deep enough to engage the fiddles, then back them out. Remove the clamps and fiddles, spread a thin coat of glue along their bottom edges, and replace them, registering them over the screw points. Then put the clamps back on, tighten them a bit, and drive the screws tight. Clean up any excess glue, and leave the work in clamps until thoroughly dry.

Attaching the Top Fiddle

Measure this section of 1½-inch molding to leave ¾-inch gaps at either end. Drill and countersink pilot holes — two in each door opening — for No. 7 screws, long enough this time to reach through the front unit's top rail, through the top board, and about ½ inch into the fiddle molding. Also drill two holes over the bookshelf compartment for 1¼-inch No. 7 flathead screws. Then attach the molding as before.

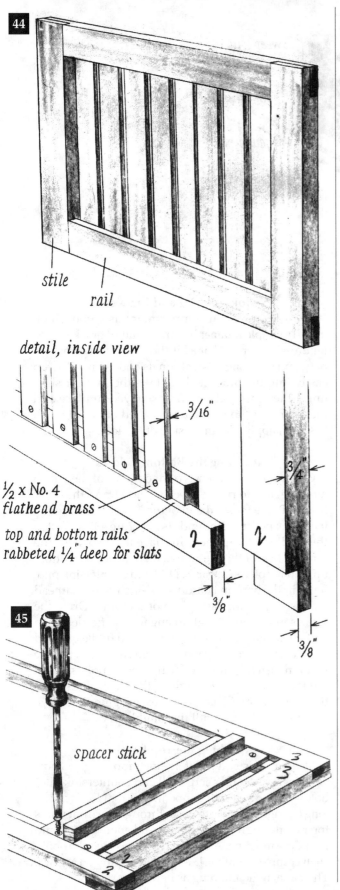

44

stile

rail

detail, inside view

3/16"

3/4"

1/2 x No. 4
flathead brass

top and bottom rails
rabbeted 1/4" deep for slats

2

2

3/8"

3/8"

45

spacer stick

3

3

2

2

Building the Doors

The doors are made of ¾-inch stock, their stiles and rails assembled with glued halved joints (no metal fastenings). The top and bottom rails are rabbeted to take the slats, which are spot-glued and fastened with a screw at each end (see Figure 44).

First, measure the door openings — individually, as they may not be identical. Deduct ⅛-inch from the height and from the width to allow about ¹⁄₁₆-inch clearance around all four sides. Then cut the stiles and rails to size, and joint them. Work the halved joints all around, numbering them as you go to avoid assembly errors. Then shoot the rabbets in the rails.

I like to start the assembly of a door by clamping all of the pieces together dry to check the fit of the joints, to make sure that their faces come flush, and that opposing members are not wound out of flat. If no further fitting is required, glue up one joint only, put on a clamp, and after fussing to get it absolutely square, tighten the clamp.

Check the square again, then set the work aside to dry overnight. With this one joint carefully put together, the others should present no problems.

Next, figure out the number and width of slats and the amount of space between them. A good way is to lay this all out on a strip of paper taped to the bench, accurately measuring and marking off the slats and spaces with a sharp pencil, and adjusting the dimensions as necessary to get it all to come out even. Then make a spacer stick milled to the exact gap width (see Figure 45), and lay it between the slats when fastening them. This is faster and more reliable than transferring the measurements to the work itself with a pencil.

Try the doors in their respective openings, shaving off a little wood at a time with a good, sharp plane, to get a uniform clearance of about ³⁄₃₂-inch on all four sides.

Hanging the Doors

Make up a few thin pine wedges tapered from ⅛-inch to almost nothing, and use them to wedge the doors into the openings, again looking for equal clearance all around (see Figure 46). If all is well, use a batten laid across the face of the locker (and a sharp pencil) to draw marks on the door stiles even with the tops and bottoms of the hinge inlets. Remove the doors and cut the inlets, a bit on the shallow side; they can be deepened if necessary. Then plane back-bevels on the doorknob edges of both doors, taking off no more than about ³⁄₃₂ inch of wood, to ensure that they won't rub when the doors are opened and closed. Attach the hinges to the doors and to the locker, but with only one screw in each hinge leaf. Test the action of the

46 hanging the doors

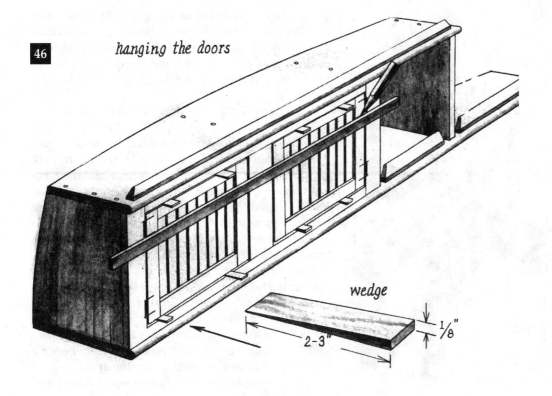

wedge

2-3"

⅛"

47

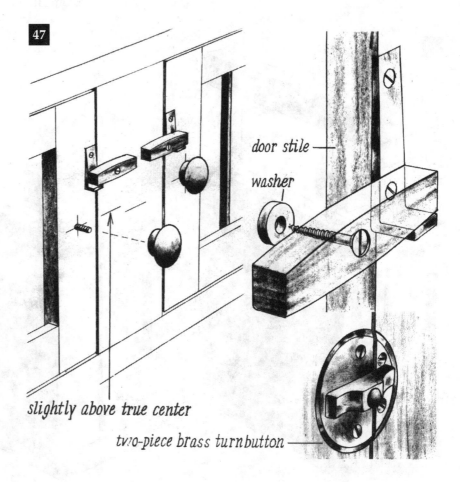

door stile

washer

slightly above true center

two-piece brass turnbutton

forward cleat

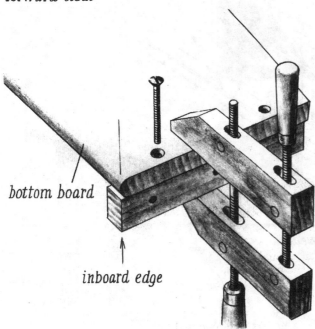

bottom board

inboard edge

doors. They should close nicely against the stops without dragging or popping open, which would indicate that the inlets are too deep. In that case, the only remedy is to glue paper shims under the offending leaf to relieve the pinching. Then drive the rest of the screws.

Attaching the Doorknobs and Buttons

The batten is also used to position the buttons and doorknobs, the knobs being optically centered slightly above true center (see Figure 47). The knobs here are stock items 1½ inches in diameter, while the turn-buttons are made up to whatever pattern you like. The L-shaped button stops are made of brass, their top ends ground to a taper (see Figure 47). They can be either face-mounted or let into the door stiles with their faces a bit proud of the surface. In either case, leather or neoprene washers should be installed under the turnbuttons to compensate for the thickness of the brass, and to provide a non-rattle closure when the buttons are seated on the L part of the stop. Stock two-piece brass turnbuttons can also be used; but after they've been in service for a while and have become worn, the buttons tend to drop into the open position unless the button half of the fixture is let into the stile to create some friction.

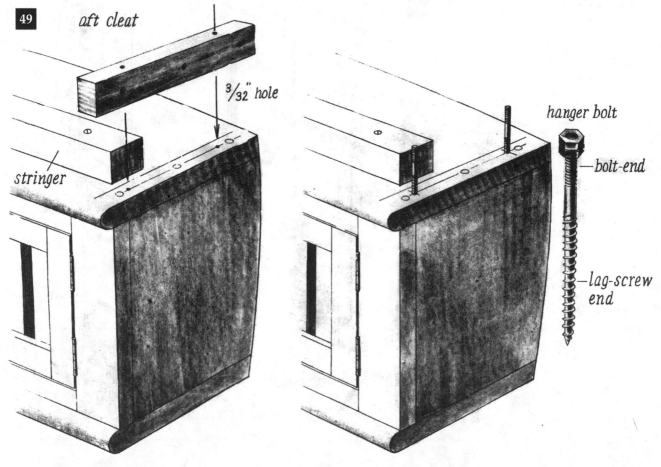

aft cleat

³⁄₃₂" *hole*

stringer

hanger bolt

—bolt-end

—lag-screw end

Finishing the Cleats

Remove the cleat blanks from the bulkheads, and cut them off at the reference marks (inboard edge of locker). With the locker upright on sawhorses, clamp the forward cleat under the bottom board flush with its end and inboard edge (see Figure 48). Drill two ¼-inch holes clear through the board and cleat, to take ³⁄₁₆-inch flathead brass bolts. Carefully countersink the holes so the head of the bolt comes exactly flush with the board's surface. Remove the clamp, and trim the cleat's inboard end back to align with the face of the locker's front unit (see Figure 32). Round the cleat's end and exposed under edge, and finish-sand all the surfaces.

To finish the aft cleat, turn the locker bottom up. Clamp the cleat to the bottom of the locker, flush with its end and inboard edge as before. Draw a pencil line on the bottom of the locker alongside the cleat (see Figure 49), and a centerline on which to locate the two hanger bolts. Then refer to Figure 32 to position these bolts, and drill ³⁄₃₂-inch holes through the cleat and about ³⁄₈ inch into the locker. Remove the cleat, and trim, round, and finish its inboard end to match the forward cleat. Then enlarge the pilot holes (in the cleat only) to ¼ inch in diameter.

Lock two nuts on one of the hanger bolts, and use a wrench to drive the lag-screw end into the pilot hole in the locker, leaving the bolt-end projecting about 1⁹⁄₁₆ inch. Install the other hanger bolt the same way.

Installing the Locker

Remove the tapes from the bulkheads, and fasten both cleats in place with two 1½-inch No. 8 round-headed screws each, piloting them into the original holes in the bulkheads. Then drive the third screw in each cleat.

Get some help to carry the locker into the boat, and if possible have a third person waiting to assist in lifting it onto the cleats. Feed the aft end bolts into the cleat holes, and, while keeping the locker level, lower it to rest on the cleats. Shove it into position against the hull.

Drop the two bolts through the forward holes; then put flat washers, lock washers, and nuts on all four bolts.

All that remains is to apply the finish and rub it all down to a nice luster, and install the interior shelf units and the bookshelf brackets. Maybe — assuming that nothing has been overlooked — this could all be done before bringing the locker into the boat. But assumptions are risky. I want to see the thing in place, make sure it fits, and know for a fact that everything's been done.

Louvered Doors

by Tim Allen
Photographs by Mariah Hughs

An opening in the jig table allows you to locate a hold-down near the cut.

As a child, I spent many hours looking through Sam Rabl's book *Boatbuilding in Your Own Back Yard* (Cornell Maritime Press, Centreville, Maryland). Although his designs no longer appeal as much to me, his enthusiasm for designing and building simple, honest boats was infectious. He described and drew interesting gadgets and ideas to help backyard boatbuilders get around expensive tools they would only need for a short time. The louver jig I will describe is of the same family of gadget. There is no reason an amateur boatbuilder or small professional shop can't make nice joinerwork using simple ideas and jigs. You may not turn out as much in an hour as a larger, well-equipped shop, but you may have more fun and take more pride in your work.

Adequate ventilation is something you should always consider for all enclosed spaces on a boat. Many areas can be ventilated through louvered doors or fixed louvered panels. There are simpler ways to ventilate lockers, or provide privacy in the head, but I think that louvered doors provide the most attractive solution. Making these doors can be time consuming and perhaps a little frightening, but the project is really no more difficult than many aspects of boatbuilding. If you understand a given process, prepare carefully, and use good material and appropriate tools, you can successfully complete louvered doors, or just about anything else.

I'll provide an explanation and plans for a simple and effective method that I use to construct louvered doors. Careful preparation is important. We can begin by investigating some of the problems that you may encounter when making louvered doors.

If you have ever built doors and upon clamping found that part of the door lifts off a flat surface, even though you carefully joined and planed flat the stiles (the vertical members of the frame) and the rails, and

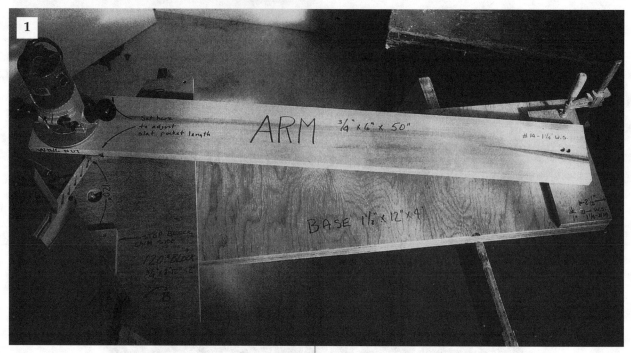

This simple jig guides a router when you're cutting slat pockets for louvered doors.

Fasten a piece of plywood across one end of the jig.

carefully cut the joints, you are well aware of a problem that is common to door-making, and particularly common to louvered door-making. You may have found a slight error, such as an inaccurately cut shoulder on a tenoned rail or a stile edge that is not square or straight. These may have seemed to have been small enough errors, but they can produce larger errors. Sometimes the problem is in the square you check

your work with, or with some other tool or jig.

A louvered door that is not flat could be the result of one or all of the above problems. It could also be twisted out of a flat plane by warped slats. We would not likely assemble a door with twisted slats, but suppose we did. We probably could pull and hold a door with one or two bad slats flat with the door rails, but as we add twisted slats, we increase the amount of holding and pulling those rails must do to flatten the door. If we were to cut the pockets that hold these slats into one stile at one angle and the opposite stile at a slightly different angle, we would produce the same problem. The slat pockets, therefore, must be cut at the same angle in both stiles. We must also cut them at uniform intervals, and their length, width, and depth must be consistent so the slats will fit well.

We can use a router to cut these pockets, and we can make a jig to guide the router (see Photo 1). If you look at the photographs of the completed jig, you can see the router mounted on a 50-inch-long arm that pivots from one end of the jig and moves over the stile, which is clamped to a block at the other end of the jig. The block edges are cut to form a 120-degree angle. A ¼-inch router bit is plunged into the stile and moved about ⅞ inch, cutting a pocket ¼-inch wide and 1⅛ inch long at a 30-degree angle to the stile edge. Although the pocket is actually part of the circumference of an 8-foot circle, it is straight enough.

I have tried to simplify construction of this jig and describe the necessary construction steps in a simple order that will allow you to make a jig that performs accurately. Some care must be taken to lay out the various parts and cut and drill accurately. A sharp No. 3

or No. 4 pencil produces a narrow mark or line on wood; having a crisp, accurate line to aim at is as important as having the proper tools to cut to that line. A 6-inch steel machinist's rule or the rule from a good combination square will also be useful. The etched marks on these rules are much thinner than the marks on a tape measure, folding rule, or stamped combination-square rule. There are only a few sections of the jig or doors where accurate measurements are important — but these are critical.

The ends of the rails must be parallel, and they must be square to the faces of the rails; otherwise, the stiles will not mate perfectly with the rails, and the joints will be partially open. Rather than having nice, crisp lines, you will have gaps or joints full of glue and sawdust. If you cut the edges out of square to the faces and your rail ends are parallel planes, the joints might be tight, but the door will not be flat. The stiles will turn up or down.

Building good joinerwork means learning to look for problems before you encounter them. Checking the various parts with an accurate square usually turns up an error that may be present; do this before any glue is mixed. Occasionally the errors we find in door-making are caused by the square used to check out the work. When you check two surfaces for square, hold the square beam to the narrower surface. This will exaggerate the amount of error; you will see more daylight between the rule and the wider surface. (By the way, if you're looking for new or used rules or squares, Brown and Sharpe, Starrett, or Lufkin have good reputations.)

This end of the jig holds the stiles while you cut the pockets.

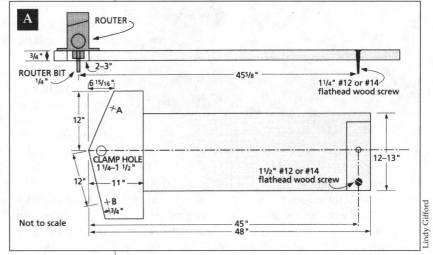

Dimensioned, schematic diagram of the jig.

Lindy Gifford

MAKING THE JIG

The Base

We can start with the base, which is about 1½ inches thick by 12 to 14 inches wide and 4 feet long. I used two pieces of ¾-inch CDX plywood, glued together against a flat surface. You could use other plywood thicknesses; the base does not need to be 1½ inches thick; 1 inch probably would be adequate. But make sure the base is flat.

Pivot Block

One end of the jig has a piece of ¾-inch plywood about 4 inches wide and 12 inches long (see Photo 2). It is fastened across the base, flush with one side and the base end, with a No. 12 or No. 14 flathead wood screw 1½ inches long, so it can be pivoted slightly. This

will allow you to make a final adjustment to the jig for your door stile thickness and to locate the pockets symmetrically in the stiles.

120-degree Block

The other end of the jig holds the stiles while you cut the pockets. A piece of ¾-inch plywood, 8 to 12 inches wide and 24 inches long, is fastened across this end of the base (see Photo 3). It should be glued and screwed so it cannot move. Be sure the screws will not interfere with the two cuts you will make across this piece and the base. Find the center of this piece at the base end. Measure along each outside edge from the base end, as shown in Figure A. Connect

An accurate method for making the necessary cuts on a table saw.

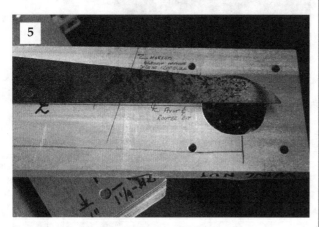

Set a 4-foot straightedge on the center of the bit.

the centerline point at the end of the jig and the 6^{15}⁄$_{16}$-inch marks at the edges; this will give you a 60-degree angle from the centerline of the base. If you use a piece that is more or less than 24 inches long, multiply half its width by 0.577, and use the decimal dimension or convert that number to thirty-seconds or sixteenths of an inch.

After you have laid out this piece, you can cut the two sides to form a 120-degree angle. There are several ways to do this. You should finish with a sharp point and the two surfaces straight and square to the top of the jig. Running with the grain of the top veneer of the plywood for this 8- to 12-inch by 24-inch piece or 120-degree block will help produce the sharp point; running the veneer's grain the other way will probably result in a chipped point. The point is useful for laying out the line that bisects, or divides in two equal spaces, the 120-degree angle. Also, it will "index" or set the pitch marks that determine the space between the slat pockets. Try to keep the point sharp.

Photo 4 shows an accurate method for making the necessary cuts on a table saw. A spare piece of plywood

is ripped so the edges are parallel and 8 to 12 inches apart. The piece is 18 to 24 inches long, and fastened temporarily to each side of the 120-degree block parallel to the cut you will make. You can lay out a separate line parallel to the cut and set the temporary piece to it. Be sure you set the blade to cut just the base and the 120-degree block. If you made them of ¾-inch plywood, you will need to cut a total thickness of 2⅛ to 2¼ inches. After cutting one side, transfer the temporary piece to the other side of the jig. As the photo shows, you feed the jig through with the temporary piece against the fence.

Alternatively a radial-arm saw might be used to make these cuts, or they can be made by hand or on a bandsaw and carefully cleaned up with a plane. Be sure the cuts are straight, flat, and square to the top surface of the 120-degree block.

Arm and Router

So far, you have the 120-degree end of the base cut and the pivot block fastened with one screw to the opposite end of the jig's base. You still need a straight, flat arm ¾ inch by 6 inches by 50 inches long to mount the router on, and you need a specific pivot point in this arm and in the pivot block where the two will be fastened together with another No. 12 or No. 14 flathead wood screw, 1¼ inches long. The router arm needs to have a 2- to 3-inch hole cut 4 to 4½ inches from one end; this hole should be large enough to look through as you cut the pockets. The router base must be mounted securely on the arm. You should remove the plastic sole on your router to get enough chip clearance and a good view of the router bit as it cuts.

After the router is in place, tighten a ¼-inch center-cutting straight bit in the collet, and set the bit ¼ inch beyond the arm. The pockets should be about ¼ inch deep for a simple 90-degree edge stile. The pockets will be deeper if you use a door set and mold the edges of the stiles. I have used good veining bits to cut the pockets, but I find the center-cutting bits clear the chips from the pockets better, stay sharper, and cut cleaner. Ballew Saw and Tool* in Springfield, Missouri, can supply these bits in solid carbide — an economical choice, especially if you intend to make your doors from teak, which is tough on edges.

With a bit tight in the collet, and the router motor tight in the base, set a 4-foot straightedge on the center of the bit and 3 inches from the edge at the arm's other end (see Photo 5). Mark this line with a sharp pencil. You will need a crisp line to check the jig's

---

*Ballew Saw and Tool can also supply a bullnose cutter manufactured by Whiteside that has a ⅛-inch radius and a ¼-inch opening. There are nominal ¼-inch bullnose cutters, such as those made by Amana, that are apparently metric rather than English. These will not work with ¼-inch slat stock.

proper alignment after you fasten the arm to the pivot block. Turn the router bit's cutting "tips" or "flutes" in line with this centerline, if they are not already, and hook your tape measure over the cutter. Measure along the centerline, and mark it at 45⅝ inches. Drill for a snug fit of a No. 12 or No. 14 wood screw, from the arm bottom (you will have marked the bottom surface) through the top, and countersink the top of the hole.

We have to locate the other half of this hole accurately in the pivot block 45 inches from the point on the 120-degree block on a line that bisects or divides the 120-degree angle into two equal parts. The 45-inch measurement is important; locating the bisecting line on the pivot block is even more important. In fact, that line is so important, we must make the extra effort to find and check it because, if it is correct, you will cut the pockets at the same angles, the stiles will lie flat with the slats in place, and you will not need to readjust the jig as you transfer from one side of the 120-degree block to the other to cut the pockets.

Photo 6 shows a close-up of the top of one edge on the 120-degree block. You need to accurately locate a point along each edge and in ¾ inch from each edge, as indicated. You can use the rule from your square, setting one end on the point and marking the other; a stick cut to 12 inches long would do as well. Set a depth gauge or square for ¾ inch, and mark across the 12-inch mark. These dimensions are arbitrary. You need a point on each side of the 120-degree block that is accurately measured an equal distance from the point and the edge, and at least 12 inches from the point. Mark a line through these two points square to the 120-degree edge and down over these edges. We will use these two ¾-inch and 12-inch points to locate the bisecting line on the pivot block, and the edge lines, to check this location once the router arm is fastened to the pivot block. Mark one point "A" and the other "B."

If you can make a large enough "compass," opening to around 4 feet, you can set the compass point on Point A and draw an arc along the back edge of the pivot block with the pencil end of your compass. If you do this again, setting the compass point on Point B, and, without changing the distance between the point and the pencil, draw another arc that crosses the first, you will have found a point (where the arcs cross) that is equidistant from Points A and B. A line drawn from the 120-degree block point through the point where the two arcs cross or intersect will represent the important bisecting line. Any point on that line will be equidistant from Points A and B, and also equidistant from the edge lines you drew. If you clamp the pivot block so it cannot move, you can find the bisecting line in the following way.

The top of the 120-degree block.

"X" marks the spot on the stick.

Photo 7 shows the end of a stick, a straight line, and two short lines that cross each other (an X) and the first line. The stick has a drywall screw driven through the other end, 41¾ inches from this end, with the sharp point sticking through about ¼ inch; that sharp point is set carefully in Point A. The pencil is held against the end of the stick at this end, and one line of the X is drawn, keeping the stick flat on the pivot block. Then the stick is moved so the screw is set carefully in Point B, and the other part of the X is drawn. The pencil, stick, and drywall screw are the compass, and the X represents the two arcs. The straight line was drawn between the 120-degree block point and the center of the X.

Next, you need to locate a 45-inch mark on the bisecting line, first hooking your tape measure over the 120-degree block point. A small taper-point drill works well to start the hole, which you must accurately drill on the bisecting line at 45 inches. If your drill wanders, try again at 45¼ inches or 44¾ inches. You will have to move the hole in the router arm also to 45⅞ inches

The bottom of the 120-degree block. The router arm shows below it.

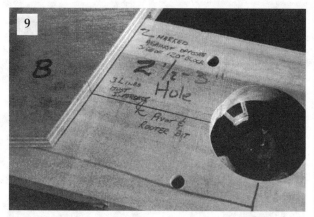

Pivot the base of the jig until the "edge line" lines up with the router arm centerline.

or 45⅜ inches, respectively. The hole should fall about 2½ inches from the end of the jig or the edge of the pivot block, and the router bit should be around ¹¹/₃₂ inch from the 120-degree block point when the router arm is in place.

Checking the Jig

Now you are ready to screw the router arm to the pivot block and check your work. With the pivot block still screwed and clamped securely to the base, locate and fasten the router arm to the pivot block with a No. 12 or No. 14 flathead wood screw, 1¼ inches long, so it will not enter the base and stop the pivot block's movement.

Turn the jig over. Photo 8 shows the bottom of the 120-degree block with the router arm (made of poplar here) below it. There are three pencil lines, two of which are drawn on the router arm. An arrow points to one line from a note "marked against the opposite side of 120-degree block." The third line is drawn on the edge of the 120-degree block. This line was drawn

over the edge, from Point A. The third line on the router arm is the centerline between the router bit and the pivot point at the far end of the router arm. The centerline and the edge line on the 120-degree block in Photo 8 line up.

Pivot the base of your jig until the edge line you drew from Point B lines up with your router arm centerline (see Photo 9). Draw a sharp line on the router arm along the 120-degree block edge. Move the base of the router so the edge line from Point A is aligned with the router arm centerline. Your lines should now look like those shown in Photo 8. You should see not only the router arm centerline in alignment with the edge line you drew from Point B, but also the line you just drew along the opposite side of the 120-degree block should be in alignment as well. If so, your jig is accurately assembled.

I am not sure how far off you can be in this alignment and still produce flat doors. If your marks line up within the width of a sharp No. 3 or No. 4 pencil, you should be in good shape. If not, try to find your error and correct it. Check and recheck your measurements for Points A and B, your arcs, the placement of the drywall screw in Points A and B, the edge lines from A and B, and the accuracy of the router arm's centerline.

You now have the router mounted on an arm, nearly ready to cut pockets, first in one stile clamped to one leg of your 120-degree block, and then in the opposite stile clamped to the other leg of that block. Before you can position the stiles, though, you need a way to clamp them to the base, a way to index or set them up for cutting the pockets at uniform intervals, and the stop blocks to limit the pocket length. To accommodate the clamps, I like to drill a 1¼-inch or larger hole in the jig, located roughly on the centerline of the 120-degree block and about 2¾ inches from the point. A 6-inch-long Jorgensen 3706 clamp works very well, and if it is temporarily fixed in place, moving and clamping the stiles is fairly easy. Of course, it must be moved from one side to the other as you cut alternate stiles.

Refer to the illustration again, and examine the stop blocks. One is fastened on each leg of the 120-degree angle block, about 8 inches apart. They should overhang about ¼ inch to ¾ inch. The stiles can be held up to these overhangs — that is, flush with the top of the 120-degree block — while you tighten the clamp. The router arm has a drywall screw on either side, which will bump the two stop blocks. These are the two screws that you will adjust to limit the router's lateral travel or the length of the slat pockets.

You are ready to adjust the jig and cut the slat pockets in the door stiles. First, however, you need to mill up the slat and stile stock, because it is easier to adjust the jig than to mill the stock to suit the jig.

BUILDING THE DOORS
Test Stiles and Rails

Before you get into milling up stock for finished doors, I suggest you try some test pieces (see Photo 10). The jig needs to be adjusted, and a few short pieces will do for this. You may also want to run off some test stiles about 3 to 4 feet long and a few short pieces of rail stock. The test stiles and rails are handy for working out suitable door sizes.

To start with, mill up about 4 to 5 feet of stile stock, pine or poplar, $^{13}/_{16}$ inch thick by 2 to 2½ inches wide. You can also mill up a 12-inch-long piece $^{13}/_{16}$ inch thick by 4 to 6 inches wide for test rails. The stile and rail stock should be planed to the same thickness; a slight difference can create serious problems in door-making, especially if you use a router or a shaper/cutter set.

You also need some slat stock to set up the jig. Again, this can be poplar or pine, or whatever you have. You only need 6 to 12 inches. If you prefer to make up a short piece and plane or sand the ⅛-inch radius, that is fine. The jig can be tested with such a piece and is easily adjusted for different slat widths. With your $^{13}/_{16}$-inch stile stock and a short piece of slat stock, you can adjust the jig.

The next goal is to set up the jig so the router bit will cut a pocket in either stile, left or right, at the same angle to the stile faces, long enough to contain the ¼-inch by 1⅛-inch slats and without readjusting the stop screws for each side. The trigonometry of the setup is shown in Figure B; you can use the same math for varying stile thicknesses. The $^{13}/_{16}$-inch thickness is a good choice, because the distance between the point and the pocket edge or ¼-inch bit edge works out to $^{11}/_{32}$ inch, an easy dimension to pick out on a good rule.

Boatbuilding and joinerwork require a fair amount of judgment. A friend of mine used to tell me to "read between the lines" of a blueprint. Drawings, tolerances, and dimensions don't tell the whole story.

Cut about 8 inches off one test stile, and clamp it in the jig as shown in Photo 3. Set the router bit over the stile, and adjust the two drywall "stop" screws to limit the length of the pocket cut to about 1⅛ inches. You will be able to adjust the screws more accurately after you have cut a pocket or two. You will need to check the $^{11}/_{32}$-inch distance between the edge of the slat pocket and the 120-degree point (see Photo 11). You can loosen the clamp that holds the pivot block and move it slightly one way or another to adjust for this $^{11}/_{32}$-inch space, and you may have to cut a few pockets before it is correct. If you are using softwood for your test pieces, the $^{11}/_{32}$-inch dimension might change slightly when you cut hardwood, or when your cutter becomes dull. Even a slight change from this dimension will significantly alter the symmetrical location of the pockets in both stiles.

Try some test pieces before working on the real thing.

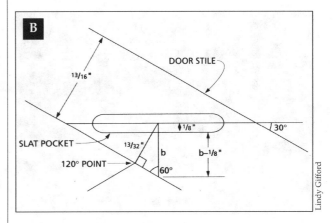

Trigonometry of the jig setup —

$$\sin 60° = \frac{13/32''}{b}$$

$$b = \frac{0.406}{0.866} = 0.469''$$

$$\therefore b = \frac{15}{32}''$$

$$\text{and } b - \frac{1}{8}'' = \frac{11}{32}''$$

Check the distance between the edge of the slat pocket and the 120-degree point.

The layout procedure is shown here.

Clamp an infeed fence to the router table.

Once you have set the pivot block for the $^{11}/_{32}$-inch dimension, adjust the drywall screws for the 1⅛-inch pocket length. It is important to cut the pocket ends equal distances from each edge of the stile. You can check this with your combination square set as a depth gauge, or by carefully measuring from each side.

When this adjustment is correct, transfer the 8-inch test stile to the other side of the jig. Keeping the same stile face against the jig, clamp it and cut a pocket near the other pockets. Since this is just a test, you can cut one pocket over another. Check the distances from this pocket's ends to the stile edge. Are they equal? If not, the $^{11}/_{32}$-inch dimension may not be correct yet. Your stiles may be a little over or under $^{13}/_{16}$ inch thick. Play with the jig to reduce the error.

You will need to develop a steady cutting technique to produce consistent pockets. Remember to "read between the lines" — in this case, pockets. You can easily adjust the stop screws so the pockets in a door are located correctly, provided this does not produce

pockets cut at significantly different angles and doors that are not flat enough for you to live with. You can easily check for consistent angles by cutting a few pockets in two short pieces of the stile stock, one left and one right. Locate a few short pieces of slat between these, and see if the two stiles lie flat (a saw, joiner, or shaper table provide a good, flat surface). If they do lie flat, or perhaps within $^1/_{64}$-inch per foot of flat, you can easily adjust the pocket locations with the stop screws. If not, you must check the critical assembly steps again — for the pivot, the bisecting line, the $^{13}/_{16}$-inch thickness, and especially the $^{11}/_{32}$-inch dimension. Try adjusting this in particular. You may, in fact, need more or less than $^{11}/_{32}$ inch.

When you are satisfied with the jig, you can mark the pitch lines for the slat pockets on your test stiles. I use a 1-inch pitch or increment, and the distance between the slats comes out about $^5/_{32}$ inch. You may want to try more or less space between the slats. The layout procedure is well illustrated in Photo 12. Locate the first pocket 3½ inches from one end of the stiles. The first and last pockets are covered by the rails. This works well for cutting the open-end mortises and locating the rail during assembly.

Slats

You want a neat fit around each slat, but you don't want too much interference in sliding the slats into the pockets. The accumulated interference from multiple slats can create problems when you attempt to pull the stiles together on the slats. You should not have any problem inserting the slats in the first stile, but when you attempt to line up the individual slats in the opposite stile pockets, any extra interference can be very frustrating. The slats are lined up carefully, one after the other, starting at either end of the door. A light clamp at each end helps, but do not force or hurry this assembly; as you line up a few slats, tighten the clamps judiciously.

I usually start with ¾- or 1¼-inch- thick stock for the slats, around 2 to 4 inches wide and 4 to 6 feet long. You can use up a fair amount of scrap in making slat stock. You start by planing the pieces to $1^5/_{32}$ to $1^3/_{16}$ inch thick before ripping the ¼-inch-thick slats. The stock pieces should be uniform in thickness. Many thickness planers, depending on their condition and setup, do not produce a uniformly thick board across the planer table. You should send the 2- to 4-inch-wide pieces through at the same place on the table or bed. Keep this in mind for planing the ¼-inch dimension, too, after you rip your slats from the 2- to 4-inch pieces, so the slats themselves are uniform in thickness. The next setup is to mill the ⅛-inch radius on the slat edges. A shaper or router can be used to mill these. You should now have slats with square edges that fit the slat pocket width, each slat measuring about ¼ inch thick and ¹⁵⁄₃₂ inch to 1³⁄₁₆ inches wide.

Set up your router or shaper with a ⅛-inch-radius bullnose cutter bit, and tentatively clamp an in-feed fence to the router table so the router bit will remove ¹⁄₆₄ inch to ¹⁄₃₂ inch from each side of the slat stock (see Photo 13). Run one edge of the slat stock into the router bit; be sure you hold the stock securely down and against the infeed fence. About 3 to 4 inches of cut is enough.

Flip the stock over, and run the other side. Measure your stock width for 1⅛ inches, and adjust the infeed fence accordingly. Once the infeed fence is set correctly (you can make the slat stock any width you choose, providing it will fit in the stiles), take a straight piece of slat stock and feed about 8 to 12 inches into the cutter. Remove the stock, turn off and unplug the router, relocate the stock against the infeed fence, and clamp it securely. You can now gently set the outfeed fence to the bullnosed edge of the slat stock. When you resume running the stock, carefully watch and make sure the stock remains tight to the fences throughout the cut. A finger stick (a separate piece of slat stock) will hold the slat tightly to the outfeed table.

Don't forget to locate something to hold the stock flat on the table, too. A small opening in the table, or a separate piece of plywood over the table with a small clearance hole for the router bit, will allow you to locate the hold-down near the cut. You can position a vacuum-cleaner nozzle behind the cutter to remove the chips.

Once you are set up, mill one side of the stock and turn the stock around, feeding the other end in first. If you are producing a slightly tapered cut (removing more at the beginning of the cut than at the end, for instance), reversing the ends of the slat should compensate for this. The stock should be uniform in thickness and width, or some of your slats will not fit in the slat pockets well. You can check the width and thickness with a simple caliper, or make yourself a gauge with two blocks 1⅛ inches apart, fastened to a third block. You can do the same for the ¼-inch dimension, although your planer should maintain it adequately. The slat dimensions are critical, and if you mill these carefully, you should produce a consistent fit in the slat pockets.

You have marked the test stiles; use these to experiment. Play around with the jig, and try setting the pockets closer to one stile face if you wish. Cut various test stiles, and don't be afraid of making mistakes on these; mistakes occasionally lead to interesting new ideas. You also have a ¹³⁄₁₆-inch by 4- to 6-inch by 12-inch piece for test rails. I like the appearance of the rails milled at a 60-degree angle, so the edges are parallel with the slats. You may want to try this, or some other configuration.

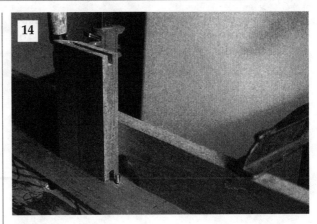

Cutting open-end mortises.

There is one advantage to the 60-degree angle edges: You can slide the rails along between the test stiles, with or without slats in place, setting the rails' 60-degree edge on a given set of pockets, and determine a suitable height for a given door, before you cut the opening for that door. I usually make the front face of the finished top rail and stiles 2¼ inches to 2½ inches wide, and the front face of the bottom rail 2½ inches to 3 inches wide. Start with the test rails wider, and figure your finished sizes from these. Be sure you cut the rail ends square.

At this point, you can make up the stiles, with pockets cut for the slat stock. Figure out the door height, the pitch dimension, the number of slats needed, and the rail heights.

Assembly

There are several ways to join the door rails and the stiles, and the method used will determine the overall length of the door rails and the slats. Because assembling a louvered door involves lining up the slats to fit neatly into the pockets, we should find a rail and stile joint that will not complicate the process. I like to fit the slats once and leave them in place while I fasten or glue the rails in place.

One simple method consists of assembling the slats and stiles, cutting the rails square on the ends, to make a simple butt joint with the stile edges. Use long screws and glue to make the joints secure. This joint allows us to assemble the door dry and check for flatness and correct door width, then slightly splay the stiles and slide the rails back between the stiles before screwing. We could use a similar joint, and instead of using screws, cut open-end mortises in the rails and stiles, using the router setup as shown in Photo 14, and slide a glue-smeared spline into the mortises after assembling the slats and stiles. We only assemble the slats and stiles once, try the rails, and glue.

If you prefer to use a more complex joint, to make the door's appearance a little more interesting, you can use a standard door-set for a router or shaper and mold the edge of the stiles after you mill the pockets — provided your cutters are very sharp and do not splinter the pocket edges. Cope the rail ends before beveling the 60-degree angle on the edges of the rails. Try a test piece. Like the spline joint, you can cut a short, open-end mortise in the stiles to accept the tenons left by the coping cutters in the door set.

I have tried various stile and rail joints, including hidden splines in closed mortises, and the method I prefer is a joint that allows me to assemble the entire door dry, check everything, slide the rails out, apply glue to the stiles and rail ends, and slide the rails back into place without disturbing the slats.

I hope you are tempted to make up the jig and play around with it. You might make larger doors and adjust the jig for 1⅛-inch-thick stiles. You might make a tiny jig for model doors. Or you might add panels to your doors. In any case, with a little experience you can design and build inexpensive doors that are durable and pleasant to look at, and turn the necessity of ventilation into an attractive virtue.

Raised Panels

by Arch Davis

A quiet anchorage at dusk. A cat's-paw murmurs along the hull; the black mass of a hill is silhouetted against the twilit sky and its reflection in the water.

An open hatchway is an island of brightness. Varnished wood gleams in the lamplight, planes and edges reflecting a spectrum of warm hues. You are pleased again, perhaps for the hundredth time, by the interplay of line and color in the joinerwork below. The boat's builder has made free use of raised paneling, and there is something particularly satisfying about the way the figured grain is thrown into relief by the subtly faceted borders and the light and the shade of the moldings.

What is it that makes raised paneling so satisfying? To me, it is that it represents an elegant solution to a particular engineering problem in wood. The problem is this: How to build, from planks of wood, a wide, flat structure — for example, a door — that will retain its shape and breadth when the planks shrink and swell with changes in humidity.

The elements of the solution are the frame (vertical stiles and horizontal rails), with tight, strong joints, the grain of the wood following the perimeter so its dimensions are stable. (Remember that, as moisture content changes, wood moves across, but not along, the grain.) In the frame are one or more wide panels, held in such a way that they can expand or contract without the frame itself moving.

The name *raised panel* is really rather misleading. The essence of the solution is that the panel is thinner at the edges, to slot into grooves in the frame. The grooves hold the panel but allow movement across the grain. The individual pieces can move, but the whole retains its size and shape.

Factories and cabinet shops use shapers to make

raised-panel doors. Special cutters make the grooves and put a decorative molding on the edges of the framing members. Cutters with a matching profile shape the ends of the rails to fit the edges of the stiles. A third set of cutters "raises" the panel by cutting back the edge to fit the grooves in the frame. A shop with properly

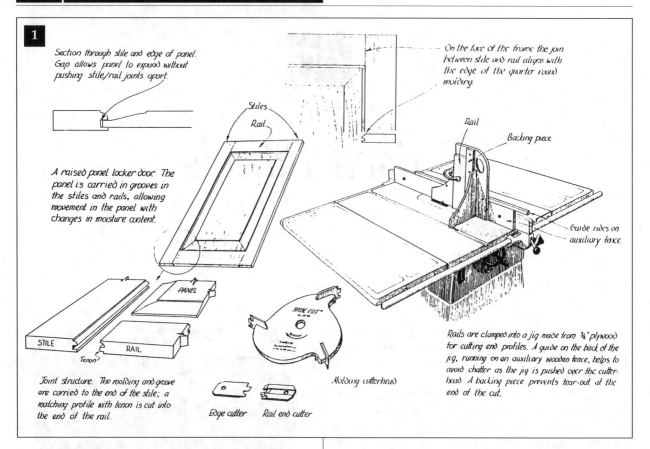

1

Section through stile and edge of panel. Gap allows panel to expand without pushing stile/rail joints apart.

On the face of the frame the join between stile and rail aligns with the edge of the quarter round molding.

Stiles

Rail

Rail

Backing piece

A raised panel locker door. The panel is carried in grooves in the stiles and rails, allowing movement in the panel with changes in moisture content.

Guide rides on auxiliary fence.

PANEL

STILE

RAIL

Tenon

TRUE CUT

Rails are clamped into a jig made from ¾" plywood for cutting end profiles. A guide on the back of the jig, running on an auxiliary wooden fence, helps to avoid chatter as the jig is pushed over the cutterhead. A backing piece prevents tear-out at the end of the cut.

Joint structure. The molding and groove are carried to the end of the stile; a matching profile with tenon is cut into the end of the rail.

Edge cutter   Rail end cutter

Molding cutterhead

set up machinery can knock out a raised-panel cabinet door in a very few minutes. The joints will be neat, and the borders of the panel will be clean and ready to finish. Nicely proportioned, the door is handsome and practical.

Raised panels are as decorative in a boat as they are ashore, and they can be used in more than just doors. The style is suitable for bunk fronts, engine boxes, cabinets for refrigeration, the end of a chart table — anywhere a relatively wide slab is needed. It can also be used to give a lift to plywood bulkheads — more on this later. Tasteful use of raised panels in a boat's interior can represent the highest quality of marine cabinetmaking.

Fortunately for the home builder and the small boatshop, it is possible to make top-quality raised-panel cabinetry without a shaper. The work takes a little longer, but this will not bother the do-it-yourselfer. Even the small yard may well find that with small numbers of paneled items of varying design, the increased labor cost is less than the investment in a shaper and expensive sets of carbide-tipped cutters.

I have used two basic methods for making raised panels with good results. Both require a table saw. One uses special, inexpensive cutters that fit the saw. The other uses a dado cutter, or just an ordinary blade, and any router in a table. In both cases, the panel is raised using a regular blade, on the table saw.

Figure 1 shows a cutter head and cutters for making cabinet doors. The cutters on the left make the grooves and put a quarter-round molding on the rails and the stiles. The cutters on the right are rail-end cutters. The drawing at the bottom left shows how the cutters work together to make the joint between the rail and the stile.

In the other method, the edges of rails and stiles are grooved on the table saw using a dado cutter or several passes with an ordinary blade. The joint is formed by cutting a tenon in the ends of the rails to match the grooves in the stiles. Figure 2 shows an open joint of this kind.

Rails and stiles could be left unembellished; carefully done, with the edges just rounded over and with a simple panel design, a pleasing, if somewhat spare appearance is achieved. Often, however, some sort of decorative molding rather than the plain arris next to the panel is desirable. One approach is to make the molding separately and glue it around the inside of the frame, mitering the corners. The molding could be a simple quarter-round beading, or something quite elaborate.

A simple alternative that I find gives a very satisfying appearance is to use a router in a table, with a bullnose bit, to put a cove on the edges of the stiles and the rails. The cove is stopped short of the corner, matching the borders of the raised part of the panel,

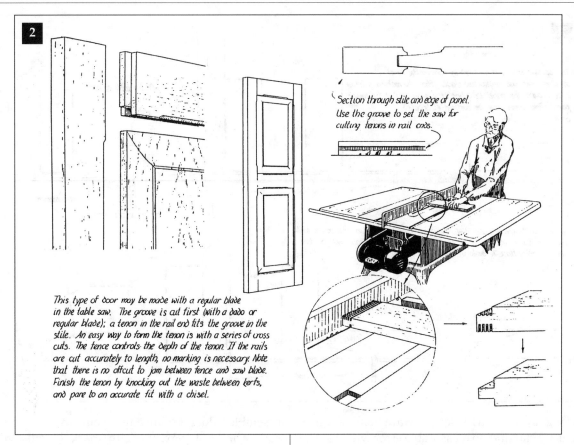

2

This type of door may be made with a regular blade in the table saw. The groove is cut first (with a dado or regular blade); a tenon in the rail end fits the groove in the stile. An easy way to form the tenon is with a series of cross cuts. The fence controls the depth of the tenon. If the rails are cut accurately to length, no marking is necessary. Note that there is no offcut to jam between fence and saw blade. Finish the tenon by knocking out the waste between kerfs, and pare to an accurate fit with a chisel.

Section through stile and edge of panel. Use the groove to set the saw for cutting tenons in rail ends.

which also have a small cove. This method is very versatile, since details and proportions can be varied endlessly. It can be used on doors of any thickness, is suitable for larger sizes, and doesn't have the limitations of the cutters illustrated.

Designing Door Panels

Now, let's make some doors — say, a ¾-inch-thick locker door, using the cutter head, and a pair of 1¼-inch doors with raised panels on both sides, for the companionway. The locker door will have one panel, the others two.

First, we have to design the doors. Scale drawings will help us to get pleasing proportions. Cabinet doors can have stiles and rails of equal width. I find 1¾ inches to 2¼ inches about right for most purposes. Larger doors may call for wider stiles, with rails wider again. Frequently, the bottom rail will also be wider than the others.

The width of the edges of the raised panels will depend on the size of the panels. Draw a full-sized cross section through a stile and the edge of the panel; this will give the correct setback and width of the groove for the panel. A setback of ¼ inch to ⁵⁄₁₆ inch seems to be right for most doors. The thickness of the edge of the raised panel also determines the size of the tenon in the rail end, and probably should not be less than ¼ inch. The depth of the groove must like-

wise be enough to give a decent-sized tenon, and to allow for movement of the panel.

Figure 3 shows the stages of raising the panel. The shapes that can be achieved with a regular blade can be made more elaborate by running a molding with a router. With some hand work, it is possible to reproduce almost any profile that a shaper can produce. Note that any profile that tapers right at the edge will become tighter in the grooves in the stiles as the panel swells; a little slack should be allowed to accommodate this.

Achieving really good joints is easy — if your table saw is accurate. If you haven't been using it for this kind of work, now is the time to check it over. Does it have a suitable, sharp blade? (Even carbide blades get dull eventually. The doors I have illustrated were made using a 10-inch combination blade with 50 teeth.) Does the blade run true, parallel to the slots for the miter gauge and perpendicular to the table? Are the stops on the miter gauge correctly set for a 90-degree cut? Is the fence straight, parallel to the blade, and perpendicular to the table? Crosscut a piece of wood with one edge dressed straight, and put your square across and along the end. Is it exactly square both ways? (While you are at it, do you really trust your square?)

Remember that tiny errors can accumulate, causing troublesome gaps in your work. I get good results by

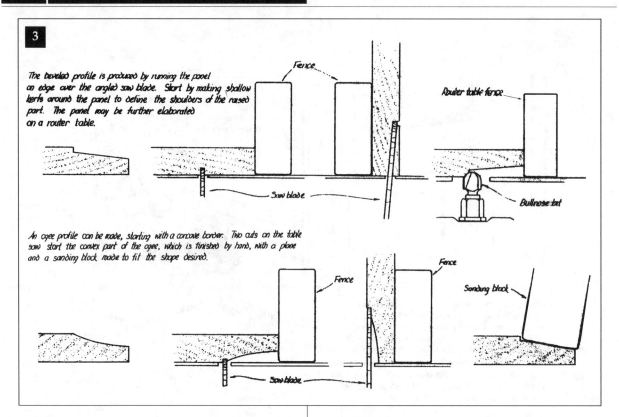

3

The beveled profile is produced by running the panel on edge over the angled saw blade. Start by making shallow kerfs around the panel to define the shoulders of the raised part. The panel may be further elaborated on a router table.

Fence

Router table fence

Saw blade

Bullnose bit

An ogee profile can be made, starting with a concave border. Two cuts on the table saw start the convex part of the ogee, which is finished by hand, with a plane and a sanding block made to fit the shape desired.

Fence

Fence

Sanding block

Saw blade

checking my saw and try-square with a framing square in which I can find no measurable error with a scribe and a straightedge.

Making the Parts

A good way to start building the door is by gluing up boards for the panels, if the width of your stock requires it. Then rip the stiles and rails from stable, straight lumber. Cut the stiles and rails approximately to length, remembering to allow for the tenons in the rail ends. Dress one edge of each piece straight and square. This edge will go inside the frame, next to the panel. The outside edge will be trued up when the door is finished. It is particularly important that the inside edges of the stiles be square across, to avoid gaps in the joints with the rails.

Lay out the stiles and the rails for each door in their correct relative positions, matching the grain with the panels for best appearance. Mark each piece on the face, showing clearly its position and orientation.

The next step is to machine the edges of the stiles and rails. If you are using a molding cutter head, this will cut the groove for the panel and the decorative molding at the same time. If you are using a dado cutter, or will be making several passes with a regular blade, make the groove only. To ensure uniformity, all cuts should be made with the face of the workpiece against the fence.

Now cut the rails to length, allowing for the tenons in each end, plus 1/16 inch for finishing the edges of the

assembled door. Because these cuts must be exactly square and of the exact length, mark the rails with a scribe, rather than a pencil, as it is more accurate.

The next job is to form the ends of the rails. A jig to hold the rails is needed if you are using a cutter head (see Figure 1). Carefully adjust the height of the arbor, using pieces of scrap, to form the end correctly without removing excess material. Once you have the jig and the machine adjusted properly, don't alter the setup, or the rails will no longer be of the same length.

If you are not using a cutter head, the tenons on the rails can be cut with the miter gauge and fence as in Figure 2 (these two accessories can be used safely together in this situation, as there is no offcut to jam between the blade and the fence). The miter gauge will ensure that the cut is square, and the fence will ensure that the tenon is of the correct length. (You can make the tenon a hair shorter than the depth of the groove so it will not quite bottom out when the door is assembled, in the interest of hairbreadth gluelines on the face of the door.)

Next, cut out the panels. Remember that you have to allow for expansion and contraction. This requires an estimate of the moisture content of the wood and likely changes in the piece in service. You also need to take into account the width of the piece, the type of wood you are using, and the orientation of the grain. A flat-sawn panel is likely to swell twice as much as one that is quarter sawn. Teak and mahogany move less than most woods. Sealing the wood with several coats of varnish helps limit moisture transfer and movement.

This sounds like a lot to think about. In practice, if you allow for ⅛ inch of movement on each side in moderate-sized panels (providing for ¼ inch total movement across the panel), you will be pretty safe. This assumes that the wood is "dry" — i.e., at equilibrium with the moisture content of the atmosphere. In summer, the moisture content will be high; allow for more shrinkage than expansion. In winter it will be low, so allow for more expansion.

Raising the panels comes next. For a beveled profile (see Figure 3, top), start by making shallow cuts on the face of the panel to define the borders of the raised part. Then set the blade at the correct angle and depth, and cut the wedge-shaped strips off the edges to raise the panel (see Figure 4, top). A featherboard will hold the panel tightly against the fence for a uniform cut. If the panel is raised on both sides, however, it may be best to do without the featherboard on the second side, to prevent the panel from being pushed out of perpendicular.

A concave profile, or a cove, requires a special fence clamped diagonally across the table. The shape of the cove is determined by the angle of the fence, and the height and the diameter of the blade. Use featherboards to hold the panel down firmly on the table (see Figure 4, bottom). You will probably have to make several passes over the saw, raising the blade a little each time. Practice on scrap lumber until you are satisfied with the results, and to check the fit of the panel with stiles and rails. After raising the panels, use a router table to add any moldings that may be required, such as the small cove in Figure 3, top right.

Finish the edges of the panel with a molding plane, if required, and sandpaper. At the ends of the panels, you have to work across the grain. I start with 80- or 100-grit sandpaper, and work by stages to 220-grit. Then, to get rid of any traces of marks across the grain, I finish with a scraper. (Actually, a chisel. This may be an abuse of a chisel, perhaps, but it does the job.) This part of door making can be tedious and time-consuming, or quite quick, depending on the profile you have chosen, how sharp and accurate your saw is, the wood you are using, and the like.

A question you may now answer is whether you want the face of the panel to be flush with the frame,

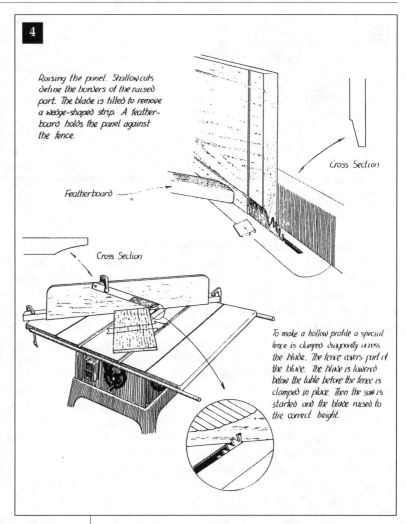

4

Raising the panel. Shallow cuts define the borders of the raised part. The blade is tilted to remove a wedge-shaped strip. A feather-board holds the panel against the fence.

Cross Section

Featherboard

Cross Section

To make a hollow profile a special fence is clamped diagonally across the blade. The fence covers part of the blade. The blade is lowered below the table before the fence is clamped in place. Then the saw is started and the blade raised to the correct height.

or slightly inset. If the latter, you can skim the stock for the panels with a thickness planer. If you don't have a thickness planer, a little vigorous work with a No. 4 or 5 plane will take ¹⁄₁₆ inch off the panel. I think this looks right, and it simplifies finishing, as we will see. At this point, complete the whole panel so it's ready for varnishing later.

If you used a molding cutter head to make the frame, the door is now ready for assembly. If you used the other method, you will have to put the molding on the edges of stiles and rails. The doors in the drawings have a ³⁄₁₆-inch cove. With a ⅛-inch cove on the panel, the effect is very attractive.

The cove is put on the rails and stiles with a router in a router table. Assemble the door, and mark where the cove is to start and finish. Make your marks clearly visible — it is fatally easy to go too far on the router table, especially on a stile of a multi-panel door, and ruin the piece. To avoid splinters tearing out ahead of the router bit at the end of a cut, stop each cut short and do the last part backwards. Again, a little practice on scrap will show how best to handle this.

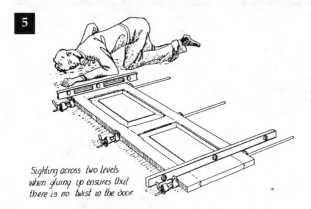

Sighting across two levels
when gluing up ensures that
there is no twist in the door.

Assembling and Finishing the Door

Now, assemble the door. Start with a dry run. Mark the position of the rails on the stiles, so the door is the correct height (allowing an extra ¹⁄₁₆ inch for finishing the top and the bottom) . Check that the door lies flat in the clamps (see Figure 5), as any twist will be permanent after the glue has set. Keep glue out of the grooves, except for a dab in the middle of each rail to secure the panel. Use a framing square to ensure that the door is square.

After setting the clamps, clean up any glue squeezed into the corners of the door; it is easier to do this now than when the glue has set. Try not to get epoxy anywhere but in the joints. It is difficult to clean off and does not show up until the door is varnished, when it can be unsightly.

The last stage of construction is finishing the door surface to get it ready for varnishing. I start by dressing the edges so they are straight and parallel, and the door is the correct width. Then, I cut the stiles flush at the ends, plane them square, and check that the door is the correct height. The final job is to clean up the face of the door (excluding the panel, which has already had its surface smoothed).

Most of the boatbuilders with whom I have worked use a belt sander to finish the door and get excellent results, but I prefer a No. 4 plane. Using a plane, you have to inspect the joints carefully to establish the run of the grain in each piece, and work diagonally across the corners. Vary the direction of your strokes to achieve a smooth, flush face at the joint. Keep the plane very sharp, set fine, and with the backing iron close to the cutting edge to avoid tearing out contrary grain. Take great care to avoid hitting the raised panel with a plane or a sander (this is easier if you made the panel a little under flush). After sanding, the door is ready for varnishing and hanging.

Raised Panels Throughout the Boat

Using raised panels in other items of cabin furniture requires only minor variations on the above methods. Provision has to be made to fix the paneling in place as part of the entire structure; when two sections of paneling meet at a corner in, for example, an engine box, a half lap or a corner post could be used to make the joint. Cleats can also be used; a bunk front might be fixed to the cabin sole by a cleat screwed to the sole and the back of the paneling, and the bunk top might be fixed to the front in a similar fashion.

In doors, the stiles run top to bottom, the rails butting against them. In other applications, a different pattern might be appropriate. For a bunk front, for example, it might be better to make the rails full length, cutting the stiles short and butting them against the rails.

Plywood has long been the almost universal choice for bulkheads. It is recommended by its stiffness and dimensional stability, and the speed and ease with which it can be cut to irregular shapes. Plywood, however, is plain to look at. A structural bulkhead made from raised paneling, while lovely to behold, lacks plywood's strength in the diagonal direction and would be limited by the strength of its stile-to-rail joints. (The panels themselves add little strength.) Plywood is very strong in all directions along its surface, and structural bulkheads made of plywood can add greatly to the stiffness of a hull. To give a bulkhead beauty as well as strength, plywood can be teamed with an overlay of raised paneling. The combination introduces some new considerations, however.

Designing the paneling may give the builder food for much thought. In most cases, the area to be covered will be irregular in shape. Figure 6 shows how raised panels might be used on the main bulkhead of a moderately sized sailboat. The problem is to achieve a satisfactory layout of the panels that fits neatly into the space and harmonizes with the rest of the interior. The builder needs to be able to visualize the overall effect he is striving for, which cannot easily be rendered in drawings.

Rather than being carried in grooves in the frame, panels on bulkheads can fit into rabbets cut with a router. You may feel that with one face of the frame held tight by being glued to the bulkhead, simple butt joints between stiles and rails are adequate. Remember, however, that the other face of the wood can still move slightly, enough to open up a gap at the joint if the glue has only end-grain to grip. If the frame is thicker than about ³⁄₈ inch, which barely gives enough for some thickness and setback at the edges of the raised panels, I feel that the joints should be reinforced — for example, by dowels or half-laps.

There are two approaches to assembling the paneling. One is to pre-assemble the frame, trim it to fit the bulkhead, then fix it in place, the raised panels

6

going in at this stage. The other is to assemble the pieces on the bulkhead, in the boat.

The first approach is easier if it is done early in construction, before the cabin trunk is on, and perhaps before building the furniture adjacent to the bulkhead. The latter option requires good planning; all the decisions regarding interior finishing must be made in advance. It may be more practical to build most of the cabin furniture with the deck, but not the cabin trunk, in place (this is efficient in any case, because it provides easy access). Fitting the pre-assembled paneling without the cabin trunk to contend with should not be too difficult. The bulkhead with attached paneling is cut to shape before building the cabin trunk.

The frame for the paneling will probably be glued to the bulkhead. How can it be held there until the glue sets? You can use screws, driven from behind, through the bulkhead, where possible. Screws through the paneling, countersunk and covered with matching plugs, may sometimes be acceptable. Around openings in the bulkhead, C-clamps can be used. Sometimes a cleat can be clamped to, say, a bunk top, allowing the paneling to be wedged against the bulkhead. Toms and wedges can be used if there is something handy such as another bulkhead, to set them against. Beware of creating a nightmare basketwork of sticks and wedges, tuned to the pitch of a concert violin, forcing a bow into the bulkhead, and ready to collapse like a house of cards if one wedge is driven too hard. In practice, a combination of methods usually works, taking advantage of seat cushions, doorway moldings, and the like to cover fastenings as much as possible.

Assembling the paneling on the bulkhead may be the only practical approach with the cabin furniture and the cabin trunk already in place. At first sight, it might seem in any case to be the easier method, but there is one disadvantage. When the frame for bulkhead paneling is pre-assembled, pipe or bar clamps can be used to pull it together. This snugs up the joints, and with good cutting techniques, provides the invisible glueline that we have been striving for. Applying lateral pressure when assembling the paneling on the bulkhead may be difficult. When screws are used to fix the frame to the plywood, pilot holes must be drilled with great care to avoid the joint being pulled slightly apart when the screw is driven. Even with the greatest care, the joints in this kind of construction can be disappointing unless some way is found to pull them together.

If there is a convenient opening in the bulkhead, such as a door, where a C-clamp can go, the following technique sometimes works:

Assemble the pieces on the bulkhead with glue and screws. Drive the screws until they just pull up. Then put a C-clamp, with wooden pads, on the piece you want to snug against its neighbor. Tighten the clamp fairly firmly. Then, one judicious tap with your hammer may be enough to tighten the joint. Hitting too hard may cause the pieces to bounce apart again. When you have it right, give another twist to the clamp, and the screws, and there you are. Failing this, you can try toms and wedges, or perhaps a pipe clamp can be made to work if a locker door gives something to pull against. The key is as much planning as possible, a careful dry-assembly run, a glue that gives plenty of working time, and perhaps some custom clamping devices.

It is important to remember, of course, that the raised panels themselves should not be fixed to the bulkhead. Just as they needed room to move in the grooves in the doors, they must be able to expand and contract with changes in moisture content while the plywood behind them remains stable.

Interesting and attractive paneling can also be made in other ways — for example, with tongue-and-groove panels, or with plywood, with or without decorative moldings. The uses to which they can be put in boatbuilding are limited only by the inventiveness of the builder.

A Strong and Stowable Table

by Kendall Williams

When I bought *Moonspinner*, a 36-foot 6-inch ketch designed by L. Francis Herreshoff, she had a gimbaled table located amidships in the main cabin. This table was nicely constructed and had served the previous owner well during weekend use and short cruises, but I planned to use *Moonspinner* as a liveaboard, and I soon decided that I needed a more open feel to the main cabin.

I wanted a strong, rigid table that could be easily disassembled and quickly stored away when the starboard bunk was in use. *Moonspinner*'s layout is fairly conventional, and my table solution is one that could be duplicated on most boats. All it requires is a strong bulkhead and/or an enclosed head at the forward end of the main cabin where a knee brace can be fastened to hold the folding, stowable table when it is in use.

On *Moonspinner*, the folded table stows away vertically in the lavatory, on the reverse side of the bulkhead. Setting up or stowing away takes less than 40 seconds. The knee brace is permanently bolted to the bulkhead with a ¾-inch oak backing block to distribute the loads, and in this particular installation, the bulkhead/passageway corner has been reinforced with a strip of glued oak. The table attaches to the knee with a tapered key fitting.

The table has a single folding leaf that is held up with a simple leg that fits into a notch in the cabin sole. When the leaf is in the down position, it rests vertically against the side of the knee, with its forward edge snug against the bulkhead, held in position with a wooden toggle. In this position, the table can resist a great deal of downward force should someone stumble against it while the boat is underway. The leaf is flush with the passageway (i.e., the face of the lavatory enclosure) and allows easy access to the head and forward cabin. It is sized so there is also adequate passage when it is in the "up" position, leaving about 10 inches between the port settee and the leaf.

The table and the knee brace are both white oak. The knee is 9⅝ inches tall, 10⅜ inches long, and 4¼ inches wide. Leaf up, the table measures 33½ inches by 26½ inches, with the leaf itself measuring 33½ inches by 16½ inches.

The table and leaf are simply ¾-inch boards, edge-glued and hinged together with flush-mounted cabinet hinges. The knee was fabricated by gluing ¾-inch and 2-inch oak into an extremely strong and rigid structural member. What is unusual and makes this table so successful is the attachment method between the knee and the table.

A rectangular block of oak is let into the underside of the smaller table section at the forward end in an

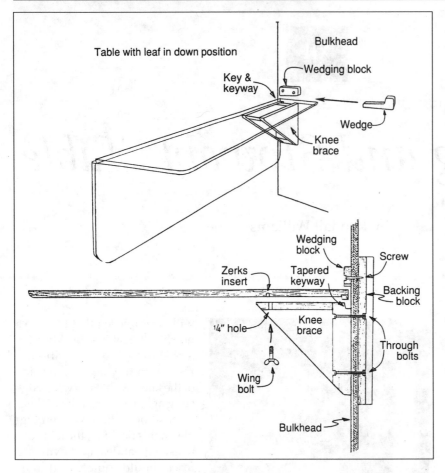

Table with leaf in down position

Bulkhead

Key &
keyway

Wedging block

Wedge

Knee
brace

Wedging
block

Screw

Zerks
insert

Tapered
keyway

Backing
block

¼" hole

Knee
brace

Through
bolts

Wing
bolt

Bulkhead

approximately 1¾ inches above the knee, and its lower edge is cut to the same slope as the wedge so the downward pressure is equally distributed as the wedge is inserted.

The taper of the key ensures that the forward edge of the table is pressed firmly forward against the bulkhead. The tolerances are adjusted so the underside of the table meets the upper surface of the knee at the same time that the forward edge of the table meets the bulkhead. The table is now firmly attached to the bulkhead and resists sideways or downward forces.

In case someone should inadvertently lift up on the table, a ¼-inch hole was drilled through the after upper surface of the knee and a wing bolt was inserted and threaded into a Zerks insert screwed into the underside of the table. To disassemble the table, the wing bolt is unscrewed, the wedge driven out, and the table is removed. It

athwartships position and glued. It projects from the table's underside surface about ⅜ inch. This projecting portion is tapered on its after face and fits snugly into a tapered slot of slightly smaller dimensions that is formed in the top surface of the knee, just where it meets the bulkhead. This creates a tapered keyway, with the bulkhead forming its forward side. A strong mating of the two elements is ensured by a wedge pushed between the tabletop and a small block bolted to the bulkhead above the knee. The block is set

is folded in on itself with the key-shaped block fitting into a cavity chiseled into the leaf. In the lavatory, where the table is stowed, it is held against the bulkhead with toggles.

This simple table has proven to be strong and easy to use. Although the knee remains bolted to the bulkhead when the table is not in use, it is small enough not to be in the way; perhaps I'll think of another use for it, so in the future even this small drawback will evolve its own purpose.

A Fold-Up Table and Shelves

––––––– by Joel White –––––––

*S*weet Olive is a 43-foot cruising cutter designed by me and built by the Brooklin (Maine) Boat Yard. When we launched her in the summer of 1991, almost the only job left to do on her was to build the cabin table. I had already thought about this at some length and had made sketches of how it might be done.

After many years of cruising, I have come to the conclusion that in a small- to medium-sized boat, a fixed cabin table with drop leaves wastes more space than anyone wants to give up. Such a table is not in use much of the time, but the floor space under it is in great demand. For that reason, *Sweet Olive*'s table is designed to fold up out of the way when not needed, yet it is instantly available for use. It is large enough to seat the boat's cruising complement of up to six people.

Sweet Olive has a conventional layout below, with high pilot berths to port and starboard and extension berths inboard. The latter act as seats most of the time but can be pulled out and made wider for use as bunks, if needed. At the forward end of the main cabin, the toilet room bulkhead makes a vertical wall extending out to the centerline. Just aft of this is the mast. I had planned to put bookshelves on the after face of this bulkhead, but it also seemed to be the logical place to hang a folding table. The drawing and photos show how we managed to combine the two. In practice, this table works very well.

I don't believe there's any truly original thinking in this design; rather, it is an amalgam of many ideas observed over years of working on yachts. Making sketches for the carpenters to work from was complex enough, so it seemed a good idea to draw up the final table accurately to scale. That way, the carpenters would have a clear idea of what they were to

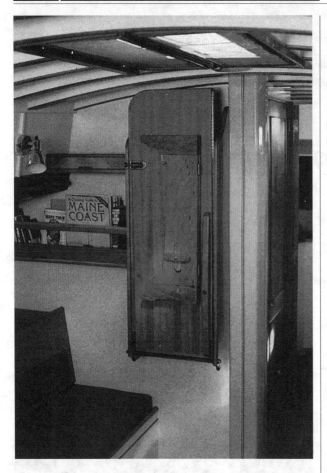

build. The finished drawings might help others facing the same problems.

There are several criteria that I considered important when designing this table: It must be firm and strong, not at all rickety. It must be easy to put into position and to fold away. If possible, it should be usable both with the leaf folded up or extended. And it should not be an eyesore in the cabin.

Since the interior of *Sweet Olive* is trimmed in varnished cherry, we built the table of the same wood. A number of other wood species — such as mahogany, oak, walnut, or teak — would be equally suitable. The tabletop and the shelves are ¾-inch cherry plywood, with their exposed edges banded with solid cherry, as shown in detail on the plan. Everything else is solid cherry. All hardware — hinges, pivot pins, and fittings — are bronze or brass.

When making cabin furniture, it is important that the boat's interior trim style be reflected in the design. We had earlier picked an ogee shape made by a router bit for all the exposed edges of the shelves, the chart table, and other interior trim throughout the boat, and this same treatment was used on the table and shelf edges. The fixed fiddles on the shelves are the same pattern as used elsewhere in the boat. The legs of solid cherry were made with square corners,

rounded slightly with sandpaper, for simplicity and eye appeal.

Decorative moldings and shaping must be done with great restraint, lest the overall effect be one of fussiness and over-ornamentation. If you use these plans to build a table for your boat, be sure to alter the detailing to conform with the style used in your cabin's trim style.

You must also alter the dimensions shown to conform to the space available in your cabin. First, the height of the table above the seat cushion is critical for both comfort and knee room. Usually, 10 to 12 inches is about right. This determines the pivot-pin height above the cabin sole. The limiting factor on the length of the table then becomes the height from the pin to the cabin overhead. Don't forget to allow for the crown of the cabintop.

In *Sweet Olive*, we had to contend with the mast being just aft of the bulkhead, so the folding leaf was shortened enough to clear the mast when opened. If your mast is elsewhere, both leaves can be the same length. The width of the leaves also depends on the available space. For instance, if the mast on *Sweet Olive* had not been in the way, I would have placed the hinged edge of the two table leaves on the centerline, rather than offset to port. This would have allowed the leaves to be several inches wider than they are, and the table to be centered between the two extension berths. On *Sweet Olive*, the starboard berth can be extended to come closer to the table edge for more comfort.

A few of the table's details are worth mentioning. The two bronze fittings that attach the table to the pivot rod were brazed up from ³⁄₃₂-inch bronze plate to form a bronze angle. This allows for four wood screws in each fitting and makes a strong and lasting attachment. The plate was rabbeted flush into the bottom of the table, while on the sides it was not left proud so as to give some clearance when the leaves were folded up into the box on the bulkhead.

The sturdy legs, attached to the underside of the tabletop with heavy bronze T-hinges, also contribute to the table's steadiness. Large brass butt hinges would work equally well. The ¾-inch vertical legs are connected to the 1¹⁄₁₆-inch upper and lower feet with a glued mortise-and-tenon joint. The port leg is anchored when open by a brass pin protruding from its base, which sockets into a brass plate let flush into the cabin sole. We found the second leg did not need any such provision. The swinging arm, which pivots on a ⁵⁄₁₆-inch bronze carriage bolt, supports the forward end of the leaf when open.

When the table is in the folded position, there must be a device to hold the legs tightly against the leaves. We chose to do this with a cherry button protruding through an oval hole in each leg, but there are obviously other ways to accomplish this. A magnetic catch, some sort of friction catch, or even a hook and eye would serve. Use your imagination.

The table itself is held in the folded position by a brass barrel bolt. This works well, and there is no chance that the table can come crashing down unexpectedly.

The cherry box, which attaches to the bulkhead, not only houses the table when closed, but also allows for four shelves located behind the table. The shelves must be narrow enough so the table will house into the box without interference. We compartmented the bottom shelf with an egg-crate divider of ⅜-inch cherry for the stowage of liquor bottles or small table items, such as salt and pepper shakers. The three upper shelves have regular shelf fiddles and are useful for any number of small items — even paperback books. Access, however, is limited to when the table is down.

If you are dissatisfied with the present table arrangement on your boat, think about adapting the plan for this table to improve the situation. It makes a nice carpentry project. With accurate measurements from the boat, the entire unit can be built in the shop and then installed with only six wood screws through the bulkhead.

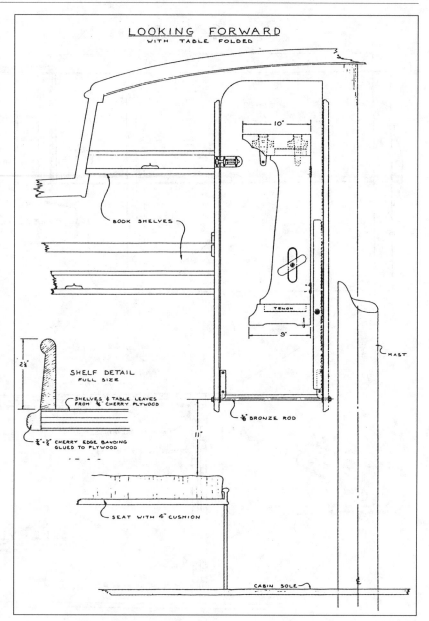

LOOKING FORWARD
WITH TABLE FOLDED

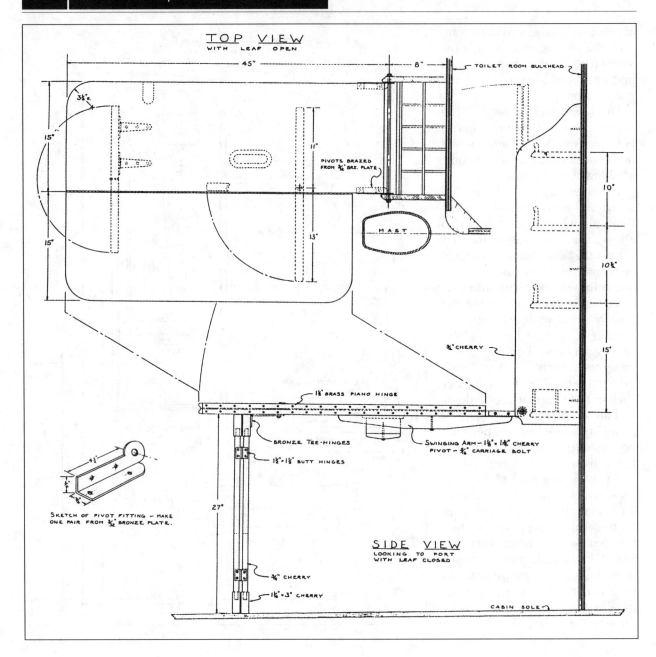

TOP VIEW
WITH LEAF OPEN

45"

8"

TOILET ROOM BULKHEAD

3½ R.

15"

11"

PIVOTS BRAZED
FROM ¼" BRZ. PLATE

15"

13"

MAST

10"

10½"

15'

¾" CHERRY

1⅛" BRASS PIANO HINGE

BRONZE TEE-HINGES

1½"×1½" BUTT HINGES

SWINGING ARM—1⅛"×1¼" CHERRY
PIVOT—⅜" CARRIAGE BOLT

SKETCH OF PIVOT FITTING — MAKE
ONE PAIR FROM ¼" BRONZE PLATE.

27"

SIDE VIEW
LOOKING TO PORT
WITH LEAF CLOSED

¾" CHERRY

1½"×3" CHERRY

CABIN SOLE

A Stowable Gimbaled Table

by Michael Kortchmar

*I*f you like to eat reasonably civilized meals at sea, particularly aboard a heeled-over sailboat, a gimbaled table is *sine qua non*. Just such a device was on a client's list when he brought his New York 32 *Dolphin* to our boatshop, Kortchmar & Willner, for a new interior.

In its conventional form, a gimbaled table is quite straightforward. It is basically a "T" in section, pivoted at the top center, with arms that are the table leaves and a leg that consists of a case·containing about 25 pounds of lead (see Figure 1). As the boat heels, the lead weight swings, so it is always below the pivot and the leaves are always horizontal. The soup stays in the bowl, and the bowl stays on the table.

Our task wasn't going to be that simple. *Dolphin* was quite narrow, and our client wanted to be able to remove and stow the table. Since I no longer feel that lifting heavy objects has any particular connection with manhood, I found the idea of dismantling the table and stowing the lead and associated joinery — perhaps in the midst of thrashing seas — less than appealing.

One day I idly suggested to my client that the gimbaling mechanism could be placed below the cabin sole. The table itself could be nothing more than two leaves, easily removable and taking up little space. To my surprise, he went for it.

"You realize that I have no idea what this is going to cost," I told him. "Are you sure you want to do it?" He was.

Thus we embarked on our journey upon the Sea of Research and Development. What follows is the record of the trip, complete with notations on the several times we went aground, the better to guide those souls who may choose to follow.

Most gimbaled tables have a bulky weight mechanism below the table but above the cabin sole. The gimbal mechanism on this table is below the sole and remains out of the way when the table is removed and stowed.

Design

In outline the scheme was this: The table leaves would slide into pivoting bronze channels attached to a pair of 1½-inch brass pipe posts running from the sole to the coach roof. Below the cabin sole, a trapeze of some sort would be suspended from sole beams to carry the lead weights. A link would connect the weights to what we used to call (when I built model

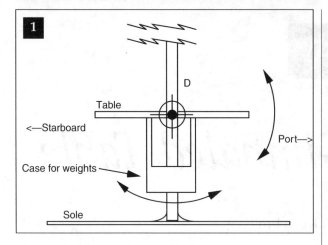

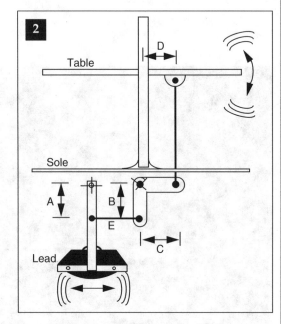

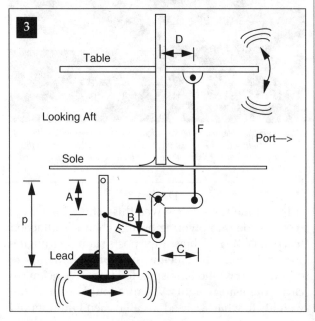

airplanes) a "bellcrank," where the horizontal swing of the weights would be changed to a vertical motion. A pushrod — designed to be easily removable — would carry the vertical motion up to the leaves. The basic idea is shown in Figure 2.

The simple swinging "T" design is more or less infallible, but when you depart from it a number of things can go wrong. I remember a delivery trip aboard a fancy new yawl. The designer of the boat had decided that only the table's leaves would move and the center section would remain fixed. It's not a bad idea in principle, because the narrower the moving leaf, the less motion there is at the outer edge. However, the linkage that made this possible was not well thought out, and the movement of the leaves doubled the angle of heel. On the windward side the food fell in your lap, and on the leeward side the food slithered away from you while the table edge clubbed you on the chin.

Not wishing to do this to the man who was paying my bills for the winter, I sat down with a pencil and paper to work out a way in which the angular motion of the table, after traveling through the linkage, could duplicate the angular motion of the weights. One achieves this by adjusting the lengths of the lever arms A, B, C, and D, shown in Figure 2. If all four arms are the same length, and if all the angles are 90 degrees, the angular change in the weights is transmitted exactly to the crank and then to the table, which is what we want. If arm A = arm B and arm C = arm D, the same is true. In both cases, the link and the pushrod keep their respective orientations throughout their travel, which is desirable for the setup to work accurately. Variations can be made to work, but things can get complicated.

In a boat, the simple way is often not an option. In the first place, we wanted the weights to pivot from as high as possible under the sole. The crank would have to be lower, however, for clearance when the boat heeled to port (see Figure 3). This means that the link (E) is not perpendicular to the weight arm when the boat is upright. If you can visualize the weight swinging 20 degrees first to port and then to starboard, you can see that the amount of travel of the vertical pushrod would differ drastically from one tack to the other.

One solution is shown in Figure 4. The main disadvantage of it was that I thought of it after the project was finished. (R&D does not always proceed smoothly on the cutting edge of gimbaled table technology.)

The only way to keep the link E at right angles would be to make arm A longer, but this violates the rules established a couple of paragraphs above. If A is longer than B, then the crank arm rotates through a greater angle than the weight. Not only that, but as the angle of heel gets greater, the ratio itself changes.

Not to worry, however. Suppose we reverse the ratio on the second leg of the linkage — i.e., if A is twice as long as B, then C must be half as long as D (see Figure 5). Then — at the risk of overwhelming the reader with scientific terminology — the weirdness in the vertical motion is exactly opposite to the weirdness in the horizontal motion, and all the weirdnesses are canceled out. It might be thought of as gearing down and then gearing back up. Note, however, that in this situation, the arrangement would jam at a high angle of heel, because the smaller crank would reach the end of its horizontal travel.

Being very pleased with myself, I returned to the bilge, began measuring, and discovered that none of these alternatives would work. The weight would have to hang in the center of the boat for an unobstructed swing, and the table was to be only 9 inches or so off center, which meant that the desired proportions were impossible to obtain.

Late one night, I toyed with the idea of an idler arm way over to starboard to allow more latitude in locating the crank (see Figure 6), but in the cold light of morning I decided that adding an extra link with all that weight flying around would be asking for trouble.

Finally, on the brink of madness, I came up with a satisfactory answer. By flipping the crank (see Figure 7) I gained more room, kept the arm lengths the same, and could fit the table where it was supposed to go. It is not perfect; as the boat heels, the link arm E goes up at the weight end and down at the crank end, and therefore at high angles of heel the table will not rotate enough to stay exactly horizontal. However, the extra

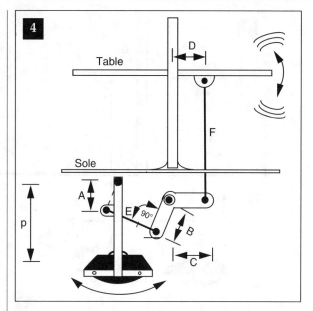

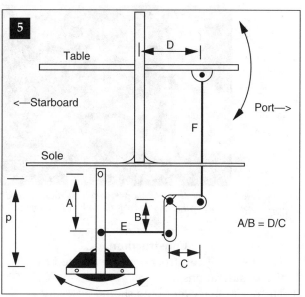

length of E minimizes this until about 35 degrees of heel, at which point the crew has other things to worry about than spilling their soup.

Another major design consideration dealt with the appropriate amount of weight needed to give the table adequate resistance to elbows leaning on it. A naval architect whom I asked estimated that the weight in a conventional gimbaled table was about 25 pounds. However, in that case, the lead hangs 2 feet or more below the axis of the table, whereas in our table the corresponding lever arm is limited to about 10 inches. To equal the righting force of the conventional setup, therefore, I guessed that our arrangement would require from 50 to 60 pounds of lead. I hedged my bet by deciding to cast the lead in four 20-pound pieces, which could be used as determined by trial and error.

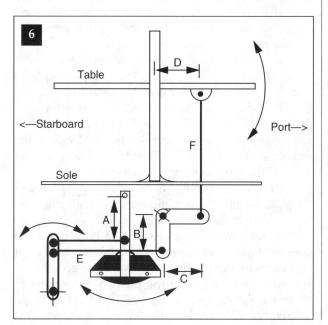

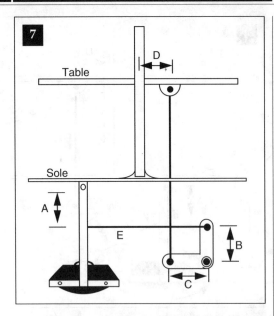

The crank mechanism, located under the sole, with the vertical pushrod in place. Note the small extra arm that holds the socket vertical when the pushrod is removed.

Construction

The details of construction were affected by three main considerations:

1. The desire that everything should be easily removable.
2. The fairly large forces generated by the weights.
3. The Guy Next Door.

In any project of this type, you need a Guy Next Door who can do the stuff you can't. In our case, the GND had a TIG welder, a metal-cutting bandsaw, and a good supply of stainless steel. Another GND worked at the local plumbing supply store. Once you figure out the relationships between the nominal sizes of plumbing parts and reality, these parts can be very handy, either as-is or customized.

The trapeze for holding the lead weights was welded up from stainless steel by the first Guy Next Door and consisted of a piece of tubing with an inverted T of flatbar hanging down at each end, joined by threaded rods. The tubing rotated on a piece of stainless rod attached to a couple of sole beams. The threaded rods

formed a cradle for the weights; I left nuts on so we could clamp them up against however many of the lead pieces we found we needed.

In searching for the lead, I was guided to a third Guy Next Door who made lobster pots and used lead for weights. He pointed me to an 800-pound piece of ballast keel and told me the deal was that if I cut it up, I could keep what I needed. He even gave me a pot to melt it in. After a couple of hours with a chainsaw, I had all the lead I needed just from the chips I made.

And how much lead was that? Lead weighs 700 pounds per cubic foot, so 80 pounds/700 x 1,728 (the number of cubic inches in a cubic foot) gave me a bit less than 200 cubic inches, or four pieces of lead 10 inches by 4 inches by 1¼ inches. The actual shape, intended to keep the center of gravity as low as possible, was that of a large truncated pie wedge, with slots at the edge to drop over the threaded rods of the trapeze.

We heated the lead with an acetylene torch and poured it into an oak mold that lasted just long enough to make the four pieces. A bent piece of bronze rod was held in place during each pour to make a handle.

I used an old turnbuckle for the link arm between the weights and the crank so the table could be adjusted to level. The crank, of ⅜-inch bronze plate, was cut originally in an L shape. As the design evolved, however, I had to remake it in two pieces in different planes to keep the two link arms from interfering with each other.

The crank pivoted on a ½-inch stainless bolt fastened to a 4-inch by 4-inch plate that, in turn, was attached to an oak post in the bilge. The high forces made it necessary to keep any slop out of the crank pivot, so a bronze bushing around the bolt allowed smooth motion. Because the bushing projected beyond the crank, the bolt could be tightened without binding the crank's motion.

So the vertical pushrod could be easily removed, I decided to screw it into a socket (a pipe coupling) attached to the crank by a fork (made from a turnbuckle end). For smooth operation, two problems needed solving. The first was that when the rod was removed, the socket would tip upside down so the rod couldn't be put back in. To hold the socket upright, I added the auxiliary arm shown in Figure 8B.

The second problem was that if I simply threaded the pushrod into the coupling with the existing tapered pipe thread, there was no guarantee that some muscle-bound bozo wouldn't twist it in so hard that (a) it couldn't be removed without a pipe wrench, or (b) it would no longer line up. To solve these problems, I turned down the end of the pushrod on a lathe so there was a shoulder (see Figure 8B) and cut a straight ½-inch No. 13 thread for both rod and socket. This way, the pushrod could be screwed easily down to the shoulder, and then it would stop. The upper end of the pushrod was left long until the height of the table was known.

The construction of the table itself was pretty straightforward. It was made in two leaves, each 15 inches by 40 inches, of 5/4 (1¼-inch) mahogany, with a mahogany border. Since gluing one piece across the end-grain of another is a good way to produce large splits when the weather changes, I fastened the border to the table ends only with screws through oversize holes.

The leaves have 1-inch brass channel let into their ends that fits into the 1¼-inch channel that pivots at the uprights. The pivots themselves were designed for motion without slop. In brief, I drilled out the channel for a pipe bushing that was welded in place, then reamed for a bronze bushing over a stainless bolt. The bolt was threaded into the clamp and held in place with a set screw.

The clamps themselves were one of the more interesting parts of the venture. At first, they were supposed to be simply cast-bronze barrels, bored out to 1.900 inches (the diameter of 1½-inch pipe) and split along one side between two ears so the clamp could be tightened around the pipe. This arrangement was designed early on, when we thought that we could simply raise the table to the overhead to get it out of the way.

After I made the pattern for the clamps, my client decided that they had to hinge open so as to be removable. I modified the pattern, adding knuckles on either side of the parting line so, after three saw cuts were made, the knuckles formed a hinge. As part of the same pattern, there was a stop ring that could be fastened permanently on the pipe so the clamp could be returned to the same height after being removed (see Figure 9).

There remained one more task: There are times when you don't want the table to swing, and so a locking mechanism was in order. It was clear that you couldn't clamp a 15-pound table and leave 80 pounds of weights free to swing, and still expect the mechanism that connected the weights to survive. The lock would have to be down below the sole where the weights were.

What I came up with can best be described as a large slide bolt. I had the first Guy Next Door weld a piece of ⅞-inch stainless tubing vertically to the trapeze. A piece of 1¾-inch stainless rod with a cross pin near the top fits in the tube. The rod cannot drop down except when it is rotated to the point where the cross

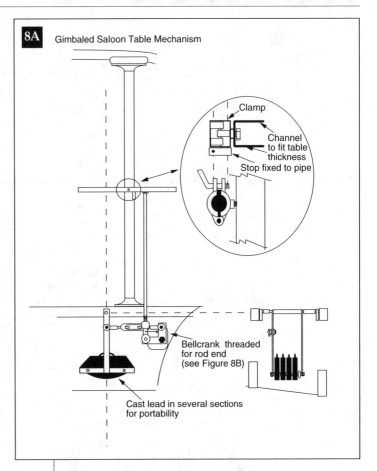

8A Gimbaled Saloon Table Mechanism

Clamp
Channel to fit table thickness
Stop fixed to pipe

Bellcrank threaded for rod end (see Figure 8B)

Cast lead in several sections for portability

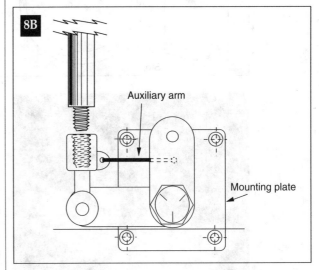

8B

Auxiliary arm

Mounting plate

pin lines up with vertical slots in the tube. Then the bolt drops 3 inches into a socket made of another piece of tube welded to a plate that is securely fastened to a floor timber.

To actuate the lock without removing the sole hatch, I made use of the T-shaped hooks that Nevins, the builder, furnished for lifting those hatches. They, too, have small cross pins in the ends that enable them to snag eccentric lift holes. After drilling out the top end

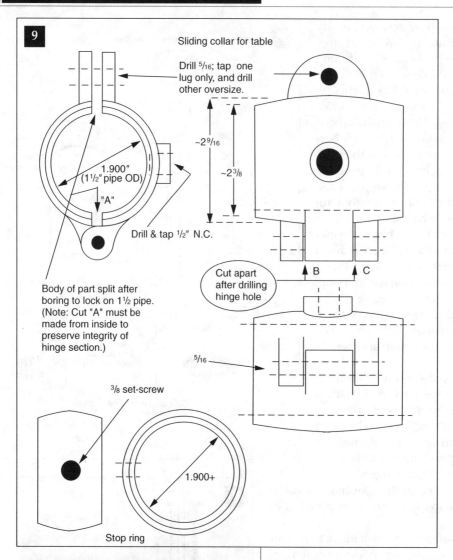

9

Sliding collar for table

Drill 5/16; tap one lug only, and drill other oversize.

1.900"
(1½" pipe OD)

"A"

~2 9/16

~2 3/8

Drill & tap ½" N.C.

Cut apart after drilling hinge hole

B   C

5/16

Body of part split after boring to lock on 1½ pipe. (Note: Cut "A" must be made from inside to preserve integrity of hinge section.)

3/8 set-screw

1.900+

Stop ring

This custom clamp, along with the channel into which the leaves slide, fastens to the table stanchions quickly.

of the rod and cutting in L-shaped slots, I had a sort of bayonet lock, by which one could lift the rod through a small hole in the sole with the Nevins T-hooks.

All that remained after that was to locate a comfortable height for the tabletop, cut and drill the top of the pushrod, and put it all together.

The table disassembles in a flash. The weight/trapeze separates from the crank with a quick-release pin, and then can be lifted out by rotating the axle a quarter turn. Even the after support pipe is designed to slip out of its flanges in seconds, leaving the saloon wide open.

At last report, the soup was still staying in the bowl.

A final word: In this project, as with any quality restoration, the most important piece of equipment was the owner. He wishes to remain anonymous, but I'd like to thank him for insisting on good work and realizing that it required time and money. He is knowledgeable enough to know what he wants but he will listen when you tell him why what he wants might not be a good idea. It was a pleasure to work with him.

A Proper Icebox

—— by Jim Brown ——

*I*n some boatshops, epoxy mixed with nonstructural thickeners, like fumed silica, is known generically as duokei (pronounced to rhyme with "cookie"). Whereas, epoxy mixed with reinforcing fibers, such as wood flour or synthetic flock, is called schmutz (this word rhymes with the apparent plural of foot, i.e., "foots"). If the epoxy is mixed with both thickeners and fibers, which is often the case, it becomes, logically, duokeischmutz. (Yes, it rhymes with "cookiefoots.")The two roots often are used singly and interchangeably.

As we shall see, the concoctions bearing these names can be mixed to a spreading consistency like that of mayonnaise or even peanut butter. With a tool such as a tongue depressor or a rubber cake spatula, the stuff can be sculpted into concavities, where it forms something akin to a bead of weld, but with some "beads" having a radius as large as that of a baseball or even a dinner plate. This technique, which can join wooden components together astonishingly well, is sometimes called "liquid joinery."

What can you do with this technique? Well, you can build amazingly complicated artifacts just by hanging the pieces together with tacks and masking tape, and then coming along later to "weld" them together with duokeischmutz. And, rest assured that this material is capable of bonding disparate, highly stressed components into organic, monocoque structures. It has been used for years to build very modern wooden boats, including sprawling multihulls, in sizes commonly exceeding 60 feet in length, and the method is embodied in vessels certified for passenger carrying by the United States Coast Guard.

However, there's an easier place to begin learning how to sling duokei than at real ships; for instance, at an icebox. And an icebox, in a boat, is a good place to

A wood/epoxy icebox made with liquid joinery, installed beneath the sole in the author's 31-foot trimaran. The ice shown is what remained of the first 10-pound block after six summer days in Maine waters.

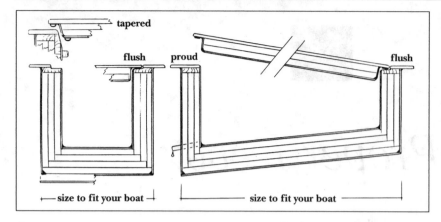

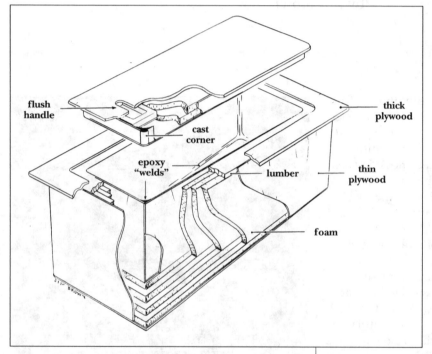

Tailor this efficient icebox to fit available space on your boat. The lid can be fit flush, tapered, or left standing proud.

can explore the myriad uses for liquid joinery in the process.

You wouldn't want to build this icebox, or any other wood/epoxy structure, out of just plain boards. For this construction, the wood prefers to be laminated. Especially, it prefers to be cross-laminated — like plywood. The joints between components, such as the corner joints in the plywood walls of this icebox, are not necessarily attached to each other in the usual manner — that is, with the likes of end-lap joints, mortises and tenons, dovetails, glue strips, or mechanical fastenings. Instead — and here's where the joinery solidifies — they are all "welded" together with coved fillets of home-grown epoxy putty. Ultimately, every surface either is coated with epoxy or is fiberglass/epoxy sheathed, and all glue joints are made with epoxy. Here's a woodworking system that really keeps wood dry!

Sloppy or loose-fitting joints in woodwork, when filled with duokeischmutz, can be stronger and more dimensionally stable than close-fitting joints, especially if the close fit is combined with sufficient clamping pressure to squeeze most of the epoxy out of the joint. You don't have to purposely perform sloppy woodwork to use liquid joinery, but you can get away with it. Even with tight-fitting joints, we usually wet the end-grain of the pieces with a preliminary swipe of straight resin-hardener mixture (no fillers or fibers) and come along a while later with a cream-thick batch of duokeischmutz used as the real glue. The fibers in this glue mix actually hold the two wooden surfaces apart, minutely, thus providing a reservoir of epoxy between so there's plenty left even after penetration; this makes for a good, juicy joint. Fiber-reinforced epoxy is that rare kind of adhesive that spans gaps well, and because no real pressure is required to make it stick like crazy, we use just enough pressure on the joints to obtain proper squigment, as evidenced by a bit of squeezed-out schmutz all around.

To build an icebox, we're not going all the way with this discipline; but even an icebox is sufficiently involved to tax your skills and judgment. It utilizes

test the long-term effectiveness of liquid joiner: because in wooden boats, the icebox is the first place the surveyor looks for problems.

Iceboxes in wooden boats have been responsible for many a big yard bill. Even the modern, non-draining, built-in refrigerator/freezer can be a threat to wooden boats; who knows what's going on behind all that insulation? However, by using the techniques of liquid joinery, you can build a wood/epoxy icebox—or even a refrigerator/freezer—into your boat, and it can be non-rotting, non-sweating, self-contained, separate from the hull, and removable. Even if you don't have a boat, or one that's deserving of a fixed fridge, you can build an elegant replacement for the usual weekender's cooler — only yours will probably keep ice for a week instead of a weekend — and you

lots more wood/epoxy know-how than the obvious corner fillets, and it utilizes other joining liquids besides epoxy, such as contact cement, squirt-can foam, and marine caulk.... sometimes all on the same piece of wood! In short, this project fully illustrates the potential of liquid joinery.

Want to try it? I'll include a step-by-step description of building the simple icebox illustrated; but first, you have to design your box. Draw it out to scale, because there are several details to be addressed.

Icebox Design

The usual minimum inside icebox volume for week-long cruising is about 3 cubic feet, but the space limitations on my boat dictated a volume of only 2 cubic feet. Be your own designer. My box had to fit into a void in my old 31-foot trimaran. We have used an Igloo on our boat for 18 years, and it kept ice adequately for weekending (the time frame for which it was designed), but it was annoyingly inefficient for longer cruises. However, it contained two plastic trays that my wife found useful for organizing storage and keeping things dry. Therefore, I was challenged to design the box to fit within existing outside dimensions, and to accommodate the trays inside — and to accommodate at least the minimum thickness of urethane foam insulation needed to keep ice for about a week. In my box, this turned out to be: 4 inches on the bottom, 3 inches on the sides, and 2 inches on top. These are minimums. Large boxes for use in the tropics, and refrigerator/freezers, need much more insulation; 8 inches on the bottom is used sometimes.

Any reasonable shape can be matched with the method described, but be sure to provide clearance for ventilation all around the box (1-inch minimum recommended).

Will your box have a door or a lid? Will it fit flush or have a lipped face? Top-opening lids are by far the most efficient for saving ice, but if you use top-opening you must decide whether your lid will stand proud of the countertop or nest flush. Proud ones interrupt counter space, but flush ones collect dirt and spills. My box actually fits under the sole in the dinette. It is usually covered with carpet, and thus the lid must fit flush and have a flush handle. Allow for gasket thickness to achieve a flush lid.

A simple icebox can do well with a weather stripping-type gasket, but refrigerator/freezers want a hollow "B"- or "D"-section vinyl gasket, sometimes available from a large appliance-repair shop. Adhesive backing, provided on some weather stripping-type gasket materials, sticks more permanently to epoxied surfaces if the epoxy is lightly sanded and pre-coated with contact cement. The point is, you need the gasket ahead of time in order to know how much to allow

for its thickness when building the box and when buying the hinges and latch.

Whether you have a door or a lid, it must be built to plug the opening, and the tighter the clearance between this lid/plug and its recess, the less space there is for air to circulate around the closure. (Hereafter, I'll call the thick outer part of the lid the "cover," and the boxlike inner part the "plug.") To avoid binding, the plug and the recess into which it fits should be tapered; the smaller the plug, the more taper is required. My lid is long, and swings up from the end; thus, very little taper was needed. But a fully tapered recess and plug can be built with the method illustrated; just schmutz the angled faces together. For freezers, a double-landing closure is desirable, with a gasket at each landing to create a dead-air space between. Furthermore, in real seagoing boats, lids, just like doors, should be secured with a hinge and even a latch, so that they cannot come adrift in heavy weather.

Boatbuilder Gordon Swift suggests that you not install a drain. He says that even if the meltwater is collected in a tank, thus preventing fresh water from entering the bilge, the drain fitting itself always sweats, providing a regular supply of rot-causing moisture to the area where it drips. Instead, Swifty installs a little bilge pump with which to occasionally evacuate the meltwater into the sink. Whatever your choice, meltwater must be removed, or the ice won't last nearly as long. If you use a drain, be sure it is easy to clean and inspect, and that there is a "gooseneck" or low spot in the line where water can collect. This prevents cold air from escaping through the drain; otherwise it will siphon warm air in past the gasket and drastically shorten the life of your ice.

The box should be easily removed intact, either laterally or vertically, for inspection behind it. Furthermore, the opening's face, like the countertop or the cabinet front, should be integral with the box. This allows the walls of the box to permanently support the opening's face, so the lid or door can have a dimensionally stable sash, a tight seat on the gasket, and no binding of the closure.

If you're building just a simple, portable cooler (as mine nearly is), many of these complications do not apply. But even a cooler will make good use of liquid joinery. The design of your box may influence the assembly steps below, but you can use my box, and the above design considerations, as a general guide.

Materials

With its double-wall construction, a wooden icebox can get heavy, so I used very light plywood — 3mm (about ⅛-inch), three-ply okoume — for both the inner and outer walls of the box, and the lid's plug. Heavier plywood — say, ¼ inch thick — would be suitable for a larger box, or on the outer bottom of a portable box. If Douglas fir plywood is used, all visible surfaces, inside and out, should be sheathed with fiberglass.

For the opening's face and the lid's cover, I used ½-inch-thick, seven-ply okoume plywood. Most counter-tops would be heavier — say, ¾-inch plywood. Whatever you use for the opening's face, and for the outer lid itself, be sure it is very stable and flat. For the lumber frame around the opening, I used a nice, straight piece of ¾-inch mahogany. My material came from Harbor Sales in Baltimore, Maryland.

For epoxy resin, I used the Gougeon WEST SYSTEM products, with the fast hardener. Controversy still rages over which resin is best, but for an "inside job" like this, where workroom conditions can be controlled and where many small batches will be mixed for the myriad, separate operations, the Gougeon stuff has the advantage of being faster curing than, say, System Three resin, especially when spread in thin films for coating. If there are no other jobs waiting to be done while a batch is curing, the faster resin helps hustle the job along. But I often use System Three resin, too, for jobs where temperature and humidity are more difficult to control, and where the structure is likely to get knocked around.

For this project I used the "Wood Flour" filler offered by System Three, simply because it was available and inexpensive. I mixed the Wood Flour about half-and-half by volume with Cab-O-Sil, which is the common fumed-silica thickening agent. When the dry powders are stirred into the resin at about two-to-one by volume, the matrix forms a fairly smooth and creamy schmutz, somewhat like Skippy peanut butter, and gives a good color match with okoume or Douglas fir plywood. But duokei doesn't have to match; the often-available, all-white, plastic fillers, or the red micro-balloons, will produce contrasting "welds," which are quite pleasing if neatly done.

Unless you're building an airplane, where "high-crush" filler components are specified, you can usually be your own Julia Child when concocting schmutz. Just be sure to mix the resin and hardener thoroughly first, scraping the sides and bottom of the container, and then follow whatever recipe is required to create your preferred schmutz. And, don't dally with it; as soon as you combine the resin and hardener, every second of working time counts for a better, more efficient job.

For insulation, your local building supply store will likely carry the polycyanurate (urethane) foam used to insulate homes. It usually comes faced with foil on both sides. That's what you want; it's the best refrigeration foam for the money. Buy 1-inch-thick sheets. Don't use polystyrene foam, or the denser urethane foams designed for structural boatbuilding.

You'll also need "squirt-can foam," the household insulation available from building supply stores (be certain to get the "non-expanding" type). I also used about a quart of contact cement, and a big tube of marine caulk, such as 3M 5200 or Sikaflex 241. You may also employ some five-minute epoxy, or even hot-glue from a gun, for making "spot welds." Use anything, even props and string and gravity, to hold your components together until you can come along with the schmutz.

For tools, you'll need the usual epoxy supplies, of course, like rubber gloves, dust masks, respirator, plastic squeegees, disposable brushes, and the solvent to clean them. Don't just throw brushes away; a used brush is far preferable to a new one, because the loose hairs have already come out of it or have been glued into the head by previous batches of epoxy. Save your used brushes in a covered container of acetone. Paint rollers, however, may as well be disposed of, because it takes so much solvent to clean them, and all but "solvent-resistant" roller covers fall apart when cleaned.

You'll need the usual assortment of hand and power tools, including sanders. In addition, your box may require special fastenings, such as nonferrous screws and nails.

Build It by the Numbers

1. Don't start cutting yet! Instead, see Step 13, and then start coating. That's right, pre-coat all the wood with epoxy and allow it to cure — both sides of your full 4- by 8-foot sheets of plywood, and all sides of your milled lumber. If you plan to leave the box with a clear finish, pre-coating avoids color discontinuities, but mostly it saves time and trouble later by ensuring that the material is sealed from the start.

Combine the resin with the hardener, following the manufacturer-specified proportions exactly; we'll call this "neat resin" from here on, because it has no schmutz in it. For pre-coating, apply just enough neat resin to wet the surface; spread it with a nearly dry roller, or scrape it almost dry with the squeegee. This thin application penetrates the surface just as much as a thick coating. When cured, it raises the grain. Indeed, it raises every microscopic sliver on the wood's surface, which facilitates a light sanding and stabilizes the substrate for subsequent coatings of anything. A "dry" coat like this also minimizes the formation of bubbles during the initial, and subsequent, coatings. Mahogany, in particular, seems prone to exuding gas from within the wood, inflating myriad tiny bubbles in resin coatings. To avoid this troublesome phenomenon, begin with a very dry coating.

Do not coat the wood and then set it in the sun to

cure. If anything, warm the wood in the sun and then take it into the shade for coating. In that way it will be cooling — not heating up — during the cure.

2. Now you can cut. Size all the box material into rough, oversized pieces per the plan for your box; leave about an inch all around for final cutting. Include all the side walls and end walls of the double box, the sides and bottom of the lid's plug, the opening's face, and the lid's cover.

3. Stack all similar-sized pieces, clamp them together, and run one edge of the stacks over the jointer. If you don't have a jointer, saw or plane at least one straight edge on all your pieces. This gives you something to "square" from, and it simplifies the layout for the final cutting of the other edges.

4. Cut the opening for the door or lid. A pocket cut with a sabersaw can be utilized for making a flush lid.

5. Cut and glue-fasten, permanently, a flat frame to the inner face of the opening. For boxes with flush lids, this frame should extend into the opening by the width of the gasket's landing (about 1¼ inches), and the frame must now be shimmed away from the face, or the frame rabbeted, to allow for the thickness of the gasket. In any case, the width of this frame should equal the thickness of the insulation in the side walls of the box — that is, the inside separation between the inner and outer walls.

Mix a batch of epoxy and schmutz powder for making internal glue joints between rigid pieces of wood. Again, follow the specified proportions of resin and hardener (more hardener does not make the stuff harden faster). Then add your duokeischmutz — about half of the neat resin's volume. When all is thoroughly stirred, you want a gluing mix about the consistency of heavy cream. This will reduce sagging and fill gaps. So, go ahead, glue on the frame.

6. Attach the side and end walls of the box to the frame, permanently, with your same epoxy-glue mixture. I decided to erect the outer walls first, and then build the rest of the box from the inside. Depending on the shape of your box, and the size of the opening, you may wish to reverse the procedure by erecting the inner walls first and building outward from them. If so, be sure to fiberglass-sheathe the inside of the walls before assembly, as in Step 20. In attaching these side walls to your frame, just the slightest mechanical fastening will suffice; use very small ring nails, or even steel staples if you plan to pull them out after the cure. Remember that liquid joinery does not require pressure, just a reasonable fit and a juicy joint.

7. You're almost ready for some real schmutz-slinging, but first, use masking tape to bring the corners of the box into the desired alignment. (In a larger box, this alignment of components can be done with "spotwelds" of five-minute epoxy or dabs from

Erecting the initial walls of the box by gluing them to the frame for the opening, which is glued to the countertop or cabinet front.

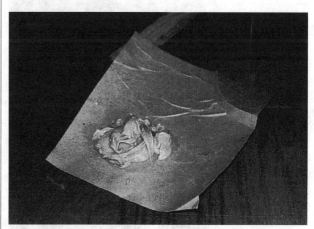

Duokeischmutz mixed to peanut-butter consistency for sculpting, and scooped onto heavy scrap paper, which is ready for rolling into a "pastry-decorating" cone.

The "pastry" cone and initial "welding" results.

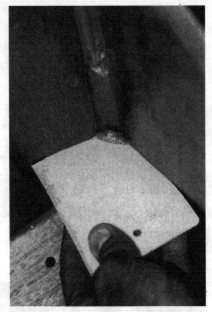

Sculpting the duokei into coved fillets with a custom-cut plastic squeegee.

Layers of foam board are installed with contact cement against the walls of the box. Squirt-can foam, the non-expanding type, is used to fill air spaces at the corners.

a modeler's hot-glue gun.) The arrangement of the overlaps, and the size of the gaps between, are not particularly important. Remember, you're soon going to join them all together with something liquid, resulting in a perfect "cast fit" at the joints. For now, cover the entire outside of the joints with masking tape.

8. Now's the time to ready your sculpting tools. For my box, I wanted a fillet radius slightly larger than the nickel-sized one produced by the usual sculpting tool, which is a wooden tongue depressor. So, I cut a plastic squeegee, as illustrated, with a radius the same as that of a quarter. Note that the sides of the squeegee are cut at an angle slightly less than 90 degrees to allow you to tilt the squeegee, and that the sides are wide enough to clean up the mess on both sides of the fillet. With a little experimentation, you'll become an expert at crafting your own schmutzers for specific jobs.

9. Pre-wet the inside corners with a little neat epoxy, wetting the end-grain of the plywood by pushing the resin with a brush through the joints against the masking tape outside.

10. Mix a big batch of duokeischmutz to peanut-butter consistency, thick enough so that only egg-sized globs will fall from the mixing stick. A batch about the volume of a stick of butter is large enough for starters. Remember, stir the resin-hardener mix thoroughly first, scraping the walls and bottom of the container before adding the fillers. You'll need a big container and a stout stick — and a dust mask on your face to prevent you from breathing the fibers.

11. Working quickly, scoop the mix out of the container onto a piece of Kraft paper about twice the size of a letterhead (like a split-open manila envelope). Roll the paper into a cone, and double over its top, as if you were going to decorate a cake by squirting frosting from the nozzle of the cone. Then, squirt the schmutz into all the inside corners of your box. The important thing is to get the stuff out of the cone as quickly as possible; otherwise it will heat up in there and harden before you're finished. Once duokei-schmutz is extruded into those relatively small beads, however, it doesn't insulate itself as much — it can stay cooler, extending your working time. But if it starts to heat up in the cone, discard it without hesitation and concentrate on the step below. You can mix another batch if it is needed to complete the job. Be certain to squirt enough schmutz into the corners. Experience, and the size of the radius desired, will determine how much to apply. If you apply too much, the sculpting tool will remove any excess. Have a palette of scrap plywood handy for collecting the excess from the squeegee. The stuff can be reused if you spread it out thin on the palette to keep it cool.

12. Now, sculpt! Notice how your best fillets are

made in one swipe with the filleting tool. That requires applying about the right amount of material in the first place. When it comes to compound or complex cavities, where the bead of weld branches out in two or three directions, don't begin your stroke quite at the apex of such corners; leave enough duokei there so that you can come back after the long strokes are made, and simply drive your sculpting tool around the corner with very light pressure. Any messy ridges left at the sides of the radius can be scraped up with "chisel sticks," which are scraps of thin wood or veneer whose ends have been sanded to a chisel shape. Make a handful of them before you start.

13. This should really be Step 1, but to avoid confusing the initial steps, it seems to fit better here. Yet, this is critical: Always get everything ready before mixing epoxy: containers, mixing sticks, gloves, brushes, squeegees, rollers, hand cleaner, brush-cleaning solvent, paper towels, chisel sticks....

Sweep your workbench neat, and provide in advance for the disposal of waste material. Mixed epoxy left in a container can heat up during cure, possibly even catching fire. Dump waste in a metal container expressly for the purpose, located where the noxious vapors exuded by hot duokei will disperse outside the shop.

14. So now the first walls of your box, except for the bottom, are erected and "welded" together. After the fillets have cured, no further structure is necessary inside these joints. If you're building a portable cooler, you may want to apply fiberglass tape to the exterior edges and the corners later. For applying the 'glass, see Steps 20 and 31.

15. When the fillets of my outer box were cured, I cut and dry-fitted the foam insulation inside it. Of course, your box may be coming along the other way, from the inside out. If so, this may require more use of the "blind duokei" technique, as described in Step 17. In any case, by buying 1-inch-thick foam sheets and using them in multiples, you can graduate thickness as necessary. Stagger the end-lap joints. During this dry-fitting step, scribe the pieces of foam board where they protrude beyond the next layer, to denote areas where the foil facing is to be removed. Mark all dry-fitted foam for later relocation. Remove the foam from the box, and skin off the foil by running the foam edgewise through a table saw. I was not able to devise any way to peel the foil off efficiently, so I sawed it off, and depended on the squirt-can foam to fill any air spaces in the joints. Where necessary, chamfer the edges on the foam boards in way of the fillets.

16. Reinstall the foam, permanently, using two kinds of adhesive as follows: Apply contact cement to the large, flat areas, and squirt-can foam in all the corners. Apply the contact cement to both surfaces to be

The foam board has staggered end-lap joints, ready to receive bottom foam. Foil is removed at the joints.

"Blind duokei" technique involves chamfering the outer edges of the foam to create a small void, which is filled proud with epoxy putty, transferred from a palette of scrap plywood.

The outer plywood bottom has been schmutzed into "blind duokei" and held with tape until cured. All outer corners are bullnosed later and sheathed with fiberglass if desired.

Pre-fiberglassed inner box walls are installed using contact cement on the wide flats, marine caulk behind the corners, and epoxy glue at the upper edge-to-frame joints, each adhesive having a different purpose.

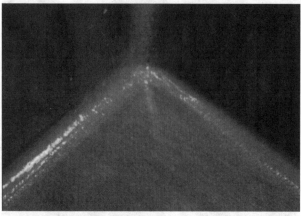

A corner of the inner box after filleting.

Making the lid's plug over tape shims for clearance.

bonded (between all mating surfaces of foil-to-foil and foil-to-box), and allow it to dry. Then run a fat bead of squirt-foam around the edges of the box where each foam piece will go. Install the foam boards by locating them with extreme care, for once the contact cement touches itself, there is no chance of adjusting the foam's position. It is critical that the squirt-foam be the non-expanding type; even this will swell slightly during cure (which takes an hour or so), easily filling all the air spaces at the joints. The full-blown expanding type could distort, and maybe even burst, your box.

17. Now, here's an application for so-called "blind duokei." With all the foam in place, including the bottom-most or outermost layer, install the outer plywood bottom with contact cement and "blind" fillets. How? Just chamfer the outer edges of the last layer of bottom foam to produce a small void all around, and fill the void proud with duokeischmutz. Lay the bottom on (cut slightly oversized), and weight it or tape it down during cure. Presto! A "blind" fillet/joint. With this technique, you can build practically anything!

18. Now, you have the outer box built. When it has cured, you can clean up the edges with a sander, and/or run the router around the corners to bullnose all the edges, and apply an initial coat of neat resin to these raw areas. Turn the box over, and prepare to install the inner walls. Note how rigid and lightweight the box is.

19. Because my box was built from the outside inward, now was my time to dry-fit the plywood walls of the inner box. I fit the sides first, then the bottom, so the bottom could be used to press the sides outward against the foam.

20. Then I removed these inner walls, and sheathed them with fiberglass while they were outside the box. In this type of operation, don't pre-cut the fiberglass cloth to match each panel; it will move around on you during wetting-out with epoxy. Instead, lay out all the panels over polyfilm and sheathe them all at once with an oversize piece of fiberglass cloth. We call this process "gang sheathing."

Six-ounce cloth is sufficient, but you may wish to put two or three (extra-large) layers on the inside bottom panel, to resist jabs with the ice pick. Lay the cloth over the dry panels, and apply the neat epoxy directly to the dry cloth with a roller or squeegee. (You can even wet through the two or three layers of fiberglass on the bottom panel all at once.) Make this first application fairly dry — just enough resin to turn the cloth transparent, with no white spots.

When this first application is done, the surface should not look wet or glossy anywhere; rather, it should look like honey soaked into hot toast. Too much resin in this bonding application will cause the fiberglass to float above the wood and leave lumps, so work lean.

When this bonding application has cured just "cheese-hard" (don't wait overnight if you can help it), apply a second coating of epoxy, and this time flow on plenty. You're working on a horizontal surface here, which is the best reason for not trying to fiberglass the inner walls of the box after assembly, when it has vertical surfaces. You can really flow the resin onto a horizontal surface, which saves applying several thin coats, plus it saves you the drudgery of sanding out the inevitable sags associated with vertical surfaces. You don't want puddles on the flat, but the epoxy should completely bury the weave of the cloth.

When the final coat has cured cheese-hard, trim the edges with a knife, separating the panels.

21. Wash these fiberglassed panels with water. Notice that the glossy surface is covered with a slightly greasy film. This film is called "sweat-out." It is evidence of the epoxy's hardener attempting to react with water vapor in the air — the more humid and cold the day, the more sweat-out. Sweat-out can inhibit the bond between successive coatings (especially if the initial coat is cured hard), and it can weaken the "weld" in the corners of the box. So, wipe it off with a wet rag. That's all, just water. It'll jump right off onto the rag. Because you'd like to avoid wetting the end-grain of these pieces, a few passes with a damp rag will suffice, if it is wrung out in a bucket of water between passes.

When the glossy surfaces are dry, notice that they are no longer "greasy." That's good; but, just to make sure, you should sand off the gloss from these inside walls with 120-grit sandpaper. If you don't wash first, the "grease" could clog your sandpaper.

22. If you have built from the outside inward, you're ready to install the inner walls of the box. For good practice, we'll use three, or even four kinds of adhesive. Use contact cement on the big flats to hold the inner walls against the insulation foam; use squirt-foam to fill any large dead-air spaces in the sheet foam; use epoxy glue around the frame to structurally bond the box walls to the frame around the opening; and use marine caulk behind the corners to fill and seal any small air spaces there. Note that all of these liquid joiners serve a different purpose. The only mechanical fastenings used are masking tape and maybe a few small nails or staples around the frame, and they can be removed later. Any gaps in the vertical corners were simply schmutzed into oblivion by the final, inside fillets.

23. Here, in the actual service area of the box, is perhaps the place to get fussy with your final fillets. If you want, you can wait until they get "Jell-O hard," and wipe them with a sopping, acetone-soaked rag.

They'll come out super smooth, and needing not one swipe of sandpaper. After everything has cured, you can round the upper corners at the frame and apply the initial coat of resin to this raw joint.

24. Install accessories, such as runners for trays or shelves, and perhaps a drain. This can be just a nipple of plastic pipe, sanded and bonded in with duokei to extend outside enough for attaching a drain hose to a meltwater tank — such as a collapsible plastic jug.

25. Apply another thin coat of neat resin to all the raw joints, allow it to cure, and give everything a light sanding. Repeat as necessary. Don't sand through to raw wood. Get at least two full coats on everything, three on end-grain plywood.

26. Now you can apply a final, thin coat of neat resin everywhere, inside and out. But, watch out for those vertical surfaces! Just the lightest coating of resin is in order, perhaps thickened with a little Cab-O-Sil at about one-tenth the resin's volume, or else the stuff will sag like crazy, leaving you to sand and re-coat. I think there's nothing like a roller for spreading coatings thinly and evenly. A paintbrush, if used to apply resin, seems always to produce sags and brush marks, but a dry brush can be used to "tip off" the stipple of a rolled coating, if you wish; make vertical strokes.

No, you're not finished. The lid, or door, is a box in itself, and it has to be fitted into its opening with a minimum of air space created around the plug.

As mentioned earlier, a tapered recess and a tapered plug are required in most installations, but their construction is similar to what's been described so far — just stick them together with that old devil, duokei. The techniques of liquid joinery permit the plug to really fit its recess. Here, with the numbers continuing, is how to "cast" your plug with wood/epoxy:

27. Erect a shore or platform inside the box on which to drop the lower, inner surface of the plug.

28. Apply at least two layers of masking tape to the sides and corners of the recess, where the plug's side walls will engage the recess. Smear paste wax on the surface tape, especially in the corners.

29. Using more masking tape, fit the plug's side walls in place against the recess. If the plug is tapered, these pieces must stand proud of the gasket's landing by the thickness of the compressed gasket, or about two-thirds of its relaxed thickness. Note that these plug pieces must end short of the corners, in order to allow room for the corner radii that you made inside the box (they are now lurking beneath the waxed masking tape).

30. When you're sure the above conditions have been met, go ahead and fillet all the plug's concavities, actually casting the corners of the plug with

The lid's plug ready to receive insulation, and the outer cover with flush handle.

The lid's plug with "cast" corners, before filleting against the underside of the cover.

The completed icebox, with an interior plastic tray on runners, and a gasketed, flush-fitting lid.

duokeischmutz against the waxed tape.

31. If you're worried about these large corner castings, you can apply small fiberglass patches, cut round to about the size of a plum, against their inside surfaces. Note how the round patches will contort to complex shapes; they can be applied even while the casting schmutz is still wet. Round patches, several layers of them in staggered sizes, can also be used to reinforce the outside corners of a portable box.

32. When the epoxy has cured, separate the plug's box from its recess, just to be sure it hasn't stuck. Then, return it to its position in the recess and fill it with foam board. To avoid distorting the shape of the plug, these pieces must be sized to fall in place of their own weight; be sure this foam exerts absolutely no pressure against the side walls of the plug. Then, install the foam with contact cement. No squirt-foam should be used here, however. Marine caulk is okay, but don't use anything that could swell and cause the lid to stick.

33. Attach the thick cover (the actual lid or door) to the plug's foam with contact cement. If the cover is flush like mine, extreme care must be used in locating the cover on the plug, with shims fitted into the kerf all around the cover to ensure clearance everywhere. Remove the assembled lid, and apply small schmutz fillets at the plug-to-cover joint. Shape the assembly, making sure it will fit into the recess without binding, all before the double masking tape is removed.

34. After removing the tape, proceed through final coating of the lid or door, and install the gasket and hardware. Does the closure stick anywhere? Is the gasket squeezed all around? If not, fix it now or forever lose your ice.

35. Well, you're close to buying your first block of ice, but before you do that you must install this unit in the boat and hook it up to the drain — if you have either. And, maybe now's the time to decide if you want to paint the box. The clear, new epoxy finish is attractive, but it will dull with use, and coolers exposed to the sun must be painted white, at least on top. Otherwise, you'll broil your ice and frizzle your epoxy; neither one lasts in ultraviolet light. As for the insides, maybe it would be nice to be able see where the mildew is growing, eh? We use two-part epoxy primers, over freshly sanded resin coatings, and any kind of topcoat over that.

There are other things to say about the wonders of liquid joinery. It's messy and fabulous. Also, the materials can be dangerous to handle; you must learn to work clean with this stuff to avoid exposure to potentially dangerous materials. Solvents are the worst.

The fabulous part of liquid joinery will be evident

from even your initial projects. It makes things that are almost rot-proof, and wonderfully strong and lightweight.

There are lots of things to say about refrigeration systems afloat, too. A real fridge on a boat can be troublesome and expensive, and, like liquid joinery, fabulous. There are relatively new technologies available, such as the engine-driven Sea Frost system offered by C.F. Horton & Co., Inc., of Dover, New Hampshire, and the solid-state, thermoelectric process offered by the Cool Corporation of Minneapolis, Minnesota.

Whether you just decide to buy ice, or opt for the Freon frenzy, the right place to start is with a good box, and duokei will do it. Have a cold one!

XVI

Crooked Drawers

—— by Jim Brown ——

his is not about what happens when one sus-
pender breaks. Tim Allen doesn't even wear
suspenders. It is about how to make dovetailed
drawers and other storage structures that fit into
skewed spaces.

In a boat, cabinets often are not "square." They may
have a parallelogram shape, their fronts conforming
to the varying breadth of the hull and their sides running straight athwartships. These skewed cabinets
may enclose angled voids that refuse to admit "square"
drawers and leave gobs of precious stowage space
unused.

Tim Allen doesn't leave anything unused. In his
woodsy combination of home, workshop, and kid cas-
tle, he produces cabinetry for some of the local Down
East Maine production boatbuilders. His creations

range from louvered doors to complete cabinet mod-
ules. Tim feels it is a virtue to have several different
ways of doing things (including making a living), so
he doesn't specialize. He points out that working at
a single, year-round job is fairly rare in Maine, so in
the summer he teaches at WoodenBoat School. It was
there that he discovered how a simple demonstration
and discussion can sometimes open an exciting new
area of woodworking to his students. One such area
is dovetailed joints.

When you ask Tim, "Why use dovetails?," he
responds: "They stay together. They're lightweight.
They're attractive, and...they're fun." When you ask
him, "Why use angled dovetails?" he responds: "To
increase storage by fitting drawers into angled spaces,
and...they're more fun."

The final drawer stock is resawn from flat-glued material to produce edge-glued stock that is really flat and stays that way.

Indeed, building a crooked drawer with Tim one afternoon was just that. It was fun partly because it was challenging. It was challenging because it required precision, judgment, and experimentation, all elements of an enjoyable workshop project. And it was fun because it was the real thing. Of course, angled joints in cabinetry can be made by other methods, such as simple finger joints that are rotated out of square to the desired angle. But Tim points out that real dovetails are strong, and they set their own, pre-cut angle during assembly. They enjoy a greater bond area for gluing, they're self-clamping during assembly, and they will actually hang together even without any glue at all.

With Tim's inventiveness, making such wonderful joints, at any reasonable angle, does not require a lot of special equipment. Several tool manufacturers offer "dovetail machines" appropriate for the home workshop, but Tim has determined that a simple wooden jig, together with a few accessories for your router can be quite adequate for making even crooked, not 90-degree, dovetail joints — which most store-bought dovetail machines won't produce. Tim's dovetailing jig is nothing more than a 2 by 8 of well-seasoned hardwood, joined flat and square, with husky strips ripped off the edges at whatever angle one wishes the corners of the eventual drawer to have. That angle can be square, or anything up to the extreme 30-degree/60-degree drawer in the example illustrated here. One

cuts both the 30-degree and the 60-degree dovetails with the same jig, simply by turning the jig upside down.

The router accessories needed are: A fingered dovetail template, a router guide for that template, and the appropriate router bit. The fingered template is something usually supplied with the above-mentioned dovetail machine. The complete machine is expensive, but the template, available separately, is not. In fact, if you already have a router of about 1 hp and are willing to make Tim Allen's simple jig, you can start cutting precision dovetails for about $30 (1991 price), invested in the likes of the following Porter Cable parts: dovetail template #48016, template guide #42027, and router bit #43640.

Guiding Principles

With the equipment in hand, you'll be anxious to start cutting, but be forewarned that plenty of experimentation is in order. Don't chop into prime stock or attempt to make a finished drawer the first time.

The arrangement of the clamps on the jig, the template, and the stock, and the positioning of the template, plus reversing the jig for opposing angles — all can influence the outside dimensions of the drawer produced. As Tim says to his students, "Start with something, and if it doesn't work, figure out why." Experiment to see how dovetails influence the dimensions of a square drawer, and then repeat the experiments for angled drawers. It's particularly tricky if you are fitting drawers into existing openings; it is better to make the drawers first and then cut the openings.

Here are a few additional tips:

• When setting up, think in terms of locating the template over the workpieces, not the workpieces under the template.

• When positioning the workpieces in the jig, offset one piece from the other by half the distance ($\frac{7}{16}$ inch) of the pitch ($\frac{7}{8}$ inch) of the template. To do this, cut the stock extra wide, and make the drawer ends wider than the sides by at least the template's pitch distance. This approach allows alignment of the sides with the ends, and helps keep drawers flat during assembly. After assembly, trim off the excess width resulting from the above pitch offset. A common pitfall is loss of flatness, or the tendency for the sides and the ends to form an ascending spiral during assembly. The above approach of offsetting the extra-wide workpieces for dovetailing, and trimming the assembled drawer down to its desired depth, will avoid a lot of layout problems for the uninitiated.

• Start right, cut left. That is, begin by passing the router between the right-hand fingers of the template, and work toward the left.

• If the drawer is angled and has a lipped face, install the face after the drawer has been trimmed to its finished size.

• It is the location of the template — its distance back from the edge of the workpieces — that yields drawers of a specific, final size. The position of the template for square drawers should be the same for all joints. For angled drawers, template location will differ between the acute and obtuse joints. However, the position of the template should not be changed for the two like corners of an angled drawer, or the resulting parallelogram will be untrue.

• Mark mating pieces after cutting and before removing them from the jig, so they can be assembled in the way they were cut — as mating pieces.

• Drawer bottoms can be ¼-inch plywood, let into the drawer's sides and ends. Locate the dado cut in a "tail" area of the joint, to hide it from view at the corners after assembly.

The Proper Wood

Having a machinist's background, Tim likes to work in wood with real precision. Once he has experimented with scrap stock, he prepares laminated stock for real drawers. Not only does laminating stabilize the material dimensionally, resulting in a drawer that is easier to assemble, but he feels laminating produces drawers that retain their shape over time, avoiding the sticking and jamming so common in boat cabinetry.

The problem is flatness. Simply running the stock through a thickness planer doesn't necessarily make it flat, because most planers won't take out warp and twist. Therefore, Tim starts with two-by mahogany stock, surfaces it, and laminates it with epoxy. That's right, he glues up a stack of planks about 12 inches high (12 inches being the width of his thickness

The dovetailing jig is simple "two-by" hardwood. The edge pieces are ripped at any angle desired to a given set of drawers, from the usual 90 degrees to this extreme 30 degrees/60 degrees. Opposite angles are cut simply by turning the jig upside down.

The dovetail template is carefully located and clamped over the workpieces. Note that the drawer's sidewall piece, here clamped horizontally under the template, is made wider than the end-wall piece, clamped vertically in the jig, by at least half the pitch-distance of the template.

An obtuse-angled dovetail joint. (The template has been removed for the photograph, but in practice it is not "dislocated" until all angled dovetails have been cut.) The template is clamped in position at the sides, so the workpieces can be exchanged beneath it.

An acute-angled dovetail joint. In extreme-angled joints like this one, the "pin" portions of the joint can become delicate, requiring careful positioning of the template.

A crooked drawer, shown before being trimmed to its final dimensions. If lipped faces are to be used, install the faces after trimming.

A crooked drawer assembled and trimmed, with bottom panel installed. Consider cutting the opening in the drawer's cabinet front after this final assembly and trimming. Note that the dadoes for the bottom panel are located in "tail" portions of the joint to make them invisible after assembly.

planer), and when building the stack he alternates the slash angle of the grain in the planks.

When the epoxy has cured, the glued stack is resawn perpendicular to the glue lines. The first bandsaw cut is made to a straight line drawn down the middle of the stack. The two resulting surfaces of the halved stack are passed over the jointer, and the rest of the stack is resawn into ½-inch to ⁹⁄₁₆-inch slabs. These slabs are then thickness planed. Now, you have produced edge-laminated drawer stock, which is somewhere around ⁹⁄₁₆ inch and really flat.

This procedure, incidentally, results in a substantial saving of wood: Less is lost to planer shavings than when resawing and surfacing two-by material.

Given the experience of the aforementioned experiments, and now having this very fine stock to work with, it is time to really enjoy producing dovetailed drawers or other structures, with no hesitation about angles.

By now you will have noticed that Tim's simple jig can be used to cut dovetails at either angle, that is, for drawers whose plan view describes a parallelogram, or drawers which, when seen in section, have walls sloping inward or outward. And yes, it is possible to cut dovetails for compound angles, as in a combination of the above. While there seems to be little practical application for such compound joints, consider the impractical applications. For instance, why not try to make something like a three-sided, or even a five-sided, pyramid!? With all its joints dovetailed and converging perfectly at the apex... just for the fun of it.

The North Woods Paddle

— by Rick Waters —

*M*any a paddler has stood in mystified silence watching a skilled team of North Woods travelers plying their seemingly delicate paddles across the waters of canoe country. Somehow it seems impossible, or at least improbable, that large, loaded traveling canoes could be propelled with so little apparent movement by the paddlers, with such fluid grace that scarcely raises a ripple to hint of the path of the paddle. Yet the canoe, as if governed by a mystical force, not only behaves, but behaves quickly, cleanly — the way an arctic char might use the water of its realm.

Much of the secret lies in the paddle, and the technique best suited to its use. With practice, much that is mysterious at first settles into a sophisticated balance of properties that blend canoe, paddler, and paddle into graceful harmony.

— Garrett Conover

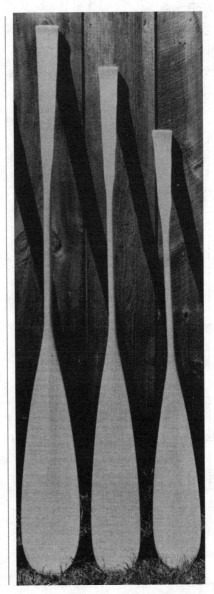

While the eerie cry of a loon cascades across a lake in northern Maine and the sun becomes a golden glow in the west, I help our guides Garrett and Alexandra make camp. I am sore and aching from a day of paddling, while Garrett claims only to be "pleasantly tired." He explains that the difference in our degrees of fatigue is not due to conditioning but, rather, due to the paddles that he and Alexandra make and use, and the North Woods stroke they employ while paddling. I had noticed a difference in the movement of their canoes — no bobbing and weaving like my canoe but a smooth, straight, silent path while their bodies rocked slightly back and forth.

Garrett and Alexandra Conover, Maine canoeing guides, learned many of their skills from the late Mick Fahey, a noted veteran of the North Woods. Perhaps the most obscure of all knowledge that Mick passed

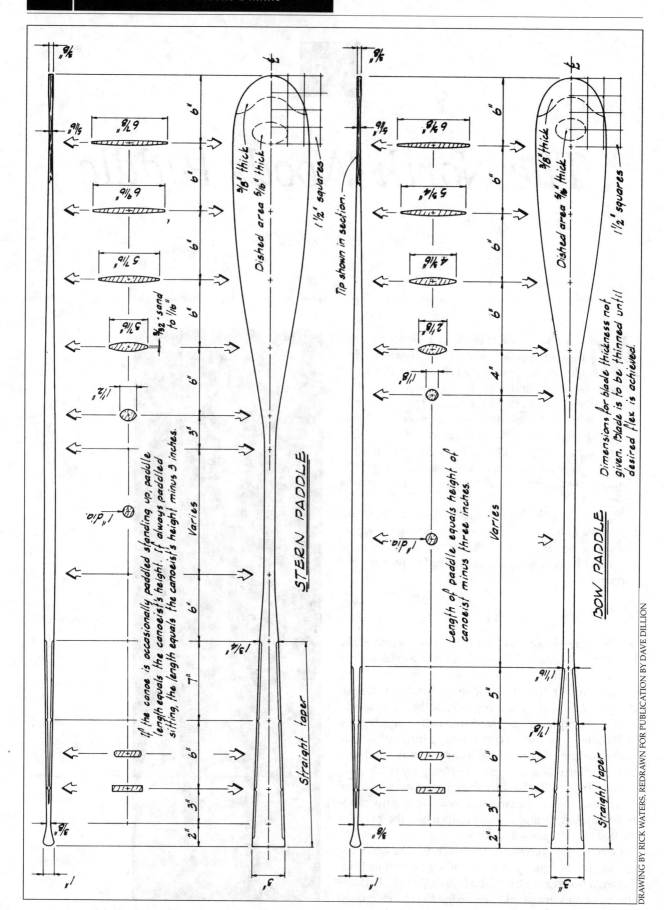

DRAWING BY RICK WATERS, REDRAWN FOR PUBLICATION BY DAVE DILLION

on to them was the North Woods stroke, the paddling stroke employed by the Indians, voyageurs, guides, trappers, and anyone else involved in serious canoe travel. Yet in a sense, the North Woods stroke and the North Woods paddle epitomize Garrett and Alexandra's life's work and all that Mick passed on to them. For they have not only preserved the knowledge of how the North Woods were traveled and the skills to make and use the paddles, but also through guiding canoe trips they are also preserving the need for efficient canoe travel.

The North Woods stroke is considerably different from the J-stroke we all learned at camp. After camp has been made and dinner has been eaten, Garrett sits near the campfire and, to illustrate the differences, he mimes paddling a canoe. "The J-stroke overuses a few muscles and expends a lot of needless energy," he explains. "In addition, you need to compensate continually for not heading in the direction you want to go. You end up crabbing down the length of a lake."

He shifts on his fireside perch to illustrate the oblique sitting position used in the North Woods stroke, and his voice rises as he sings the virtues of a stroke evolved over generations of constant use. "The North Woods stroke places all your muscles in a line and uses them all a little bit. It is a very efficient stroke involving subtle arm and body movements that enable you to paddle all day with little fatigue. The paddle flexes instead of your back."

The paddles that Alexandra makes are works of art. They blend graceful, delicate lines and flexibility with strength and utility. Comparing a store-bought paddle to one of Alexandra's North Woods paddles is like comparing a fast-food hamburger to a gourmet meal.

The first thing one notices about a North Woods paddle is that half of the shaft is handle. The paddle can be gripped at the end or any one of three "grips" carved along the side of the handle. This allows the paddle to be used as a long or a short paddle with equal comfort. The edge of the handle is scalloped to allow the canoeist to find the "grip stations" without looking. The shaft is narrow (1 inch in diameter), and the long, narrow blade is slightly dished near the end to reduce weight and increase flexibility. The paddle can be used from a standing, sitting, or kneeling position and in any type of water. Each paddle is custom made to fit the height of the owner, and each blade is carved to get the proper strength and flex from a particular piece of wood.

Alexandra is remarkably adept with an axe, and with it she can literally split a pencil line. Using an axe and a crooked knife, she can make a paddle in a day, but she is not bound to an ethic that prohibits the use of power tools. She has made paddles with a bandsaw and a power plane as well.

The North Woods paddle described in this chapter can be made by following the plans shown here.

Ash and maple are the two types of wood to use when making a North Woods paddle, and it makes little difference which is used. Choose whichever species is available. If you are starting in the woods, fell a tree 16 to 18 inches in diameter. Cut a clear section 5 to 6 feet long, depending on the length of the paddle, and split it through the center. Split this half-round in half, and you will have a quarter-round approximately 9 inches a side. You should get out the piece near the outer growth rings but inside the sapwood, where the growth rings are the flattest. This is the same piece of wood to look for if you are buying a blank from a lumberyard or a mill. Paint the ends of the blank with hot linseed oil, or red lead to prevent checking, and allow the wood to dry for as long as possible. The blank should measure 1¼ inch in thickness so you can get a straight paddle, even if the board warps slightly while drying.

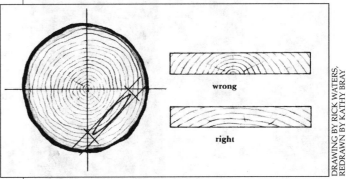

wrong

right

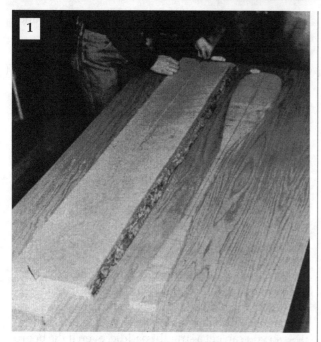

Build It by the Numbers

1

With a suitable blank laid flat, snap a chalkline along its length parallel to the direction of its grain and approximately centered across its width. The pattern, which shows to the right of the blank in the photo, and which should be made from the accompanying plans, is then laid on the blank so its centerline aligns with the chalkline. The paddle profile is then traced from the pattern. (If you want to avoid driving nails into the blank, you can use a small block of wood with a nail in it to hold one end of the chalkline as shown.)

2

If you elect to hew out your paddle by hand, begin at the bottom corner of the blade, but don't shape the blade tip until later. Remove wood by splitting it away, working your way in toward the marked outline. As you cut away wood where the blade begins to narrow, you'll have to take shorter cuts so as not to split off part of the blade. Continue this hewing process up the shaft to the handle, reversing the direction of cut by turning the blank end for end as necessary to take advantage of the grain runout or to shape the handle itself.

3

Hew away the other edge of the blank to its marked line, and your paddle really begins to take shape. If you have access to a bandsaw, you can reach this stage simply by sawing around the line, but leaving the tip square until later.

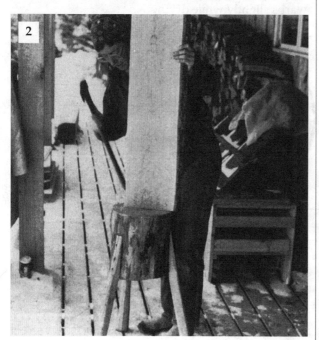

4

Now set the paddle on edge, holding it there with weights against its sides, and stretch a string above it. A C-clamp just beyond the ends of the paddle can be used, as shown, for holding the string.

5

Sight vertically downward and place the middle of the paddle's edge directly under the string, then make marks for a centerline at intervals along this edge. Connect the marks, using a flexible batten or straightedge, to give a continuous centerline all along this first edge of the paddle. Sight in from each end to confirm that the centerline is straight.

6

The next step, that of marking a similar centerline on the opposite edge, has to begin by establishing end points for that centerline — a process that results in the blade and handle being in the same plane; to put it another way, this is a process that assures there will be no twist in your paddle.

7

After you've marked a centerline on both edges, mark the paddle measurements out from these centerlines and connect them with a straightedge.

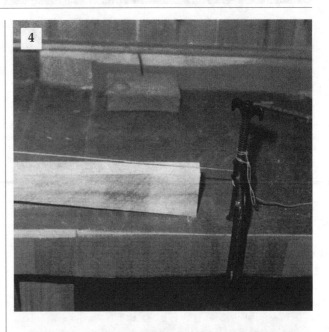

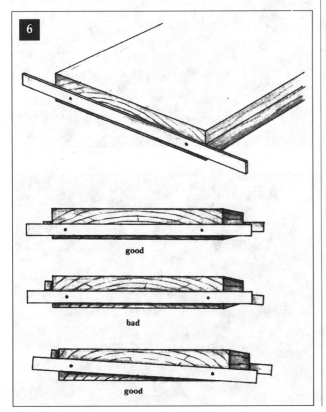

good

bad

good

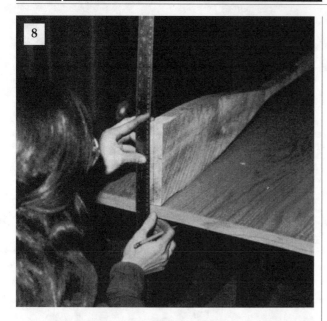

8

Continue the paddle outline markings across both ends of the blank. (This is the reason why the blade tip was left square.)

9

Taper the blade by hewing to the lines, just as you did earlier for the profile. A portable power plane, a hand plane, or a spokeshave can help out here. Note that at this stage there is no crown to the blade: all surfaces are flat across the paddle.

10

Continue thinning the blade and handle. Crown the blade, as shown in the drawing, by removing wood on each side of the centerline.

11

The thickness of the grip — anywhere from ⅝ inch to 1 inch — can be made to suit your hand. Hollow out the area just below the grip with a gouge, a spokeshave, and a rasp until it is comfortable.

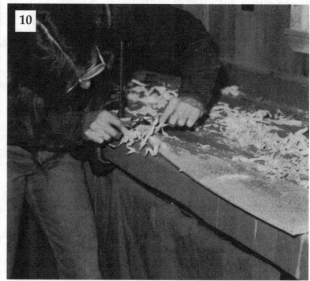

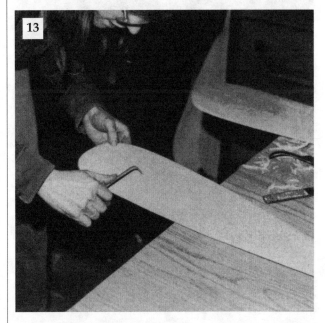

12

Now you can mark the rounded tip of the blade from your pattern, cut it out with bandsaw or coping saw, and rasp it fair, square, and smooth.

13

Continue shaping the blade, including the dished-out area, as shown in the drawing. Calipers that are a tight fit at the blade tip will just rattle when the dished area is shaved to the right thickness.

14

Round off the sharp corners along the blade's outline, and fair in the blade tip.

15

Start rounding the shaft by planing its four corners to 45 degrees until all eight faces are of equal width, just as you would when making a round spar. Then plane off the eight corners. Continue shaping until you produce a 1-inch diameter round shaft, all the while checking for straightness and uniformity.

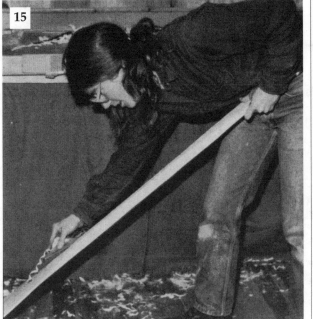

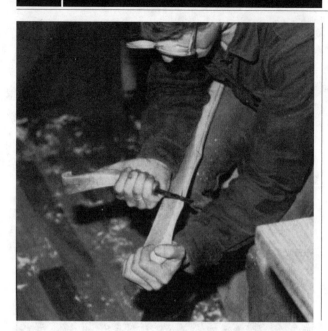

16
When you are satisfied with the shaft, fair it in to the blade handle with a gradual transition as shown in the plans. Scallop the corners of the handle for grip stations, using a crooked knife (shown in use here) or a spokeshave. Then smooth the entire paddle with a rasp, sandpaper, and a scraper.

The paddle can be finished with either oil or varnish. If varnish is used, it is best to just oil the handle to ensure a good grip.

A Double Paddle

by Peter H. Spectre
Illustrations by Kathy Bray

Gail Wills

The double paddle, used for propelling kayaks and some canoes, is a wonderful instrument. In fact, once you get used to it, you will never go back to a single paddle, except perhaps when maneuvering in tight quarters or controlling your craft when fishing. A double paddle, in effect, makes a single paddler twice as effective — the bow man and stern man rolled into one — and the struggle to master the J-stroke or the North Woods stroke becomes a thing of the past. Also, it makes going into the wind significantly easier, especially if you are using a feathering design.

The double paddle does have a drawback, however. Because of its extreme length — approximately twice the length of a single paddle — it can be unwieldy at times; for example, when transporting it in a car or storing it in the bottom of a canoe. But this problem can be eliminated by putting a joint in the middle of the shaft so the two halves can come apart. I never did that with mine, though, because the joint has a tendency either to bind, making the unjointing a struggle, or to become too loose, making paddling awkward to say the least when the shaft comes apart in midstroke. Since I have no experience with jointed paddles, this discussion assumes the building of a continuous-shaft model. If you want to put a joint in yours, see Chapter 19.

Feathering and Nonfeathering

There are two types of double paddle: feathering and nonfeathering. The nonfeathering has blades that are in the same plane, while the feathering has blades that are at an angle, usually a right angle, to each other. A nonfeathering paddle is deceptively easy to use, but when you take a stroke with it, the up blade is flat to the wind and has a tendency to act like a sail. This can

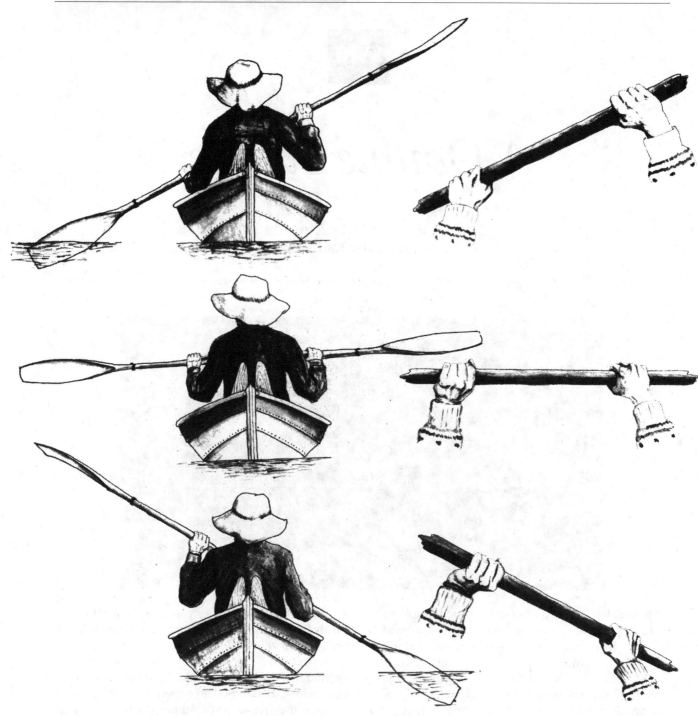

work to your advantage when going downwind, but in a light canoe or kayak going upwind, it can stop you cold and make paddling a muscle-rending chore. The feathering paddle is the choice of experienced double-paddlers, because the up blade presents its edge to the wind, virtually eliminating windage. If you don't think the latter is worth achieving, try slogging your way upwind on a long lake in a brisk breeze with a nonfeathering paddle. You'll see the light.

A feathering paddle is used by rotating the shaft between strokes so first one blade and then the other goes into the water at the correct angle. The shaft is rotated by turning it with one hand — just a slight twist of the wrist is required — and allowing it to turn freely in the other hand. Which hand does the rotating and which hand allows the free turning determines whether the paddle has right- or left-hand control. Left-hand-control paddles are rotated with the left hand, and right-hand-control paddles are rotated with the right hand.

The type of control you use for your paddle is up to you, but contrary to most people's expectations, it

blade with one-direction spoon   blade with total spoon   blade with no spoon

has nothing to do with whether you are left- or right-handed. For example, I am right-handed but use a left-hand-control paddle, simply because that was the type I first used. After a number of years with a left-handed paddle, I could never switch over to a right-handed one. It has something to do with old dogs....

If you are building a straight-bladed double paddle — one without spoon blades — whether it is to be used for right- or left-hand control is immaterial. But if you are building a spoon-bladed model as described here, careful consideration has to be given to the direction of the spoon of the blades. I could go into a long impossible-to-understand description of this, but the drawings describe this better than words ever could.

Blade Shape

There have been endless debates about blade shape, and I'm sure there will be many more in the future. Like any other design work for waterborne craft and implements, determining blade shape is a question of priorities and compromise. Are you looking for maneuverability? Speed? Slippage? Cruising distance?

I'm no expert on the subject, but so far I have learned that wide blades with lots of area get a good bite in the water but tend to sap my strength on the long haul. Long, narrow blades have more slip in the water and seem to be more reasonable for long-distance cruising. Short, fat blades are good for maneuverability, especially when moving sideways and most especially when using the paddle as a rudder.

Since I do a lot of paddling in widely varying conditions, I chose for myself a compromise — my blades are not too long, not too wide, and have a moderate amount of area. The configuration is one that is pleasing to the eye (mine, at least) and doesn't have sharp edges that can be damaged or broken. You might have other thoughts on this, or your paddling needs might be more specialized than mine. To make your choice, borrow paddles of different configurations and try them out. You will find, as I have, that even the slightest change in blade shape can give your paddling a substantial difference in "feel." Only you can tell what's right for you. (I might mention that my latest paddle, shown here, is loosely based on a design by L.F.

Herreshoff, presented in his book *Sensible Cruising Designs*. LFH was an experienced double-paddle man, and like all of his designs, his paddle is a careful blend of scientific and artistic considerations.)

Another consideration is the amount of spoon you give to your blades. My first paddle was rather wide and had considerable spoon, which caused more bite in the water than I wanted. My second paddle, shown here, has less spoon and is narrower, and I find it almost ideal. My blades have concavity going in one direction only — simply because I don't have the proper gouges to work in both lengthwise and athwartships concavity — but I have tried paddles that almost literally look like spoons and haven't found them to be superior.

Paddle Length

Still another consideration is the overall length of the paddle. This is determined in part by the width of your canoe or kayak and the height of the coaming or gunwale, and in part by your attitude about the length of oars. People who like long oars tend to like long double paddles and vice versa. This has a lot to do with gearing; long paddles are high gear, short paddles are low gear.

Being a compromiser, I chose a moderate length for my paddle: 8 feet from tip to tip, which allows me to get the blade into the water without striking the shaft on my canoe's coaming yet doesn't give me an overly long up end to wave in the breeze and catch the wind. I have used a long paddle, 9 feet, and felt as if I were working with a flagpole, and I have used a 7-footer and felt as if I were playing table tennis. Again, the choice is yours.

The most critical consideration, of course, is the weight of the paddles. A double paddle is held aloft by your arms all the time you are using it, so the lighter you can make it, the less strength will have to be expended holding it up and the more will be left over for actually propelling the boat. On a short haul, a heavier paddle isn't much of a problem, but on a long haul, a couple of ounces of excess weight can wear you down quickly. Every shaving you can take off a paddle without affecting its strength is weight worth losing.

Scantlings

Naturally enough, this leads into paddle scantlings, which is an impossible subject. My second paddle has substantially lighter scantlings than my first, and is consequently much lighter, yet I can see that I could still pare away at the thing and not diminish its strength. On the other hand, light scantlings can mean a whippy paddle, favored by some, but I prefer a stiffer one, if only for peace of mind. Scantlings are also determined by your selection of wood stock. The stronger the wood, the lighter the possible scantling. For example, cedar can be used for paddles, but needs thickness of section to provide strength. I use spruce, because it is both relatively light and strong, and because it is easily obtained.

As you can see, much goes into a double paddle's design. There is no science to it; rather, figuring out a design is mostly art, feel, and experimentation. You build a paddle, try it out, modify it, build another, etc., etc. It's cheap fun.

Build It by the Numbers

1. Pick your stock. This paddle is built from two lumberyard spruce 2 by 4s — one for the shaft and one to build up the sides of the blades. Look for straight, dry, clear-grained pieces, which may be impossible to find, but do your best. Small, tight knots are okay, but straightness is an imperative. In today's lumberyard, dryness of stock is debatable and can be the cause of heated argument, but your 2 by 4s should be air-dried anyway, so you needn't be too fussy.

2. Air-dry your stock. Rest the 2 by 4s on evenly spaced sticks in the room where you will be building the paddle. Leave them to dry — a week, a month, 6 months, whatever it takes, however long you can wait — but keep coming back to check them. If they start to curl one way, turn them over the other way. You want them to dry as straight as possible.

3. Rip one 2 by 4 right down the middle. Pick the clearest half for the shaft of the paddle. Keep the other half for your next paddle. The half that you are using is to be kept square for the time being, but cut it down now to the eventual thickness of the paddle shaft. In other words, if the shaft is to be 1¼ inches in section, make your piece 1¼ inches square by ripping it with a saw or planing it with a thickness planer.

4. Glue pieces of the other 2 by 4 to both sides of the ends of the shaft. Make these pieces slightly longer than the total length of the blades so they can be faired into the shaft later, and pay attention to the direction of the grain. You want the annular rings to cup with the blade if there is to be athwartships spoon, and you want the tendency of the grain to be the same on each side of the blade to facilitate carving. Remember to glue up the side pieces so the blades are at right angles. Use any glue you are comfortable with as long as it is waterproof.

5. Make a paper pattern of the blade and trace its shape onto the glued-up stock. Use the same pattern for both ends.

6. Cut out the profile of the blade. Use a bandsaw, sabersaw, coping saw — whatever you have that will do the job.

7. Draw the curve of the spoon along the edges of the blades. I do this by eye, but you can use battens and tacks to ensure accuracy. Make the blade as thin as you dare.

8. Cut the curvature of the backs of the blades. I use a drawknife for the rough work, a spokeshave for the rest, and finish up with wood files and sandpaper. Some people use Surform tools. Some also leave a ridge partway down the back of the blade for strength, but I don't think it is necessary (some put a ridge on the inside instead, but I don't do that either).

Remember: Whatever you do to one blade, do the same thing to the other. The goal is to obtain evenly shaped blades of equal weight for proper balance.

9. Cut the inside curve, or concavity, of the blades. This is the hard part and requires patience and careful work because of the run of the grain. If the blade is to be spooned both ways, use shallow gouges. If not, use the same tools you used for the back.

10. Round off the shaft. Do this the same way spars are made — use a plane and a spokeshave at the throat to make the shaft first 8-sided, then 16-sided, then round.

11. Fair the profile of the blade into the shaft. Note that the sides of the shaft at the throat are pinched in. This is to pare off a little excess weight and also to give the paddle a little extra stylishness. The thickness there is not needed for strength.

12. Sand the paddle carefully and apply your finish. I give my paddles four coats of spar varnish — the first thinned down — and I sand lightly between coats.

Tip Protection

Because the tendency is to use the paddle as a pole at times, especially when shoving off from shore, the tips should be given some type of protection. The organic way is to glue hardwood strips on the tips before varnishing. Another method is to fiberglass the tips. Still another is to cut copper tips and tack them in place. If you do this, drill for the tacks to prevent splitting the blades and clench them on the other side.

Drip Guards

Double paddles can be annoying at times because water can drip down from the up blade onto your arms and into the canoe. Skilled paddlers develop a little flipping motion that flicks off most of the water, but drip guards are helpful for getting rid of the rest. You can buy rubber drip guards, but your paddle must be jointed so you can slide them on. An alternative that is just as effective and much more decorative is to make Turk's heads with thick twine. To preserve them once they're on, soak them with pine tar.

pattern of blade drawn on stock, then cut out

inside curve cut

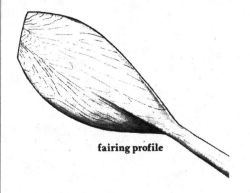

fairing profile

A Double Paddle Jointed in the Middle

by Donald MacKenzie

Drawings by the author   Photos by R.G. Whitelaw

The ideal material for a double-bladed paddle is spruce, a wood combining light weight with stiffness and strength. It is widely available as inexpensive construction lumber. Go to your local lumberyard and search in the piles of 2-inch framing stock for clear pieces. (Leave the piles neatly stacked when you are done; you may want to come back for more.) You might have to buy what seems to be a large board to get the small amount of good stock that is needed, but there will be use for the scrap.

If your local lumberyard does not carry spruce, substitute what is available. In general, moderately close-grained, lightweight boards are preferable. Although Southern yellow pine and Douglas-fir are on the heavy and splintery side, hemlock and white fir are acceptable when dry. A good piece of white pine or red cedar, although weaker, will be lovely; add a bit extra to the designed thickness to compensate for the weakness. Most of the second-choice softwoods are heavier than spruce, but they are stiffer, so some of that extra weight can be removed by working to thinner dimensions.

I prefer to use vertical-grained wood for oars and paddles. It is less likely to warp or split and places the

stiffer grain in opposition to the thrust. If the material is stiffer, you need less of it. Put the extra weight in your anchor, not in your paddle!

Look for planks whose end-grain is square to the plank's width, or those that have been slab-sawn from a large enough tree that the end-grain is fairly straight and parallel to the surface. Pieces cut from such a board and turned 90 degrees for lamination produce a finished blank with vertical grain.

Much construction lumber is sawn with the heart of the tree close to the center of the plank; there will be vertical grain on each side of the heart, which is perfect for use in a paddle. Stay a couple of inches away from the unstable wood in the very center of the tree, however, and always check the edges for spike knots, which may be invisible on the faces. Plan your layout to avoid knots as much as possible. Small, tight knots are acceptable, as they do no real harm.

The paddle described here is made in two pieces so it will fit in the trunk of a car. I prefer to make one-piece paddles in halves as well and then join them together with glue, because shorter lengths are much easier to handle when carving the blades.

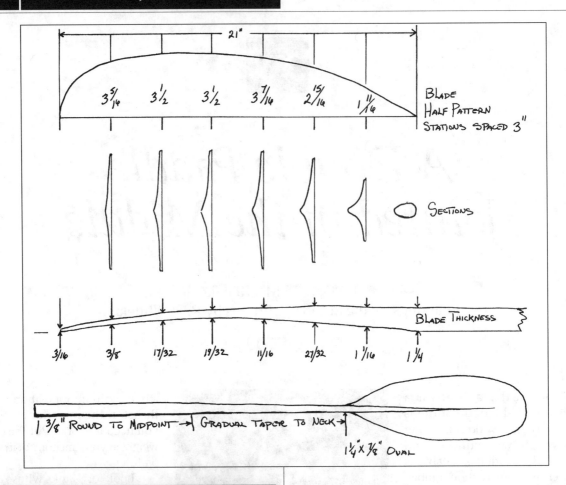

BLADE
HALF PATTERN
STATIONS SPACED 3"

21"

$3\frac{5}{16}$ $3\frac{1}{2}$ $3\frac{1}{2}$ $3\frac{7}{16}$ $2\frac{15}{16}$ $1\frac{11}{16}$

SECTIONS

BLADE THICKNESS

$\frac{3}{16}$ $\frac{3}{8}$ $\frac{17}{32}$ $\frac{19}{32}$ $\frac{11}{16}$ $\frac{27}{32}$ $1\frac{1}{16}$ $1\frac{1}{4}$

$1\frac{3}{8}$" ROUND TO MIDPOINT → | GRADUAL TAPER TO NECK →

$1\frac{1}{4}$" × $\frac{7}{8}$" OVAL

The tools shown here — combined with spruce, practice, and patience — can produce an elegant paddle.

Getting Started

For a double paddle 9 feet long, with blades 7 inches by 20 inches, you will need the following material:

For the shafts, you'll need two pieces 1½ inches square and 5 feet long. To build up the blade width, you'll need either four pieces that are 1½ inches by 3 inches by 20 inches, or eight pieces that are half that width. Also, to protect the edges during clamping, you'll need two pieces of scrap wood, ¾ inch by 1½ inches by 20 inches. (You can alter these dimensions as necessary to make a paddle that will suit you and your boat.) A table saw is ideal for rough-cutting this material, although other saws will also serve.

After rough-cutting, the wood may need drying. Here on Cape Cod, where I work, construction lumber is sold as "surfaced dry." "Dry" means the moisture content of the lumber is 19 percent, which is a bit wet. However, once cut, the small pieces required for paddle making will dry very quickly indoors, particularly in the winter. A week or two will easily do the trick. In the summer, if the wood is left in the sun, it will dry even faster, sometimes so fast as to lead to end-checking. Either rough out the pieces extra long so you can cut off the end checks, or paint the ends to prevent rapid moisture loss. Turn the pieces at intervals, and don't leave them in the hot sun for more than a few hours at a time.

Keep the final shape of the paddle in mind while you make a trial assembly of the blank. Try to place any knots in areas that will be removed. When you are satisfied with the arrangements, record them with a bold, diagonal registration mark across one set of pieces and two marks across the other set. Begin jointing the gluing surfaces with your longest hand plane set to take a moderate cut; finish truing with a finer cut.

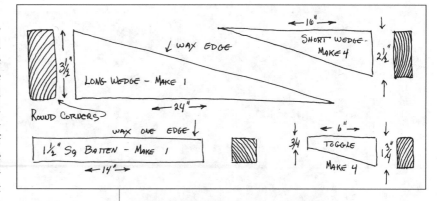

Test each joint by eye and by placing the pieces in contact. Try to swivel them; try to rock them diagonally. You should feel some resistance at the ends but no rocking. An easy swiveling shows that the joint is pivoting on the center and open at the ends; diagonal rocking indicates a twist in the joint. Avoid these conditions! You may be able to correct them with clamps, but that will be only a temporary solution; the joint will invariably open later. (On the other hand, a joint that is slightly open in the center will stay tight if it can be brought together with moderate force.)

To correct a joint with open ends, make a couple of short swipes with your plane on the surfaces that will be in the center of the joint, followed by cuts of increasing length; finish with a full-length cut. A twist is taken out by sliding the plane sideways from one high corner to the other during the stroke.

Gluing and Clamping

Now, glue the "wings" to the shaft. I use Weldwood plastic resin glue. It's cheap, strong, and easy to mix. Even though I don't follow the mixing instructions to the letter — I measure by eye, and shop temperature is often less than that called for — this type of glue has always worked. Close fitting and good clamping are required.

The saying "You never have enough clamps" is all too true, particularly concerning the larger size clamps. If you have them, use them. However, there are ways to make do without clamps — and make do we shall, without any clamps at all!

Before the screw, there was the wedge. And indeed, the screw is only a wedge wrapped around a shaft. With a combination of wedges and rope we can get all the clamping pressure we need to glue up our blank.

If you've done any gluing at all, you have seen the perversity of wood and glue. The glue becomes a lubricant, and if the clamps are set just a bit askew, none of the pieces want to stay aligned. So, how are we ever going to control seven pieces of wood, all slimy with

The blades of the paddle can be glued up without big, expensive clamps. This method, perfected by Spanish guitar makers, uses inexpensive polypropylene rope, and homemade toggles and wedges.

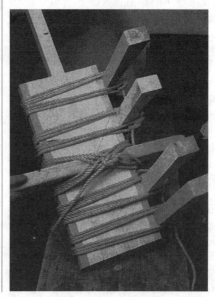

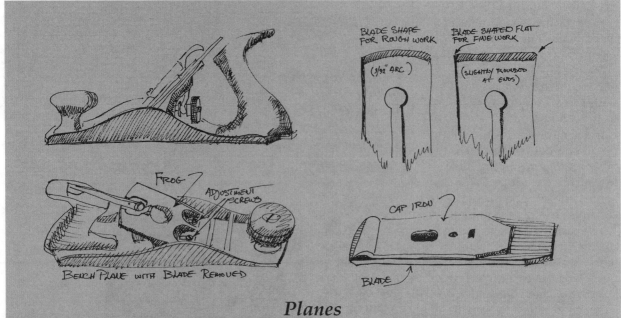

BLADE SHAPE FOR ROUGH WORK

(3/32" ARC)

BLADE SHAPED FLAT FOR FINE WORK

(SLIGHTLY ROUNDED AT ENDS)

FROG

ADJUSTMENT SCREWS

CAP IRON

BENCH PLANE WITH BLADE REMOVED

BLADE

Planes

I expect to find a plane or two in even the most modest tool kit, but rarely is one of these planes in usable condition. That's too bad, for once mastered the plane becomes a most versatile tool. Some of the basics of hand plane use are:

1. Sharpen the blade.

2. Check the cap iron, if there is one; be certain that it closely fits the blade; sharpen it if it is dull.

3. Adjust the plane to suit the work; set the cap iron very close to the cutting edge for finishing cuts and up to ⅛ inch back for rough-cutting. Also, adjust the throat to match the work — tight for fine cuts, open for coarse work.

4. When using the tool, take a good stance and use your whole body, not just your arms; transfer your weight forward with the stroke.

5. When planing a straight edge or flat surface, start with downward pressure on your leading hand, shift your weight back during the stroke, and end with most of the pressure on the trailing hand. To avoid rounding off the ends, imagine you are trying to plane a hollow.

glue, while we try to force them together with rope and wedges?

As it happens, the guitar makers of Spain figured out years ago how to clamp thin pieces of wood with string and wedges. Their method is still the best way I know to clamp thin boards. It will keep the pieces subdued while you finish the job with a high-powered version of the same technique.

Prepare the wedges, toggles, and batten as shown in the diagram. Wax one side of the batten. In addition, you will need about 75 feet of ⁵⁄₁₆-inch line. Polypropylene is cheap and doesn't stretch very much. There is nothing absolute about the size. Almost anything smaller than hawser and bigger than thread will work. Larger rope may need fewer turns; smaller stuff will require more.

Start every gluing job with a dry run. Now is the time to discover and correct any problems; this is never easy once the glue has been applied. After checking the fit, spread the glue on the mating surfaces. Then place a couple of scrap spacers on your workbench and lay the batten on top with its long dimension across the bench. Be sure to have the waxed side of the batten up so the glue doesn't stick to it. Balance the parts of the blank across the batten, placing them in order as shown by the registration mark. Shim up the other end of the shaft so it is approximately level. Proceed to truss the blank to the batten with three or four complete figure-eight turns of your line. Secure the ends with a square knot.

Hold the long wedge with the rounded edges up and the waxed side down; slide it in the lower eye of the rope figure eights, under the crossings of the rope and out the upper eye. Give it a good shove, and it will pinch the pieces between the batten and the wedge, aligning and clamping simultaneously. I know that it doesn't look as though it should work, but it really does! Tap the ends of the parts into proper alignment, then blast the wedge home with a good-sized hammer.

The real pinching power comes from rope shackles paired with toggles and wedges. Place a toggle across the edge of the blank. Draw the rope from the toggle down the side of the blank, pass it underneath, and bring it up the back side, going over the other end of the toggle. Return the line to the other side, passing over the front of the toggle. Repeat this route for a total of three complete loops, and join the ends with a square knot. Push a wedge between the toggle and the blank. Rest the end of the toggle on the workbench as shown, and drive the wedge with your heavy hammer. Four such units will be sufficient.

Remember this technique; it has many uses in woodworking and a lot of power. I should emphasize that all assembly and clamping ought to be practiced before spreading the glue — not just to check the fit, but also to learn the techniques.

Shaping the Paddle

After 24 hours, knock the wedges out of the rope shackles and reuse them to glue the next blank. You can start carving the first blank while the second is drying. Firmly secure the blank to your bench with clamps, stops, or a vise.

Your workbench is a tool, just as important as any other in your kit. Benches that are crooked, twisted, or flimsy will transfer these qualities to your work. If necessary, straighten the top of the bench, and brace the legs with diagonals or plywood. Attach the whole unit to a wall. A few nails properly placed will introduce amazing rigidity to a flabby bench.

Rough shaping of the concave curve of the paddle blade is easily done with a hand plane; you don't need a bandsaw. Grinding the plane iron to a strong curve (see diagram) makes your hand plane a veritable beaver for rough work. Open the throat of your plane by moving the frog back. If you have an extra plane to leave set up this way, so much the better. A Stanley No. 4 plane is ideal.

Rapid stock removal from the face of a board is best done across the grain. With the blade set to take a generous bite, begin cutting straight across the center of the blank. As the sides of the plane's body contact the surface, the blade will cease cutting. Move the plane to the right and to the left, then back to the center. Continue in this manner, gradually working out to the ends, and you will almost automatically create a nice curve. The depth of the hollow should be about $\frac{5}{8}$ inch. This dimension can be checked with a straightedge and a rule. You can test the fairness of the curve by eye and with a small batten sprung into the curve.

When the concave curve of the blade is satisfactory, turn the paddle over, and with the same cross-planing technique rough out the shape of the back of the blade. Holding the plane at an angle to the stroke may help to get a clean cut. Rough the tip down to about $\frac{3}{8}$ inch in thickness, and work back in a curve for about half the length of the blade. Check this curve by eye and with a batten.

Sketch the outline of the blade on the face of the

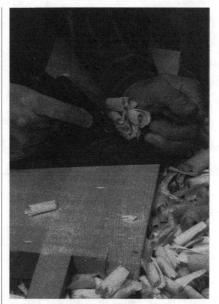

Roughing out the concave surface of the spoon blades with a Stanley No. 4 plane. For fast removal of stock, work across the grain.

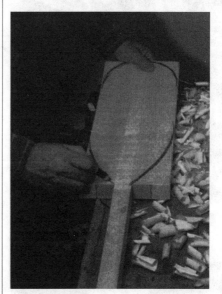

Sketch the outline of the blade on the face of the blank.

Smooth the blade surface with a scraper. Here, a scraper is being pulled, but pushing can be effective as well.

Cut the profile of the blade with a drawknife, using a slicing motion for improved control.

Using a knife to shape the shaft. Here, the author uses a pulling stroke, with his left-hand thumb serving as a safety stop.

blank. With the blank firmly clamped in the vise, cut close to the line with a drawknife. Hold the drawknife at an angle to the direction of cut and slide it sideways as you pull it forward. Make a series of short, controlled cuts, twisting the handles up at the end of each cut to split away waste wood. As you near the neck of the paddle, where the shaft and the blade join, use great care with the drawknife. You can avoid accidental deep gouging of the neck by increasing the amount of sideways sliding of the blade. The resulting shearing cut requires less downward pressure and provides more control.

Now finish the concave face of the blade. A flat wooden plane with a toothed blade takes off the high spots left by the iron plane, and it allows cutting in all directions without tearing the wood. Plane in many different directions, crossing your strokes. Check the curve by eye and by feel. Help your eye by illuminating the work with a strong, raking light. Early-morning and late-afternoon sun is great for carving. Run your hand over the surface to reveal hollows and hard spots. Any irregularities that you can't see and can't feel probably won't bother you too much in the finished paddle.

Perfect the concave surface of the blade with a flexible scraper. I made mine from an X-ACTO #239 razor saw. The steel from this inexpensive backsaw makes a fine tool. The blade of the saw has been reinforced by a steel stamping held on by two punched dimples. This stamping can easily be pried open to release the blade. Use a flat file to remove the saw teeth, round the corners, and sharpen what will be the scraping edge to a slight angle — say, 75 degrees for general use. But, for a fine cut, sharpen the scraper square and turn the edges with a burnisher in the classic manner.

This is a tool for shaping as well as smoothing; use it that way. Experiment with it. Vary the angle of attack; try different strokes; use one hand or both hands; bend an arc in the blade or use it straight; push it and pull it. When you have the shape of the scraper right, use a light touch for a smoother surface, one that accentuates the grain lines in a slight corduroy pattern that is pleasant to see and feel. Sanding is optional.

With a pencil, using your fingertip as a guide, mark a parallel line around the edge of the blade about ¼-inch from the finished face. Also make a centerline down the back of the blade. Roughly shape the back of the paddle with a bench plane, working from the edge to the center as well as lengthwise.

The neck-to-blade juncture has more concavity than the plane can handle. Here, turn to a knife, a tool of generally unrealized abilities. The work calls for a knife with a blade 3½ inches to 4 inches long — it must be sharp! — with a bit of convexity to the end. My knife was made in Sweden of laminated steel; available from Woodcraft Supply, it is inexpensive and tough.

Using the knife with both hands provides control. The position of the thumb of the left hand (right hand for a left-handed carver) is particularly important. Use it against the right-hand thumb to push, as a fulcrum, and as a safety stop when cutting toward the left hand. The right hand furnishes some of the cutting force, but, more importantly, it is the steering mechanism — the tiller — that turns the blade in the cut like a rudder. With some practice you will learn to roll thin shavings off the surface of a piece of wood. Often a small sideways motion of the knife gives the cleanest cut.

Some shaping of the shaft should come next. Pencil in guidelines for eight-siding the currently square shaft. For 1½-inch stock, measure ⁷⁄₁₆ inch from each corner. Remove the bulk of the waste wood with a knife and finish with a block plane; I prefer the Stanley No. 60½. In the usual way for rounding a square, take the shaft down from eight sides to sixteen to round. A strong, low light to one side helps to exaggerate irregularities. Running your hand over the shaft will reveal more. Set the plane for a finer cut as the shaft nears round.

Begin tapering the shaft at the neck so it will flow into the blade. A knife and a small wooden plane are used where things are too tight for the block plane. Sighting down the length of the shaft will help you to achieve the proper taper. As you go, refine the curve down the back of the blade with the block plane.

Use the half-blade pattern, made from thin cardboard, to establish the final outline of the paddle blade. Trim to the line with the block plane. Indicate the finished edge thickness of ³⁄₁₆ inch with your pencil, and re-mark the centerline down the back. Use a small wooden plane with a convex base to shape the back of the paddle as shown in the pattern. Plane diagonally and lengthwise.

Finish the back of the paddle with a scraper. This requires both hands to spring the scraper into a curve that matches the hollows along the back ridge. The small-radius curves where blade meets shaft are handled with the curved ends of the scraper.

Complete the paddle blade with a small chamfer around the edge, then carve the second blank in the same manner.

Joining the Halves

The two halves of the paddle can be joined by a commercially available ferrule, but I prefer to use a rope-seized scarf joint. This joint is not convenient if you want to take apart the paddle after every time you use it, but it never jams and can always be tightened if it loosens. Of course, alternatively, you can glue the two halves together permanently.

To make the scarfs for either a rope or a glue joint, cut each half of the paddle to its finished length, which

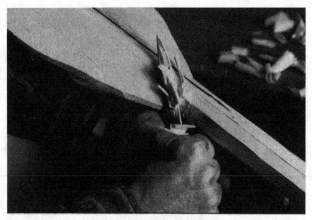
For rough work, use both hands to push the knife.

For finer work, control the knife with the right hand while pushing with the left thumb.

Seize the scarf joint by rotating the paddle while holding the line taut with your foot.

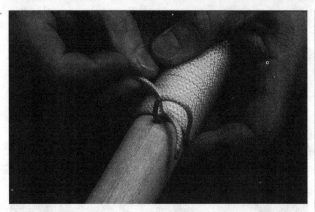

Finish the seizing by pushing the line through a hole in the shaft and half-hitching over it.

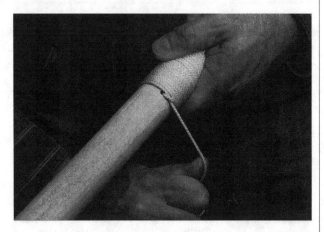

will be one-half the total length plus 6 inches. Therefore, in a total length of 9 feet, for example, each half will be 5 feet long. Determine the angle — the rotation — that you wish the blades to have relative to one another. Lay a small straightedge across the end of the shaft and sight down it to the blade. Shift the straightedge until it is parallel to the blade, then draw a light line on the butt end of the shaft. Divide the intended angle of the two blades in half and lay off the result on the shaft end relative to the first mark. This line should decline to the left; make it heavy to avoid confusion with the first. Mark the other half of the paddle in exactly the same way.

Place the two halves of the paddle end to end, aligning them with the marks, and check to be sure that the angle and rotation are correct. When you hold one blade vertically in the water, the other should face down. Measure back 1 foot from the butt end of each and make a bold mark. Hold the shaft in the vise with the heavy end mark horizontal.

Starting at the end of the shaft, plane down until you have a straight path from the 1-foot mark to the lower end. As the end is thinned, it will need hand support

from below; otherwise, it will bend away from the plane. Finish with a block plane. Before you scarf the other half, double-check to make certain that you are about to make a complement to the first scarf and not a duplicate of it. If you fail to do this, the result could be a double paddle only good for turning in circles.

If length doesn't create a problem in transportation or storage, there are good reasons to permanently join the two halves with glue. Here's how to do it:

Temporarily lash the halves together with string or tape. About 3 inches from each end of the scarf and starting on the thin side, drill an $\frac{1}{8}$-inch hole, about 1 inch deep, at right angles to the plane of the joint. Fit a wooden peg in each hole to maintain alignment during gluing. Apply glue to the pegs and the joint, reassemble, and wrap with waxed paper or plastic film. To clamp, bind tightly with cord; a constrictor knot is useful here. After the glue is dry, clean up the area with light strokes of a block plane and a scraper.

The pegs mentioned above will be needed for the rope-seized scarf, too. To complete this scarf, drill a $\frac{5}{32}$-inch hole right through the shaft about $\frac{1}{4}$ inch beyond each end of the joint. Pass one end of a 50-foot hank of $\frac{1}{8}$-inch nylon line through one of the holes. Melting the end of the line into a nice button will keep it from pulling out. Assemble the paddle, and lash the two halves together by turning the shafts in your hands. Keep tension on the line by stepping on it. Pinch the line against the shaft to prevent loosening, and rest as you get tired. When the wrapping reaches the other end of the joint, push the line through the second hole. Pull all but an inch or so through while still holding the last turn against the wood. Bring the end of the line up from the bottom and pass it under the standing part; pull everything tight. Cut off most of the excess, but leave about 2 feet. Melt the end of the line, and twist it into a taper. Lay the excess on the shaft in half hitches.

Finishing Off

In preparation for varnishing, wipe down the entire paddle with warm water. This will raise the grain and expose areas that show imperfections and may need more fine scraping. Should you want a flatter look to the finish, sand lightly with 120-grit production paper followed by 220-grit. Dampen the surface again to re-raise the grain, let it dry, and sand very lightly with the 220-grit. Don't overdo the sanding. This should be a five-minute job, maximum.

Two coats of almost any type of varnish will be enough, but I have been using my paddles quite happily without any varnish at all. Bare wood gives a much better grip than any varnished surface.

Long Oars

by Rick Cahoon

The natural feeling of grips made for your hands; the balance of the long oars as they move easily into and out of the water; the sound of leather against metal; the feeling of power that seems to multiply the effort you put into each pull; the muffled sound of the blades as they slide smoothly, gently into the water, are turned for maximum power with each pull, and are feathered for a clean exit that leaves only tight whirlpools trailing behind the skiff — all these fine qualities of well-designed and made oars reach their epitome in the long oars of Pete Culler. They must be powerful but balanced, have the right amount of spring in them without being weakened, must turn minimum effort into maximum power, and feel and look "right."

One boatbuilder who has become intimately familiar with these oars and their construction is John Burke, author of the book *Pete Culler's Boats*. As Culler taught him, "The oars being used must match the boat, and, to a large extent, the oarsman, too, in the same way a propeller needs to match hull and motor."

"The importance of choose the right type of rowing craft for your requirements and purposes has been given much coverage," says Burke. "Unfortunately, this emphasis on a proper craft does not generally extend to the oars that propel it."

According to Burke, most oars being mass produced are too short, too blade-heavy, and suffer from a lack of liveliness. Good oars should be "alive," in the same way a good pulling boat is — light, flexible, and designed and built with a specific purpose in mind. Culler accomplished this by creating light and thin blades (both in cross section and width), relatively light and thin blades (both in cross section and width),

9'·0" SPRUCE OAR

As built by John Burke from a pattern by R.D. Culler
Drawn by D.W. Dillion, May '86

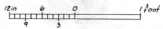

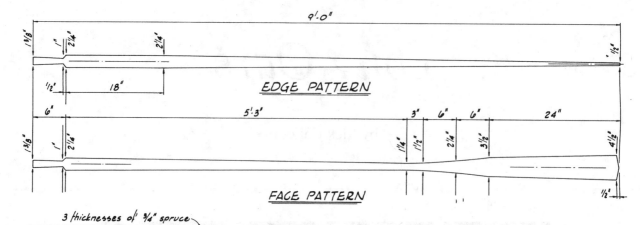

EDGE PATTERN

FACE PATTERN

3 thicknesses of ¾" spruce

EDGE PATTERN TRACED ONTO THE BLANK

FACE PATTERN TRACED ONTO THE BLANK

THE ROUGH CUT OAR

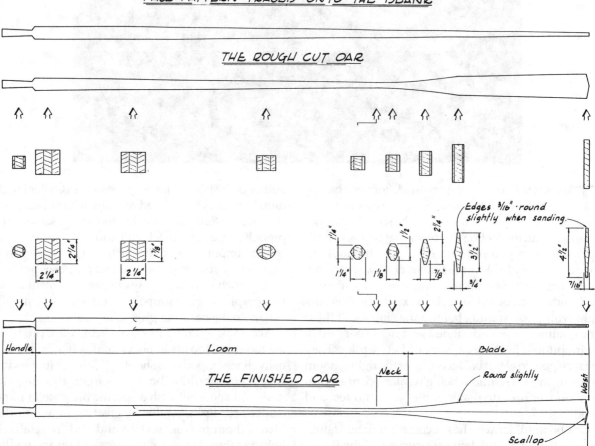

Edges ³/₁₆"·round slightly when sanding.

Handle   Loom   Blade

Neck

Round slightly

Wash

Scallop

THE FINISHED OAR

relatively light looms, heavy square sections inboard of the gunwales for balance, and a unique handle design.

There are many designs that can be made to these specifications. For the purpose of this instruction, Burke chose a set of 9-foot, flat-bladed working oars. For other types, a pattern can be fashioned from another oar or from lines taken from Culler's books, *Boats, Oars and Rowing*, or *Skiffs and Schooners*. Mystic Seaport Museum (50 Greenmanville Ave., Mystic, CT 06355; 203-572-0711) also provides plans for Culler oars.

The choice of wood for this project is critical. Strength, flexibility, and light weight are essential characteristics of Culler oars. Burke finds that Northern spruce works well for him, but cedar and pine can be used. For heavier boats, harder woods, such as ash, fir, or even sassafras, may be suitable.

Build Them by the Numbers

1

After deciding on the wood species, you'll need to select suitable pieces of timber. The best pieces will have grain that closely parallels the length of the oar and doesn't "run out" to make the oar difficult to work or weaken the finished oar.

You may also want to consider the end-grain orientation. Since so-called vertical grain is stiffer than flat grain, you can influence the finished oar's springiness by controlling the run of the grain lines when viewed from the end of the oar. For a springy or supple oar blade, the end-grain should parallel the blade; for a stiff, strong upper loom in this laminated oar, align the top and bottom layers (those that form the handle end) sawn so their end-grain is at right angles to that of the middle layer.

2

Once the pattern has been traced, three blanks are cut for each oar.

3

Each blank is then finished to a thickness of ¾ inch. Two thicker blanks can be used, but thicker stock is not as readily available as standard ¾-inch lumber. Although Burke uses a bandsaw and a planer in this sequence, he emphasizes that "a hand saw and a hand plane will produce similar results, although the process will be more tedious and time consuming." Whatever tools you use, it is very important to true up the surfaces that are to be glued, since this will create a stronger bond.

4

Each blank is weighed to determine that corresponding blanks are approximately equal. This will ensure that both finished oars will start out weighing the same and therefore will be balanced — an important characteristic. If there's a great weight discrepancy between the blanks, weigh three of them at a time in various combinations until you get two sets nearly equal in weight.

Blanks are placed together so there is no opposing grain in adjoining pieces, since this would make the oar difficult to shape. The blank with the best flat grain at the blade end is sandwiched in the middle, since most of the wood of the outside pieces will be cut away at the blade, leaving only the center piece in that section.

5

The choice of glues is not highly critical, although ease of use and aesthetics are important to Burke. "Weldwood is my choice," he says, "since it is easy to mix, is not temperature critical, has a fairly long working life, and does not show a noticeable glue line when the oar is shaped."

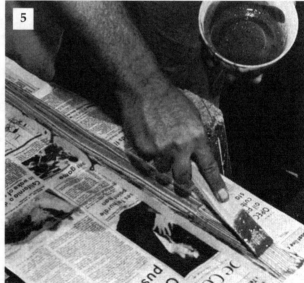

6

After covering all mating surfaces with glue, the blanks are fitted together and clamped to strongbacks, top and bottom, using as many clamps as possible. Firm, even pressure is applied, and then Burke sights down the glue lines to be sure all blanks are straight and true, top to bottom and side to side.

7

Shaping begins with rough-cutting the oars, starting with the blade. A centerline is drawn along the edge of the blade, with two guidelines for cutting on either side. These cuts, made on a bandsaw, will determine each blade's maximum thickness along the center ridge from neck to tip. Additional shaping with a hollow plane will be necessary later to produce the cross-sectional diamond shape of the blades. (If a two-way tilting-table bandsaw is available, you can eliminate much of this additional hand-shaping by making four cuts at a 2- to 3-degree angle to create the desired diamond shape.)

8

With the blade end roughed out, the oar is reversed and the handle is shaped. The grip is marked out on the wood so it will have a reverse taper — that is, the end of the grip that joins the shaft of the oar will be smaller in diameter than the free end. Most grips on commercial oars are front tapered or barrel shaped, but Culler found that the reverse taper was more comfortable and secure. Burke agrees, and says, "The shape is unusual, but I have found it to be a great advantage."

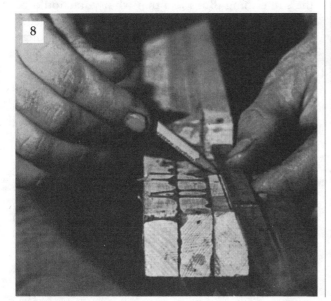

9
The grip is rough-cut on the bandsaw.

10
The round shape of the grip is drawn on the roughed-out grip…

11
…and the corners are removed with a rasp.

12
Just below the grip, the shaft of the oar is kept square and should be trued. Maintaining this square shape adds extra weight inboard of the oarlocks to help counterbalance the long outboard portion leading to the blade. This is an important feature of Culler oars, one that gives even the longest oars a balance and liveliness that adds to the pleasure of rowing. "It is a counterweight and helps in lowering the inboard part of the oar during feathering," says Burke. "Even eight-siding this part of the oar will take off weight that you need. Some people drill a hole in the end of the handle, bore it down, and fill it with lead to accomplish the same thing. But I feel that what you should be looking for is the lightest possible oar, and if you leave the inboard end of the oar square, there will be enough weight without adding any more."

13A

Starting at a point shown on the pattern, the remainder of the shaft is rounded. Rounding generally begins where the leathers will be attached to the oar. The shaft is held in place on the bench with a V-block and clamp. To round this length of the shaft (the loom) requires that it first be eight-sided. A spar gauge is used for marking the eight lines that will be used as a guide.

The gauge is a small piece of wood with ears at each end that fit comfortably over the wood at its widest dimension. Between the ears are two pins or pencils that score or mark the wood when the gauge is drawn along the loom of the oar with the ears in contact with it. The easiest way to position the pins or pencils is to draw a boxed circle on the oar stock the exact diameter of the wood at its widest point. Then, using a try-square or bevel square set at 45-degrees, mark the lines tangent to the circle. The two pins on the spar gauge should be positioned where these lines intersect the box.

13B

To use, pull gauge along the length of the oar while keeping the markers and the ears of the gauge in contact with the oar. Use the gauge on all four sides of the loom.

14

After all four sides have been marked from the oarlock location to the neck, the corners are cut down with a drawknife.

15

This is followed by a spokeshave, which makes a more precise cut to the marks.

13A

13B Making a Marking Gauge for Eight-Siding an Oar

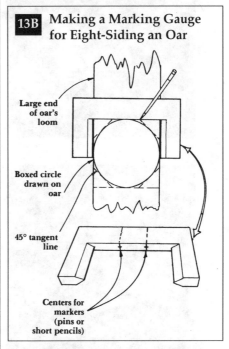

Large end of oar's loom

Boxed circle drawn on oar

45° tangent line

Centers for markers (pins or short pencils)

14

15

16

Then a hollow plane is used to round the eight-sided loom. If a hollow plane is not available, the loom can be 16-sided by using the spar gauge a second time. A spokeshave can then be used to round the 16-sided section.

17

To shape the neck and the blade of the oar, Burke uses a box scraper, although any hollow tool, such as a round-bottomed or backing-out plane, is useful for this purpose.

18

The shape being sought is a ridge that runs the length of the loom, becomes prominent at the neck, and dominates the blade. "What you're trying to do as you reach the end of the oar is take off as much weight as possible," explains Burke, "and the ridge allows you to do that. It's similar to the webbing of a duck's foot. Anything that's not being used for strength, that's excess on the blade, is weight that you don't need, particularly out on the end of the oar." Eventually, the edge of the blade is reduced to approximately ³⁄₁₆ inch.

19

The final stage of shaping is to give the oar a complete sanding. How much effort this step takes depends on how carefully the shaping tools have been used and what type of finish you desire. This step can be shortened substantially by first going over the oar with the shaping tools set for very fine cutting. This eliminates much of the rough sanding and leaves an excellent finish for fine sanding. When all visible cutting marks are removed, the oar should be wiped with paint thinner to reveal any hidden tool marks. Sandpaper with 220 grit may then be used to produce a final smooth surface.

Oar Security

To prevent the theft of your oars, you can construct a locking device from ⅜-inch bronze rod that can be secured from below a thwart with a small padlock. Simply place the rod in a vise and saw it down the middle with a hacksaw until enough metal is provided to form arms over the oars. Hammer the arms over an anvil horn or a piece of heavy pipe. Drill a hole through the other end for the lock, and polish the rough edges. Then drill a hole through the thwart for securing the device. This is not a foolproof antitheft device, but it will deter casual thieves.

In some ports even your oarlocks may be a temptation for thieves. But you can rig lanyards to each that will allow you to remove them for more secure storage. The lanyards utilize eight-strand sennits of tarred marlin. Begin by forming a splice through the eye of the oarlock. Braid the sennit until you have sufficient length to attach it to the boat. Then form an eye-splice with four of the strands and a stopper knot with the remaining four strands.

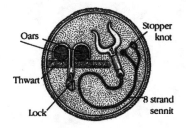

Finishing

Whether the oar is partially painted for decoration (which Burke prefers) or is left bright, Burke recommends at least six coats of varnish. The only portion of the oar to be left unfinished is the grip. A simple oil finish will adequately treat and protect that section.

Leathers must be cut and sewn to the shaft just below the square inboard section. The herringbone or reverse baseball stitch seems to work best. This stitch is illustrated in Culler's book *Boats, Oars, and Rowing* and in *The Marlinspike Sailor* by Hervey Garrett Smith. The leathers for the 9-foot oars illustrated here should be about 14 inches long and should be sewn on before the final coat of varnish is applied. Leathers should be kept greased with tallow (preferred) or Vaseline.

It should be noted that the two oars should be made together. Do not complete one oar before starting the other. At various points during the shaping process, the oars should be checked for equal weight. Although it is not necessary (or even possible) to have them come out exactly the same, their weights should be as close as possible to provide balance while rowing.

The final weight of the oars will depend on the type of wood used, the length of the oar, and your level of skill. Examples of ideal weights are: 10 to 11 pounds per pair for 8-foot ash; 5½ to 6 pounds for 8-foot spruce; and 6 to 6½ pounds for the 9-foot spruce oars illustrated here.

"Yours oars may be heavier," says Burke, "but don't be dismayed. Just remember that excess weight is something that you've got to move around with your own energy. If your oar breaks, you took off too much. If you break oars in the learning process, you're not out a whole lot of money and you've learned a lot."

The primary requirements for building oars are time and patience. Costs are usually minimal. A critical characteristic in the builder is love of wood, oars, and rowing. With that love as motivation, the requirements are easily met.

Spoon-Bladed Oars

by Rich Shew

Photographs by Dick Shew

The long, narrow shape of this spoon blade provides smooth action in rough water. A center ridge adds strength and stability.

Most oars are plainly unexciting. They are milled out on machines that make dozens like them every day. These store-bought oars will give a lifetime of acceptable, thoroughly average service. More efficient and elegant custom oars are available at a high price. You can make your own, but what should they look like? What are you going to use for patterns and for wood?

Ash is the traditional choice for oars, but it is by no means the only option. I've seen oars made out of pine, basswood, Douglas-fir, and even mahogany, but one of the best materials — in terms of strength vs. weight — is North American spruce. Not only is spruce strong and light, but also it is dirt cheap (at least it is in Maine, where I live and work). The only drawback is that it can be loaded with knots and, therefore, somewhat difficult to work with. Still, most lumberyards will allow you to look through their piles for clear stock, and if you have the time, this is definitely worth your while.

Once you've found good, clear stock, you'll need to decide on an adhesive to use. Given the excellent quality of modern glues, water resistance — not strength — is the main concern. The wood is strong enough on its own to handle most of the stress. Oars are more likely to delaminate because of a non-water-resistant glue than because of stress. I use epoxy to glue up my oars, if only because that is the type we have in the shop. A variety of other water-resistant glues will work as well.

As for tools, a bandsaw would be nice, but it is not necessary. The work of a bandsaw can be done with a bow saw. A table saw, on the other hand, is almost a necessity for ripping your stock to size before you assemble the oar blanks. (If you do not have a table saw, try to borrow the use of one, or have your lumber custom milled.) Beyond this, everything else can be done with hand tools. I recommend a well-tuned block plane, a drawknife, a spokeshave, a

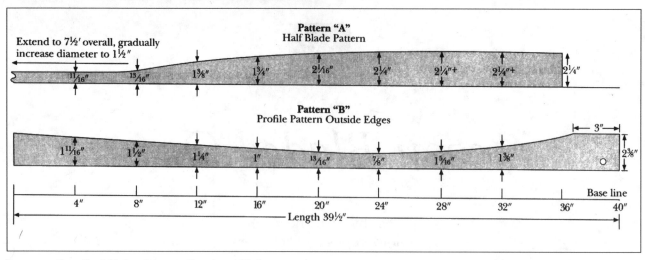

Pattern "A"
Half Blade Pattern

Extend to 7½' overall, gradually increase diameter to 1½"

11/16"   13/16"   1⅜"   1¼"   2¹/16"   2¼"   2¼"+   2¼"+   2¼"

Pattern "B"
Profile Pattern Outside Edges

1¹¹/16"   1½"   1¼"   1"   13/16"   ⅞"   1⁵/16"   1⅜"   3"   2⅜"

4"   8"   12"   16"   20"   24"   28"   32"   36"   40"   Base line

Length 39½"

You can use the author's blade patterns exactly as is, modify them, or make your own.

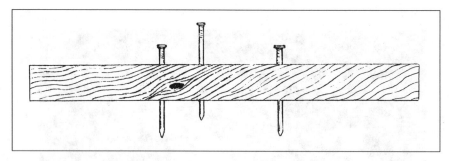

Make this simple gauge for marking the loom when eight-siding as shown in Step 15.

1½-inch chisel, and a pair of outside-bevel gouges. The larger gouge should be 1½ inches wide by ¹⁵/₁₆ inch deep. The smaller gouge should be 1 inch wide by ¼ inch deep. To some extent, the size and shape of the gouges dictate the eventual shape of the oar blades, but there's no specific formula for figuring that out. A shallower gouge will leave more wood behind when you hollow out your blades, but just how much wood you remove in the first place is a subjective matter.

The pattern drawings I've included here are for 7½-foot oars, but they can be adapted for oars that are 2 feet longer or 2 feet shorter. If you would like the blades of your oars to be a little wider than those shown and not so long, by all means feel free to draw up your own patterns.

After determining the shape of the oars, you're ready to glue up the blanks for the looms. Each of these should be made up of two pieces of spruce, 8 feet long. The larger piece should be 1¼ inches by 1½ inches. The smaller piece should be ½ inch by 1½ inches. When the loom blanks are glued up, they should measure 1½ inches by 1¾ inches.

If you're in doubt, start out with more wood instead of less. This may seem like a callous attitude in this era of environmental consciousness, but it's better to waste a little in shavings than to throw away entire blanks because you failed to give yourself enough material with which to work.

After you've given the adhesive a day or so to set, glue side pieces to the ends of the blanks; these will form the blades of the oars. These side pieces should be 29 inches long, 1½ inches wide, and 1¾ inches thick. Across the blade end of each oar blank, glue a 1-inch by 4½-inch strip of ½-inch-thick hardwood (preferably oak or locust). This will serve as a tip for the oar and will provide a measure of protection.

Now, shape the oars as shown in the step-by-step photographs.

After you have shaped the oars, sand them with 80-grit sandpaper, followed by 120-grit and then 220-grit. Finish them with a good-quality spar varnish, using two or three thinned coats before applying the final coat.

For oar leathers I recommend sections of leather hide stitched around the looms in way of the oarlocks. If you would prefer a ready-made product, most chandleries carry rubber and plastic collars that slide right over the looms and work nearly as well as leather.

Good luck, and enjoy your oars.

Build Them by the Numbers

1

A glued-up oar blank, side pieces and tip in place, prior to sawing.

2

Using Pattern A, mark out the profile on each oar.

3

Cut out the profile of the oar with a bandsaw. At this point, leave part of the waste wood on one side of the oar blank so you will have a flat surface for working across the table.

4

Mark out the shape of the spoon by making a mark 6 inches from the tip and drawing the curve with Pattern B from the tip to the 6-inch mark.

5

Draw a straight line from the 6-inch mark to the loom section of the blank.

6

Cut out the spoon shape on the bandsaw, as marked. Now you can remove the waste wood flat remaining from Step 3.

7

With a spokeshave, smooth the rough edges left by the saw.

8

Draw a curved line at the point where the oar blade meets the loom, using a cup or a bottle that is 2¼ inches in diameter. Alternatively, you could use a compass.

9

Mark the center of the blade. Put one mark on top of the curved mark made in the last step, and another mark 6 inches from the tip of the oar

10
Draw a line connecting the two marks made in the last step.

11
Using Pattern B, draw the inside curve of the blade.

12
Use the larger gouge and chisel to rough out the blade. Cut to the centerline with the large gouge.

13
Clean out the waste wood with a wide chisel.

14
Thin the center ridge with the smaller gouge.

15
Mark out the tops and bottoms of the looms with a homemade gauge. Make a mark 5 feet from the tip, and mark the sides of the looms as you did the tops and bottoms above this point.

16
Continue marking with the gauge from the 5-foot mark to the concave side of the blades. Then, draw a pencil line ¼ inch from the scribed line you have just made.

17

Shave to the lines with a drawknife and a block plane. The looms should now be octagonal in section.

18

Make a pencil mark 18 inches from the tip of the oar.

19

Make two marks ¾ inch apart and equidistant from the center of the oar.

20

Connect the last two marks with a scribed line on the top of the loom.

21
Draw a pencil line ½ inch from, and parallel to, the concave side of the blade.

22
Rough out the blade with a drawknife and a spoke-shave.

23
Shave away the transition area from the loom to the curved scribe-line made in Step 8.

24
Draw pencil lines for making the loom 16-sided. Do this only on the bottom of the oar below the 5-foot mark.

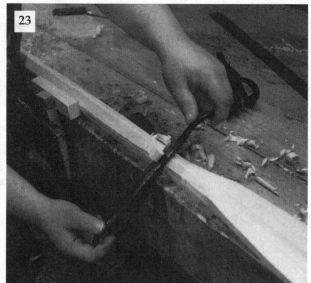

25

Shave to the lines with a block plane.

26

Mark a line ¼ inch from, and parallel to, the concave side of the blade. Shave the oar blade down to the lines just drawn, and finish rounding the loom with a spokeshave.

27

Make a shallow saw cut all the way around the loom, 5 inches from the end of the oar and ⅜ inch deep.

28

Form an inverted cone for a grip by carving to the saw kerf with the larger gouge held upside down. Sand and varnish the oars, but leave the grips bare.

Hollow Spars

—— by Maynard Bray ——

Dexter Cooper of D.P. Cooper Boat Building, Inc., single-handedly builds hollow spars in a large barn in Hartland, Vermont. Although his shop is small, it is filled with some first-class woodworking tools, all of which are on wheels. There is a 14-inch bandsaw, a spindle shaper, a thickness planer, an 8-inch jointer, a table saw, and last but by no means least, a power feed unit that is one of Dexter's solutions to working alone.

Almost everything in the shop can be easily moved. The bench

where the spars are laid out and glued up is a series of individual units, each of which can be lifted or dragged to whatever location seems best for the job at hand. Dexter has made sawhorses with tops that can be raised to whatever height is needed to support the long pieces that, ordinarily, would require a second person's help. Furthermore, Dexter has made machines that are normally thought of as being stationary easily movable by fitting them with wheels.

Wheel-equipped machines, to be shuffled around easily, must be on a smooth floor. The floor of this shop not only is newly laid and smooth, but also is kept clear of sawdust and shavings by a dust collec-

tion system. As each of the big machines is hauled to the center of the shop and put to use, it is connected to the big, flexible hose of the two-stage dust collection system. The system's ducting runs out of the way under the floor and drops large chips in a bin downstairs. The power unit, on the main floor for easy maintenance, blows fine particles into a dust bag and allows the warm shop air to return to the shop.

In addition to eight-stave hollow spars, Dexter Cooper builds conventional rectangular spars and solid ones. The handling aids and the movable machinery are used to advantage for all three types. Here is how he builds the eight-stave hollow type:

Build It by the Numbers

1

One face of the rough-sawn Sitka spruce stock is first passed over the jointer, which flattens and smooths that face. Portable infeed and outfeed tables, one end of each table being partly supported by the jointer itself as shown, carry the weight of the overhanging ends as the stock passes by the cutters. Next, the stock is turned on edge and run over the jointer in that position until that edge is straight and can be used as a reference for measuring. A thickness planer is then wheeled out to replace the jointer in the center of the shop, and the stock planed to the required thickness. Dexter shapes the individual pieces first and then scarfs them to length.

2

From a full-sized layout of the spar's largest cross section and the designer's drawings showing the taper, Dexter lays out the correct width on one of the staves. As the first step, the stations are marked along the length of the stave.

3

Widths are then laid out at each station, measured outward from a previously marked centerline.

4

A long, stiff batten, one edge of which touches each of the marks made in the previous step, is now clamped to the stock at each station and used as a guide in marking the finished edge.

5

The first stave is passed through the bandsaw, where it is cut close to the marked line.

6

After it has been sawn, the first piece of staving is now cleaned up with a hand plane and used as a pattern for marking the other seven.

7

When all the staves have been sawn to shape, their rough-sawn edges are planed smooth and close to the line.

8

Now the shaper is wheeled into position for cutting the required 22½-degree bevel on each edge of each stave. Sawhorses support the overhanging weight of the staves as they pass through the shaper, and a power feed unit ensures that the staves advance steadily and stay in close contact with the shaper cutters as well as with the shaper table. Once the shaper has been set up, the work is automatic, and Dexter has only to keep an eye on the machinery.

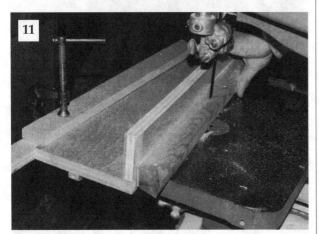

9

Here's a close-up of the business end of the shaper, with the beveling cutter head in place. The guide, clamped to the shaper table to hold it in place, is faced with Formica to reduce friction and to allow the stave to slide along easily. Here, the near edge of the stave has already been beveled, and the opposite edge is about to pass by the cutter.

10

Using another cutter head and guide, Dexter sets up the shaper for rounding the outside surface of each stave. The cutter is shaped and adjusted for properly cutting a 45-degree arc (with two passes) at the spar's maximum diameter. Where the spar is smaller in diameter, the tapering stave widths will create a peak down the stave's spine that must be planed off by hand after the spar has been glued up. Dexter uses two sets of cutters: one that will shape staves for spar diameters from 4 inches to 7 inches, and another that will work on diameters from 7 inches to 10 inches.

11

Scarfs for staves are cut prior to being run through the shaper only if they are glued to length before both shaper operations. A jig that indexes to the slot in the bandsaw's table ensures correct alignment.

12

Here the scarf is being cut in its mating stave. Although this scarf orientation is perfectly acceptable as far as strength is concerned, my preference would be to cut the scarf at 90-degrees from this, so the glue lines of the finished spar will be less conspicuous.

13

Dexter uses a router for smoothing the saw cuts before gluing. During this process, a vacuum pump is used to suck the stave down into close contact with the base of the jig.

14

C-clamps are used to hold the scarf together while the glue — epoxy for both the scarfs and the staves — sets up.

15

The completed staves are first glued together as pairs, as shown here, with sliding bar clamps providing the necessary pressure. Small pieces of plywood, notched to fit, keep the clamps from damaging the fragile corners of the staves.

16

Two pairs of staves make half the spar and are held in line and clamped together as shown. The wood scraps, temporarily screwed to each of the pairs and clamped together, prevent the assembly from spreading as pressure is applied from above.

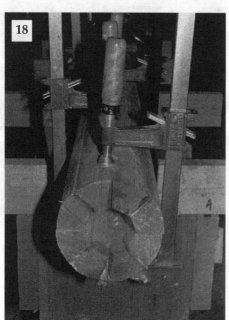

17

Two halves, glued together, make the whole, round, hollow, spar. Before spreading the glue, Dexter first checks that the surface of each half is perfectly flat so there will be an even glue line, then he spreads the epoxy quickly with a foam roller. To seal against moisture, the spar's inside surfaces have already been coated with epoxy. Any internal wiring or solid blocking that has been specified (as it often is at the spreaders and tangs) is installed before the two halves are joined. At the right is another view of the clamping arrangement for gluing two pairs of staves together.

18

Here is the final clamping — when the two halves are joined. If the fit is good, only a little pressure is needed to hold the mating surfaces in contact. After the glue has cured, some final shaping and sanding is required to round the spar and make it fair and smooth. In addition, the ends are finished and, if called for, shoulders are cut for spliced rigging. Then the spar is painted or varnished.

The Buckboard Trailer

by Jack Jagels
Drawings by Arch Davis

The Adirondack guideboat, "however fragile looking, if properly handled could ride out any storm on the average fresh water lake, carrying a load of 500 pounds." So writes Kenneth Durant in *The Adirondack Guideboat*. On land, the boat takes on a more delicate personality, and "the fragile guideboat requires protection against sharp pebbles, [and] the hot sun, which can warp the seams." Furthermore, since the guideboat has only an outwale if it is turned upside-down on a car roof-rack, the weight of the boat rests on the top strake, which is only ³⁄₁₆-inch-thick pine or cedar.

Having cartopped some guideboats, I can also affirm that the strong sny (or sharp rise from amidships to the bow and the stern, reminiscent of the WoodenBoat logo) greatly diminishes fore-and-aft visibility. This distinctly advances the level of adventure while speeding down the interstate highway. Nervous passengers tend to lean strongly to port or starboard, trying to improve their line of sight, while the driver assumes a low, painful crouch.

I finally concluded that cartopping my guideboat was less than ideal one hot summer day after I'd driven from my home, which was then in western Vermont, to Blue Mountain Lake, New York, site of The Adirondack Museum, to attend the celebration of the publishing of the above-mentioned book. Upon arrival, as I attempted to remove the stretch-rubber hold-downs from my circa-1910 varnished guideboat, I discovered that the straps had annealed

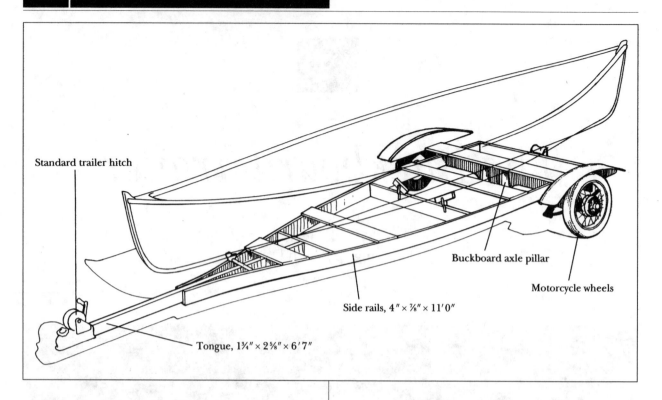

Standard trailer hitch

Buckboard axle pillar

Motorcycle wheels

Side rails, 4″ × ⅞″ × 11′0″

Tongue, 1¾″ × 2⅝″ × 6′7″

themselves to the boat's bottom. I don't recommend this as the method of choice for stripping varnish. Then, when I placed the boat in the museum pond, alongside a dozen or so other guideboats, it promptly began to leak like a sieve through its sunbaked, opened seams.

On an earlier trip to another gathering, this time to a small-craft meet at Mystic Seaport Museum, I had been permitted to view some items not generally on display at the museum. There, in among the boats in a storage building, was a Herreshoff-designed boat trailer. The sight of that beautiful boat conveyance set some gears in motion. I had always found the common galvanized boat trailer, with its tinkertoy wheels matched with springs designed for a Mack truck, not only aesthetically unappealing but also, from an engineering point of view, inappropriate for carrying my fragile guideboat over rough back roads.

The Design

Several years went by while I incubated design ideas and gathered items from auctions and yard sales. As my pile of junk grew, my designs were adjusted accordingly. The final form, shown here, was the culmination of a lot of winnowing of both ideas and accumulated "parts." Since I understand the engineering properties of wood better than those of other materials, and because I can easily work with wood and find wood aesthetically appealing (especially in a conveyance for a wooden boat), I focused my thoughts toward making maximum use of this material.

These days, wood is rarely connected to wheels, except in children's toys; but in earlier times, this was not the case. So, I began to study wagon and buggy construction when I visited museums. The classic buckboard set me to thinking about using wood for part of the suspension system. Buckboard wagons suspend the passengers between the front and rear pairs of wheels, but a trailer has only one pair of wheels. So I thought that if the buckboard were rotated 90 degrees, I could simultaneously create a suspension system and a live axle for attaching the wheels. This would give me independent suspension on each wheel.

As I thought about this wooden live axle, I realized that if I created one with enough strength to carry the weight of a boat pounding along on rough pavement, and then added a safety factor, I would end up with an axle that would be too stiff. Among the assorted stuff I had picked up at auctions was a pair of wagon seat springs. If I used these in conjunction with the buckboard, I could keep the trailer lightly sprung, and at the same time provide the necessary fore-and-aft constraint on each end of the centrally pivoted live axle.

Once the suspension system had been devised, the rest flowed smoothly, or relatively so. Among my collectibles was a front wheel from a motorcycle. After searching a few chop shops, I came up with another to match. The outside diameter of the short motorcycle wheel axle fits snugly inside ¾-inch black iron plumbing pipe. A local welding shop welded the black

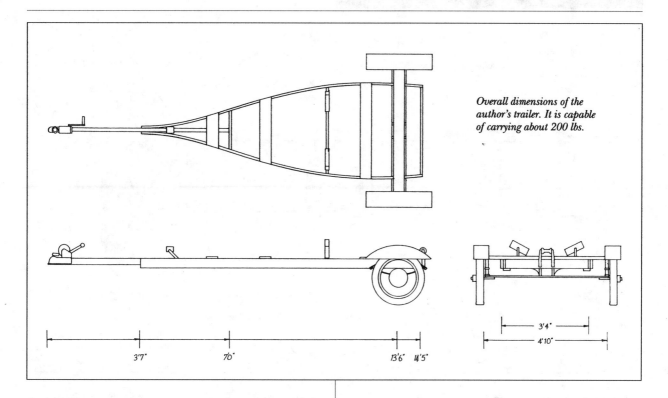

Overall dimensions of the author's trailer. It is capable of carrying about 200 lbs.

3'7"   70"   13'6" 14'5"

3'4"
4'10"

iron pipe to ¼-inch-thick, 6-inch by 6-inch steel plates. After pre-drilling, these axle plates were bolted to the underside of the live axle with carriage bolts.

Since a wooden "buckboard" axle is a very critical component, it must be perfectly straight-grained (no cross-grain), without knots or other defects. The board should be flat-sawn ash, oak, or hickory, and have relatively wide growth rings (in these ring-porous woods, wide growth rings indicate greater strength). If possible, use air-seasoned wood rather than kiln-dried.

For my trailer, I chose an axle with dimensions of 6½ inches by ½ inch by 4 feet 10¾ inches. The thickness could be increased to ⅝ inch to provide more carrying capacity. The trailer shown here should easily carry 200 pounds. The heaviest boat that I carry is a strip-built peapod that weighs about 130 pounds with the mast and other gear thrown in. However, I often stand on the trailer while loading or unloading the boat, and see no serious deflections (I weigh about 160 pounds).

Construction

I built the frame of the trailer with oak, but ash or hickory would do. The curved side rails were purchased as green lumber from a local mill and were bent to shape before they dried. Steam-bending would be preferable if a long-enough steam box could be found or made. But I was lazy and in a hurry, as usual, and the gentle curves permitted cold bending of the green oak. Laminated side rails would be another option.

The forward ends of the bent rails were drilled and bolted to the 1¾-inch by 2⅝-inch by 6-foot 7-inch tongue first, and then the after cross-member was attached (with screws only, at this stage). While the wood was still wet, the intermediate cross-members were gently forced into place, creating the curved shape. The frame was then dried, out of the sun, for about a week. This reduces surface-moisture sufficiently so the parts can then be glued (I used epoxy) and screwed. The frame will not reach its full strength until the green lumber is air dry (15 to 20 percent moisture content), which will take several weeks or months, depending on conditions. However, the frame has enough strength so that you can continue with the construction now.

The rear of the frame is now beefed up with the addition of a 5-inch by 1½-inch by 4-foot 10¾-inch axle support made of oak. The live axle is attached to this beam using an oak pillar, four struts, and oak spacers and carriage bolts. The height of the pillar and struts for this trailer is 7¼ inches, but this will need to be adjusted to match the set of wagon seat springs available. The long axis of the pillar is cut to fit snugly between the side rails.

Wagon seat springs may be difficult to obtain in your neighborhood, but a competent spring shop can fabricate something comparable from a pair of small leaf springs. Another alternative is to use a more readily available coil spring. However, coil springs do not contribute to the fore-and-aft stability of the live axle, so diagonal struts between the axle and the frame will also be needed.

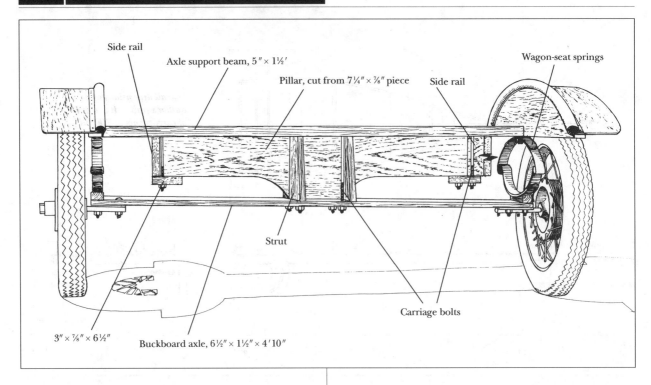

Side rail

Axle support beam, 5″ × 1½′

Pillar, cut from 7¼″ × ⅞″ piece

Side rail

Wagon-seat springs

Strut

Carriage bolts

3″ × ⅞″ × 6½″

Buckboard axle, 6½″ × 1½″ × 4′10″

Standard steel trailer fenders can be purchased, but as a compulsive wood nut, I fashioned the fenders from ¼-inch birch plywood and oak. The arc is so gentle that the thin plywood can be bent without steaming (a fortunate happenstance, since I used interior plywood, which is manufactured with urea-formaldehyde glue).

Wheel caps are 1-inch plastic plumbing pipe caps. A standard trailer hitch is attached to the central shaft, and standard boat trailer supports and a winch are added to complete the job. I chose to varnish the

trailer, but painting would provide a more durable finish.

If I were to build another trailer like this, I would extend the tongue as a central shaft to the live axle supports. I also might make the curved frame rails a bit wider. This would strengthen the frame (especially adding torsional stiffness) without dramatically affecting the "ride." The present frame is a bit willowy, although it has held up now for several years with no signs of fatigue. I always store the trailer under cover, which should greatly lengthen its service life.

This Herreshoff trailer, holding an Amphibicraft in Mystic Seaport Museum's storage building, has Indian motorcycle wheels.

A Wooden Bilge Pump

by Ed Frost

Here is a pump that will throw a lot of water, is easy to build and repair, and will fit right in on a traditional boat. Not so long ago, the wooden bilge pump was common on working craft. Outside of a bucket there's nothing simpler nor more reliable for putting water back where it came from.

This pump has only three components: a wooden barrel (with or without a spout), a flapper valve at the bottom, and a plunger. Because it is simple, there's not much that can go wrong, and what little there is can be readily fixed with a bit of leather and wood.

With the help of some muscle, a properly made wooden pump can be depended on to work when you need it, no matter the state of your boat's electrical system. It will move a surprising amount of water without much effort. A 3-inch pump will raise 12 to 14 gallons a minute at an easy pumping rate of about 45 strokes a minute. With tools and materials at hand, you should be able to build one in a couple of hours.

The Barrel

The barrel is made of pine or cedar planks (½ to ¾ inch finished), fastened with screws or ring nails, and soaked with linseed oil and kerosene. Anyone so inclined could make the barrel of plywood, rabbeted and glued at the corners, and sealed with epoxy. Either way, the inside should be greased for easy pumping action.

Inside dimensions of 3 inches by 3 inches are about right for the average person. You can go larger, but the bigger you make the barrel, the more water you'll be lifting on each stroke and the sooner you'll get tired. A smaller pump that can be worked steadily will move more water in the long run than a bigger one that will make you want to stop and rest every few minutes.

The length of the barrel depends on the depth of the boat. It must be long enough to carry water overboard from the lowest point of the bilges.

The Plunger

The plunger is a square of heavy leather mounted on a block of wood. For a 3-inch pump, the leather must be 3 inches square and the block to which it's fastened should be about 2 inches square. The block can be of any tough wood, ½ inch or so in thickness. The plunger handle is wedged into a hole that goes through the leather and the block. The drawings show two kinds of blocks; the centered square block just discussed and, for those who favor something more exotic, a cutout block with the handle offset. The leather should be greased to keep it pliable. Neoprene or something similar might be used in place of leather and, of course, would need no grease.

Whatever is used, it must be stiff enough with the support of the block under it to fit the barrel snugly and create a suction on the upstroke, but it must be limber enough to lift and pass freely through the water on the downstroke.

The Valve

The valve is simply a flap of greased leather or neoprene over a hole in a block of wood. The flap is tacked down along one side; the other side is free and lifts, allowing water to be drawn up into the barrel when the plunger is raised. When the plunger is lowered, the flap lies flat over the hole and keeps the water from running back into the bilge. Unlike the plunger leather, the flap should be smaller than the inside of the barrel so it can move up and down freely. The block must be a good fit in the barrel to prevent leaking, and it should be fastened to the barrel with screws so it can be removed easily when the time comes to

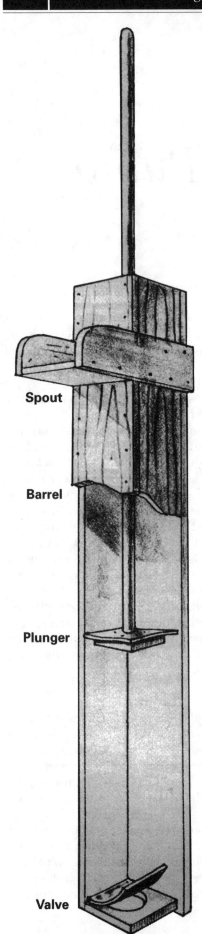

Spout

Barrel

Plunger

Valve

replace the flap. For a 3-inch pump, the hole should be at least 2 inches in diameter.

To keep the valve off the boat bottom so water can pass freely into the pump, two opposing sides of the barrel are extended about ½ inch beyond the valve block, and the projecting ends are hollowed out to allow a flow of water from all four sides. It's a good idea to put a piece of coarse screen across the bottom of the valve to reduce the chance of debris in the bilge water jamming the flap.

Spouts and Wells

For an open boat with the pump discharging directly over the gunwale, a wooden spout, as shown in the labeled drawing, is best. As the spout is the same width as the barrel, it doesn't restrict the flow of water, and being of wood, it won't make dents in your boat. If the pump is to go in a well on a decked boat, you can make the spout of pipe or tubing and run the discharge overboard through a hose. The spout can be below the deck with the hose leading to a through-hull connection in the side, or to the center-board case of a centerboard boat; or, it can be above the deck with the hose leading directly to the rail or scupper. Whatever type of spout you use, put it far enough down the barrel to keep water from surging over the top when you're pumping.

You can put a pump without any spout in a deck well and let the water run off through the scuppers. This is the simplest way; there are no leaky connections

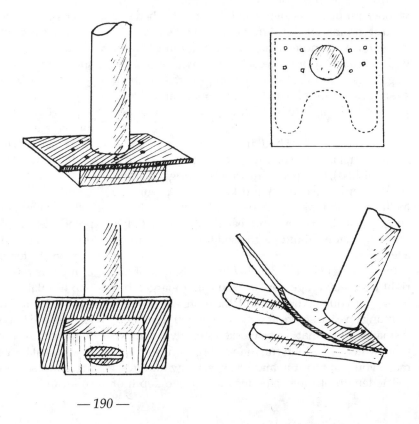

or hose to monkey with, and if your bilges are clean it's probably the best for a decked boat of any size.

If you're going to caulk or wedge the pump into a well so it can't be easily withdrawn, you should make a removable section at the lower end of the barrel so you can get to the valve in a hurry if it jams.

You'll find that this type of pump has to be primed. Just pour a little water down the barrel and start with short quick strokes until you feel it taking hold. Once you get suction, you can pump her dry, sit down, have a drink, and consider the rewards of an active life.

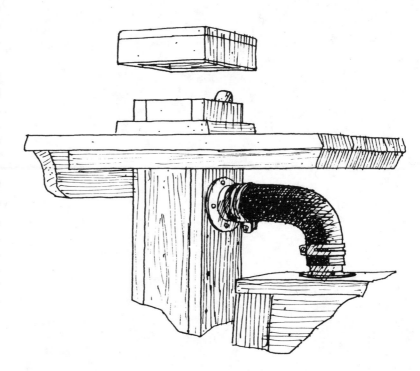

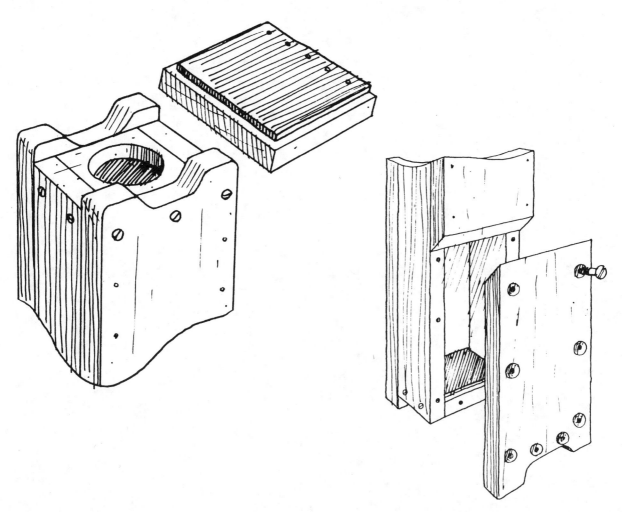

Other Ways

by Ben Fuller
Illustrations by Kathy Bray

Roller Cart
in use

H ere are a few boat-related ideas and projects collected by me over the years. I learned most of them from Josef Liener, a boatbuilder on the Eastern Shore of Maryland.

Rollers, Carts, Hoists, and Such

Boat owners moved their boats around long before the advent of modern trailers. They used rollers and winches, both devices which are easy to build, allow single-handed movement of boats weighing up to 400 pounds, and are offered here for whatever utility they may have.

Most important and versatile is a simple contraption that is either a roller or a cart, depending on its attitude. Essentially it is a platform or a frame with a small roller in its center. Roller down, it is a cart; platform down, it is a roller wherever you need one, like at the edge of a dock, a bank, or a marsh. I use mine in sliding a boat on and off a trailer. It also comes in quite handy for moving spars or pilings.

The platform can be a frame made of 2 by 4s, or plywood with a couple of stiffeners. The roller can be a solid piece 4 inches to 6 inches in diameter, bored to take a pipe axle. If you don't have a wood lathe or an old part of a mast lying around, the roller can be made from a 6-foot plastic water pipe with two wooden plugs driven in the ends that have been bored for the axle. Two cheek pieces will also be needed, sized so that the roller clears the platform if it is solid, or clears the load if a frame is used. These should be of a hard wood, such as locust. Dimensions of the whole unit can vary to suit the boat and the terrain; obviously, the larger the roller the better, especially if the ground is soft.

When used as a cart, the boat is set on the platform at the balance point, or a little bow down. A bridle, made fast to the front edge of the cart, is made long enough to reach from the cart to the hole, ring, or pad-eye where the painter is attached, and is stuck through it. The boat owner picks up or pulls on the bridle and the boat obediently follows.

If you often stick your boat in the back of a pickup or a station wagon, build a frame with rollers to fit the bed. Make it long enough to bear against the front wall of the truck bed or the back of the front seat of the station wagon. Rollers can be made from pipe with thinner pipe as axles. These should be low, only an inch or so above the bed. The boat is rolled to the vehicle (on your cart), and one of its ends is lifted onto the tailgate and the rear roller. Then the boat can be easily slid in.

Finally, if you regularly carry a boat weighing more than about 100 pounds or so on the roof of your car, or on racks on your truck, consider the merits of a block and tackle, and a tree. Look for a convenient tree limb near your launch site, reachable by standing on a car top or hood. Lash up the tackle, drive the boat underneath and hook up slings or a bridle (if you have lifting eyes). Un-lash the boat, haul away on the tackle, make fast, and drive out from under. Put your cart underneath, let her down on it, and off you go. Launching sites without trees probably should not be patronized if you depend on this system.

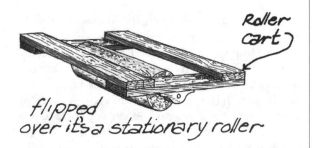

Roller cart

flipped over it's a stationary roller

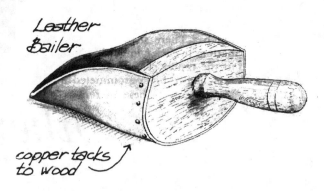

Leather Bailer

copper tacks to wood

A Bailer

So you have a nice small wooden skiff and you've made a nice set of oars to go with it. But lurking in the bilge is an old bleach bottle with the end cut off. It's your bailer and it works pretty well, but it's ugly as sin and certainly not traditional. Build an efficient bailer of wood and leather. The back is wood, with a hole bored at an angle and a handle inserted in it and tightly wedged, like a trunnel. The scoop is leather, tacked around the edge of the back. Use as heavy a leather as you can get, unsplit by preference. Go see your local leather handcrafter or shoemaker. Use long copper tacks. The back of the bailer should have a nice transom shape to it, sort of like the stern of a catboat, with a bit of tumblehome.

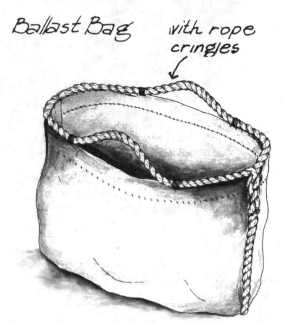

Ballast Bag   with rope cringles

A Ballast Bag

Sand or ballast bags used to be common around small boats — so common that they were sold commercially by marine hardware companies early in this century. Today's small boat racing rules prohibit shifting ballast, perhaps a legacy of the shift away from sand-baggers in the 1880s and '90s. But the non-racing wooden boat owner isn't bound by any rules, and 25 pounds of sand can do wonders for a small boat. It can hold the bow of a flat-bottomed skiff down and keep it from pounding when only one person is sailing. It can be shifted to weather to relieve some of the effort of keeping a boat on her feet in a breeze. Or the sand in it can be poured over the side when it isn't needed and an empty bag brought home.

Although sand bags are no longer sold as such in your local yachting store, one of those large canvas carryalls, originally designed for ice but now used for almost anything, serves admirably. If you want to make one, use a canvas envelope, perhaps 2 feet on the bottom and 18 inches on the side. Leave the top open. Rope it up each stitched edge, and down each side of the open top. Work rope cringles into the middle of each top rope for handles. This is the way they were once sold.

A Boathook and a Pushpole

If your boat is big enough to make a boathook useful, mark your hook in feet and use it to sound with when you are poking up a little channel. Florida sextants, they're called. Take your gouge and cut a groove down its length on the same side as the hook, and fumble no more when hooking a line underwater or at night.

without knob for use as a sprit

knob end to prevent slipping

pole length between 10 & 16 ft.

This Combination Push-Pole & Boat-hook, if long enough, can be used as a sprit for your sail.

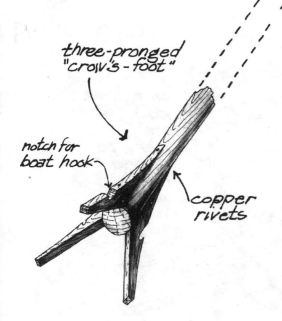

three-pronged "crow's-foot"

notch for boat hook

copper rivets

Perhaps your boat is a shoal-draft skiff and you spend a lot of time in marshes or thin water. Take a tip from the rail bird hunters of the Delaware and Chesapeake and make a pushpole. The best are spruce, but fir or even a cedar sapling will do. Pushpoles are from 10 feet to 16 feet long, about 2 inches in diameter, and have a three-pronged crow's foot at the dirty end. Anyone who has had an oar stick in the mud can appreciate the need for this pole. Each prong or toe is best made of a natural crook of locust or other hard wood, and is riveted to the pole with two copper rivets. The pole is flattened to take each toe and each is inlet slightly for strength. Cut a shoulder on the clean end and glue on a nice hardwood knob so the pole won't slide out of your hand. Or leave off the knob and slip the clean end into the peak of your spritsail. Your snotter can then be long enough to go around the foot and be tied with a rolling hitch. Unship the "sprit" when you get to the creek, strike your rig, and pole away. Your pushpole can even serve as a boathook of sorts if you cut a little notch into the top of one of the toes, and groove out your pole as with the boathook above.

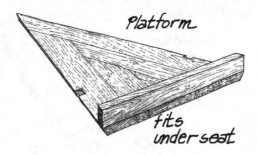

Platform

fits under seat

Stowage

Small boats tend to accumulate gear: bailers, sponges, scrub brushes, extra rowlocks, compasses, lines, foul weather gear, lunch, beer. Once it's all in, it can make quite a mess. Perhaps the most elegant solution to this problem is a dry fish well like the one that makes the amidships seat in many old-style skiffs. Another solution has been worked out in the Delaware, where gunning boxes for boats were once common. These served as movable seats when the boat was being rowed, and had a hinged top and a sealed bottom. But their use is limited to boats without center thwarts, such as Delaware Duckers and Melonseeds.

Something that can be adapted to almost any small boat is the removable tray or platform. It can be tucked underneath a stern seat in a square-sterned or double-ended boat, high enough above the bottom to be unaffected by any bilge water. In a flat-bottomed skiff, the tray can sit on the chines, while in a round-bottom boat, it can be fitted to land on the plank laps. The smooth inside surface of a carvel-planked boat, however, presents a bit of difficulty. The problem can usually be solved by a stringer across several frames. Delaware Duckers — lapstrake double-enders — carried their "lunch platforms" high underneath the stern decks, where they rested on the laps.

While thinking about the seats, why not make one of the middle boards of a stern seat removable? This will allow you to get to the gear on your lunch platform without pulling it out, and will let you get to the aftermost part of the transom and cornerposts when new oil or paint is needed.

Backrests

Seats can use backrests. These can be plain or fancy. One boat in Mystic Seaport Museum's collection has two simple ones. The stern rest is shaped like an H with a second bar across the top. The verticals have tenons in their bottom ends that fit into holes bored into the seat. The crossbar lands on chocks on the inwale.

The other backrest is especially ingenious, for it folds, and can be used for any of the amidships thwarts. Two bars run across the backrest, with chocks shaped to lock under one edge. The back of the seat is pivoted, and its posts extend a bit past the pieces resting on the seat. When unfolded they lock the backrest to the seat and keep it from swinging too far back.

Stern-Seat

a natural place for a backrest

Thwart-Seat

an ingenious locking backrest. It can be removed & folded flat when not in use.

An Awning

On a windless day with the hot summer sun beating down, rowing can be a bit unpleasant. Consider adding an awning to your boat. It should be canvas, long enough to cover most of the boat, and a bit wider than the boat's beam. A scalloped fringe adds a nice touch. There should be pockets for battens in each end. A ¾- or 1-inch hole in the center of the batten should be matched to brass-grommeted holes in the awning. These fit tenons in the tops of the awning stanchions. Tenons in the bottom of the stanchions fit into holes in the bow and stern seats.

The stern stanchion should have a brass hook that fastens into an eye in the sternpost or transom. The forward stanchion should have an eye on its forward side that can take a light line, pulled taut, to the stem head. If you prefer, each stanchion can be made longer — enough to pass through the seat and land in a small step on the boat's bottom, like a miniature mast. In either case, lateral stability has to be provided by guy lines attached to the ends of the battens. The stern guys should be crossed and might have adjustable loops to be hooked to small brass hooks under the inwale. There may be enough space ahead of the awning to lead the fore guys, without crossing them, down and forward a bit to similar hooks under the inwale in this part of the boat.

There are few things as delightful as a leisurely row under an awning on a hot day. But don't try it if you don't want your picture taken.

A Boathouse Design That Works

This boathouse design was developed by Josef Liener to house his small fleet: a pair of Delaware gunning boats and their spars, sails, oars, pushpoles, and assorted paraphernalia.

The shed is a simple pole shed, with its basic ingredient made from old creosoted telephone poles. Six would be enough for a 20-foot shed. They need not be more than 4½ to 5 feet high — off the ground — just tall enough to slip the boat and its trailer underneath, and to allow several feet of clearance with the boat hoisted. The poles should be buried about 2 to 3 feet deep. The shed is 8 to 10 feet wide to allow for

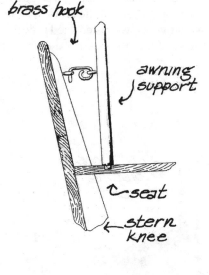

brass hook

awning support

seat

stern knee

Boat Awning

scalloped fringe

awnings are great fun — on a calm day!

more than one boat side by side. The poles are tied together with a longitudinal plate, spanned with joists and rafters, and topped with a roof. The roof ridge need not be more than 3 feet above the ends of the poles, and the roof should overhang the plate by several feet on each side so that the boats underneath are protected from a driving rain. If you live in an area raked by winter winds, some siding might be necessary.

What makes this shed unique is its built-in hoisting winch. A hole is bored in each joist to accept a 1-inch steel pipe that runs the length of the building, to be run through before you put up the front joist (which is un-bored) and the rafter. Old pipe couplings are then used to make a handle on the pipe at one end, with a swing of a foot or so. Two strongbacks wider than the width of the widest boat are made, each with a sheave let into each end. A cable is then wrapped around the pipe, threaded through each sheave underneath the strongback, and attached to a clip. A padeye

is mounted to each plate, opposite the points where the cables are wrapped around the pipe.

In operation, after a boat is rolled into the shed, the cable is unwound, the strongbacks placed fore and aft underneath the boat, and the bitter ends of the cables are clipped to the padeyes. Turn the crank and the boat rises. When it is up to the joists, pre-cut canvas slings go under the boat to additional padeyes. The cable is slacked and the winch is ready for the second boat.

If you are blessed with more than a two-boat fleet, the shed can be made high enough to accommodate boats slung one above another. The winch can also be adapted to other structures, such as garages, where a boat may need to be slung above a car or a woodpile.

The gable ends of the shed are boxed in, except for a door in the front. Through this opening you can then slide spars and oars, where they will lie on top of the joists. Here again, a relatively low-posted shed is desirable to make sliding stuff into the overhead easier.

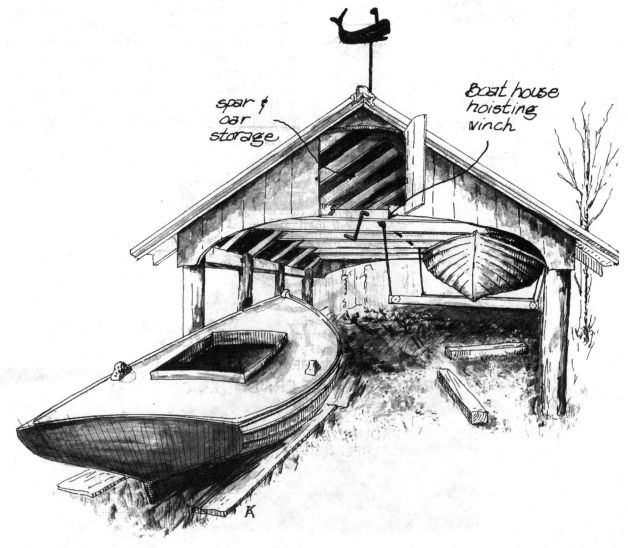

spar & oar storage

Boat house hoisting winch